MY LIFE ON THE FRONTIER
1864–1882

MY LIFE ON THE FRONTIER
1864–1882

Facsimile of Original 1935 Edition
by
Miguel Antonio Otero
Former Governor of New Mexico

New Foreword
by
Ray John de Aragón

SANTA FE

New Material © 2007 by Sunstone Press. All Rights Reserved.

No part of this book may be reproduced in any form or by any electronic or mechanical means including information storage and retrieval systems without permission in writing from the publisher, except by a reviewer who may quote brief passages in a review.

Sunstone books may be purchased for educational, business, or sales promotional use. For information please write: Special Markets Department, Sunstone Press, P.O. Box 2321, Santa Fe, New Mexico 87504-2321.

Library of Congress Cataloging-in-Publication Data

Otero, Miguel Antonio, 1859-1944.
  My life on the frontier : facsimile of original 1935 edition / by Miguel Antonio Otero ; new foreword by Ray John de Aragón.
    p. cm. -- (Southwest heritage series)
  "Facsimile of original 1939 edition" -Vol. 2, t.p.
  Includes indexes.
  Contents: [1] 1864-1882 -- [2] 1882-1897.
  ISBN: 0-86534-554-6 (v. 1 : softcover : alk. paper) -- ISBN 0-86534-555-4 (v. 2 : softcover : alk. paper)
  1. Otero, Miguel Antonio, 1859-1944. 2. Otero, Miguel Antonio, 1859-1944--Childhood and youth. 3. Governors--New Mexico--Biography. 4. Pioneers--New Mexico--Biography. 5. Frontier and pioneer life--New Mexico. 6. New Mexico--History--1848- I. Title.

F801.O88A3 2007
978.9'4092--dc22
[B]
                              2006053500

WWW.SUNSTONEPRESS.COM
SUNSTONE PRESS / POST OFFICE BOX 2321 / SANTA FE, NM 87504-2321 /USA
(505) 988-4418 / ORDERS ONLY (800) 243-5644 / FAX (505) 988-1025

The Southwest Heritage Series is dedicated to Jody Ellis and Marcia Muth Miller, the founders of Sunstone Press, whose original purpose and vision continues to inspire and motivate our publications.

CONTENTS

THE SOUTHWEST HERITAGE SERIES / I

FOREWORD TO THIS EDITION / II

FACSIMILE OF 1935 EDITION / III

I

THE SOUTHWEST HERITAGE SERIES

The history of the United States is written in hundreds of regional histories and literary works. Those letters, essays, memoirs, biographies and even collections of fiction are often first-hand accounts by people who wanted to memorialize an event, a person or simply record for posterity the concerns and issues of the times. Many of these accounts have been lost, destroyed or overlooked. Some are in private or public collections but deemed to be in too fragile condition to permit handling by contemporary readers and researchers.

However, now with the application of twenty-first century technology, nineteenth and twentieth century material can be reprinted and made accessible to the general public. These early writings are the DNA of our history and culture and are essential to understanding the present in terms of the past.

The Southwest Heritage Series is a form of literary preservation. Heritage by definition implies legacy and these early works are our legacy from those who have gone before us. To properly present and preserve that legacy, no changes in style or contents have been made. The material reprinted stands on its own as it first appeared. The point of view is that of the author and the era in which he or she lived. We would not expect photographs of people from the past to be re-imaged with modern clothes, hair styles and backgrounds. We should not, therefore, expect their ideas and personal philosophies to reflect our modern concepts.

Remember, reading their words and sharing their thoughts is a passport back into understanding how the past was shaped and how it influenced today's world.

Our hope is that new access to these older books will provide readers with a challenging and exciting experience.

II

FOREWORD TO THIS EDITION

By Ray John de Aragón

Miguel Antonio Otero was not only an author and popular territorial governor of New Mexico from 1897-1906, he was also a major presence in the rough and tumble days of New Mexico politics and Wild West turmoil.

He once stood up against the infamous Santa Fe Ring which was a shifty group of land grabbers and speculators who were stealing Spanish and Indian land grants throughout New Mexico. Otero had inherited a ranch of nearly a million acres from his father and the Ring was trying to lay claim to a portion of it by expanding the boundaries of an old Spanish land grant they had swindled. Otero, along with an armed group of his companions, chased off the Ring's men when they tried to squat on the land. The Santa Fe County sheriff arrested Miguel Otero and threw him in the Santa Fe jail until a group of Hispanic cowboys from Las Vegas busted him out. The rapid pace of this exciting episode would be reflective of this daring governor's career. He even claimed he had broken bread with the notorious outlaw Billy the Kid.

Miguel A. Otero was born on October 17, 1859, in St. Louis, Missouri. His father, who bore the same name, and who was born in Valencia, New Mexico in 1829, had built up a stellar career in the East. He was noted variously as a college professor of Latin and Greek, an attorney for the law firm of Trusten Polk in St. Louis, as a successful merchant on the Santa Fe Trail, as a bank president, and railroad president. The elder Otero also served as a delegate to the Congress for the New Mexico Territory and was appointed Secretary of the Territory by President Abraham Lincoln.

Young Miguel Antonio Otero, Jr. was brought up in a family of wealth and influence, but he also experienced the hardships of growing up in a household that was always on the move. His family's sojourns took him from one town to another across Missouri, Kansas, Colorado, and New Mexico. At one point Miguel Antonio was left at a boarding school, the likes of which he compared to Dickens' *Oliver Twist*. Needless to say, he escaped with a couple of companions but they were turned in to the law after purchasing a train ticket to New Mexico. They were given a choice of going to jail, or returning to the boarding school. They opted for a return to the school and were severely punished. He later wrote that it would have been much better to have spent time in jail than to have been back at the school.

During Miguel A. Otero's travels and frequent stopovers in Wild Western towns he came into contact with notorious outlaws like Clay Allison and popular lawmen such as Wild Bill Hickok, Pat Garrett, Elfego Baca, and other well known figures including Doc Holliday, William F. Cody ("Buffalo Bill"), General George A. Custer, and frontiersman Christopher "Kit" Carson. In fact, Miguel Antonio was such an adventurous soul that he always sought out, or was in close contact with, anyone making headlines during the turbulent era he lived in. He even published a short lived newspaper called the *Otero Optic*, which eventually became the *Las Vegas Daily Optic*.

The family finally settled permanently in Las Vegas, New Mexico in 1879. Miguel A. Otero worked for his father's mercantile business, Otero, Sellers and Co., and he also helped his father establish the San Miguel National Bank and the first telephone company in New Mexico. Otero's father was busy paving the way for a railroad system through New Mexico while he, in turn, began an illustrious career in politics as Las Vegas City Clerk, San Miguel County probate clerk, county clerk, and recorder, and district court clerk. Then in 1892 President William McKinley appointed Miguel Antonio Otero as governor of the New Mexico territory where he served until 1906.

Miguel A. Otero rightly distinguished himself as a political leader in New Mexico where he raised a family and lived out his life as a champion of the people, but he is also highly recognized for his career as an author. He published his legendary *My Life on the Frontier, 1864-1882*, in 1935, followed by *The Real Billy the Kid: With New Light on the Lincoln County War* in 1936, *My Life on the Frontier, 1882-1897* in 1939, and *My Nine Years as Governor of the Territory of New Mexico, 1897-1906* in 1940.

These books are filled with the raw power and intrigue of the Wild West written by one who lived it. One would expect no less from such a vibrant personality who filled the pages of his monumental history with the passionate memories of an exciting era.

III

FACSIMILE OF 1935 EDITION

My Life on the Frontier
1864-1882

MIGUEL ANTONIO OTERO

My Life on the Frontier
1864-1882

*Incidents and Characters of the Period
when Kansas, Colorado, and New
Mexico were passing through
the last of their Wild and
Romantic Years*

BY
MIGUEL ANTONIO OTERO
*Former Governor of
New Mexico*

ILLUSTRATED
BY
WILL SHUSTER

1935
The Press of the Pioneers
Incorporated
New York

Copyright, 1935, by
The Press of the Pioneers, Inc.

DESIGNED BY LEWIS C. GANDY
PRINTED IN THE UNITED STATES OF AMERICA

Dedicated
to
Miguel A. Otero, Jr.
My Son
With Love and Affection

Contents

	PAGE
Chapter I	1
Chapter II	11
Chapter III	25
Chapter IV	35
Chapter V	47
Chapter VI	57
Chapter VII	66
Chapter VIII	78
Chapter IX	91
Chapter X	103
Chapter XI	116
Chapter XII	128
Chapter XIII	141
Chapter XIV	157
Chapter XV	164
Chapter XVI	176
Chapter XVII	187
Chapter XVIII	200
Chapter XIX	210
Chapter XX	219
Chapter XXI	234
Chapter XXII	243
Chapter XXIII	268
Index	289

List of Illustrations

Miguel Antonio Otero.	*Frontispiece*
	FACING PAGE
"*Don't shoot him in the back; he is drunk.*"	20
We boys would dress quickly and run to the bridge and look up to see if we knew any of them.	28
Indian attack on a covered wagon train.	36
The old bull buffalo charged the ambulance.	68
Duke brings Kiowa home.	84
Otero, Sellar & Co. at El Moro, Colorado.	100
Clay Allison.	116
The duel in the grave.	124
Steamboat landed on her ample frontage, high and dry and squarely on top of the wriggling heap of men and women.	132
Uncle Dick Wooten.	148
"*The Court takes positive delight in sentencing you to death.*"	164
George Howe as General Washington — a Christmas prank at Las Vegas, New Mexico, in the early days.	180
Jimmy Morehead shot by a waiter — for ordering eggs.	196
Doc Holliday shoots it out with Charlie White in Las Vegas, New Mexico.	212
Miguel Antonio Otero (1), the author's father.	276

My Life on the Frontier
1864-1882

My Life on the Frontier
1864-1882

Chapter I

AS the railway lines pushed their way westward through Kansas, I migrated from one rough and sporadic terminal town to another, scraping acquaintance with Westport Landing, Leavenworth, Ellsworth, Hays City, Sheridan and Fort Wallace in quick succession during my boyhood. In like manner, I followed the Kansas-Pacific Railroad into Colorado and sojourned in Kit Carson for over three years. Then when the Atchison, Topeka & Santa Fé Railroad began to build west from Topeka to Granada, Colo., at the crossing of the Arkansas River, I transferred my nomadizing to that line, first locating at Granada in the fall of 1873, then at West Las Animas, La Junta, El Moro and Trinidad, and when it eventually continued its lines into New Mexico, I left El Moro and Trinidad and became part of Otero and Las Vegas. Naturally, I saw much of the last phase of frontier life in America.

My father, Don Miguel Antonio Otero I had declined a renomination as New Mexico delegate to the United States Congress because of a determination to retire from politics. He had also refused the appointment as Minister to Spain which President Lincoln tendered him at the close of the 36th Congress. It was my father's strong conviction that he should devote his time and energies entirely to the business partnership he had previously formed with David Whiting. The firm of Whiting & Otero was engaged in the multiform and very profitable activities of banking, outfitting, wholesaling and retailing, which were, in the old days, included under the designation "Wholesale and Retail Grocers, Forwarding and Commission Merchants." Westport Landing on the Missouri River was the first location of the firm.

It was my father's intention to take his family at once to Westport Landing, but circumstances necessitated his postponing this move for over a year. Though my father did not feel that he could give further time to politics, his public spirit would not permit him to turn a deaf ear to any appeal for his services coming from his native home, New Mexico. The illness of Governor Henry Connolly had resulted in many serious complications in the Territory, and there was great need for a strong and experienced hand to take the helm. Judge John S. Watts, a Republican, who had succeeded my father in Congress as territorial delegate, urged President Lincoln to appoint my father, a Democrat, Secretary of the Territory. This appointment carried with it the office of Acting Governor. When the post was offered my father, he felt that he could not refuse. This delayed his going to Westport Landing until the summer of 1862.

At the time, our family consisted of my father, my mother, my older brother Page and myself. On first going to Westport Landing, we took rooms in the old Gillis House on the levee, facing the Missouri River, but during the summer of 1863 we moved to a small brick residence some distance from the river on the old wagon road leading to Lawrence, Kans.

Since this was during the Civil War, conditions were anything but pleasant on the border line separating Missouri from Kansas. My mother came from one of the most prominent Southern families, and had grown to womanhood in Charleston, S. C. Her pro-Southernism underwent many trials while we were living in the vicinity of Lawrence, one of which I shall relate:

My father had gone to the office, leaving my mother

at home with just my brother and myself and the servants. At noon a troop of Federal cavalry drew up in front of our home and decided to pitch camp. Immediately, they hitched their horses to our picket fence. This was too much for my mother. Hurriedly putting on her white linen sun-bonnet, she rushed into the yard and unhitched every horse tied to the fence.

Some of the officers and a few of the soldiers came up and objected in unbecoming language. But my mother stood her ground, declaring aggressively:

"I want you to understand that no Yankee soldiers can hitch their horses to any fence of mine."

Her manner and her words were effective, for the soldiers forthwith took their horses to a clump of trees some distance down the road.

Our next move was to Leavenworth, Kans. In 1864 it seemed as though Leavenworth, on the west bank of the Missouri River, was destined to become the metropolis of the region, rather than Kansas City.

It was also a current belief that Leavenworth would obtain the deciding advantage when the proposed railroad bridge was built across the Missouri River. Everyone seemed to concede this bridge to Leavenworth.

So secure were the large business interests in Leavenworth in their feeling that they had landed the bridge that they relaxed their vigilance. But not so with the business men of Kansas City. With a determination little short of desperation, they continued to campaign for the coveted prize, and at last their efforts were rewarded: they secured the bridge. This settled the question of which city was to predominate. Kansas City moved ahead into its present greatness, while Leavenworth sank farther and farther back.

But in 1864 everything seemed favorable to Leavenworth and people flocked thither from all directions. My father yielded to the lure of Leavenworth, and in that year associated himself with the firm of C. R. Morehead & Co., which had been in business in Leavenworth for several years.

One of the strongest recollections I have of Leavenworth is the large number of Union soldiers, both infantry and cavalry, I saw there, largely due to the fact that Fort Leavenworth was only a few miles north of the city. They literally seemed to fill the streets of the city and the entire country thereabouts. No doubt their presence was necessary, for the animosity between the anti-slavery and the pro-slavery factions in eastern Kansas was still red hot. As I look back to those early days, it occurs to me that much of the hatred and bitter feeling might have been avoided had those in authority on the border between Kansas and Missouri used cooler judgment and more temperate means.

It certainly was a stupid policy on the part of the commanding officer at Fort Leavenworth to place, as he sometimes did, negro officers with the rank of lieutenant, captain, or even major, in command over Southern sympathizers who might have been arrested for merely expressing an opinion. I recall one such officer in particular, a Major Douglas, who was not only arrogant but insulting both in his demeanor and language. Such appointments as those were unfortunate and probably unnecessary, and only served to inflame the pro-slavery people. They also became the direct cause of many of the killings that marked those years.

Shortly after our arrival at Leavenworth, we had an experience with the military authorities at our home. One day six soldiers called and inquired for my father. My mother went to the door, and at the sight of the soldiers naturally concluded that some embarrassment, or possibly harm, was in store for my father. So she replied to their inquiry: "Mr. Otero is not at home."

The soldiers were about to accept her statement and take their leave, when I, thinking that my mother did not really know the truth of the matter, ran to her side and blurted out:

"Why, yes, Mama! Papa is upstairs."

Hardly had I let the cat out of the bag than my father, who had been standing in the hall upstairs, came quickly to the door and submitted himself to the soldiers, who took him to headquarters to answer a summons they had for him.

What had happened was that some of my father's political enemies in New Mexico had preferred certain charges against him to the military authorities at Leavenworth. Fortunately, my father had with him in his pocket the findings of the Santa Fé Military Court, as well as a personal letter from General Canby, which completely exonerated him. No sooner had the commanding officer at the fort examined these than he apologized for the arrest, and smilingly remarked:

"Mr. Otero, you are all right. You may return to your home without an escort."

In the fall of 1866 my brother and I were sent away to boarding-school in Topeka, Kans.

As we drove up Topeka's Main Street, we saw what was more or less typical of all main streets in the new towns of the West: there were a row of nondescript business houses of all kinds facing south on open country ... the church and schoolhouse were small stone buildings, with gable roofs of wood shingles, standing side by side in a fenced enclosure a short distance west of the business center ... on a little farther were a few scattered dwellings.

The school proved to be a detestable place and its horrors are still fresh in my memory, though nearly seventy years have passed since then. I can only compare my experiences at this frontier boarding school with those of which Dickens relates in *Oliver Twist*. The discipline was harsh and brutal; in fact, I do not think I would be overstating if I said that we were at all times treated more like vicious dogs than human beings — and much worse than prisoners in jail.

The letters from our parents were opened and read before

we even saw them; those we wrote home were inspected before being sealed, and we were always forced to write that we were happy and contented — a downright lie. Boxes sent us from home containing turkey, chicken, ham, pie, cake, candy and the like, were actually opened and devoured by the faculty, and if any part of the contents of the box reached the boy for whom it was intended, it was received in such condition as to remind him of the passage in the Bible about the crumbs that fell from the table.

Our reaction to such treatment was the age-old one of the boarding-school boy: we decided to run away. I suppose that something particularly harsh had made us more desperate than usual; at any rate my brother Page and a boy named Edward Thomas took the lead in fomenting a conspiracy to take French leave. After some discussion, eight of us pledged ourselves to make the break together. The most opportune time, we decided, was just after our miserable supper immediately before we were called to the church for our evening prayers. At an agreed-upon signal from our leader — a low whistle — we would gather at the outside corner of the schoolhouse.

Everything worked as we had planned, and on a certain evening all eight of us slipped away from the school premises and headed for the toll-bridge, our only outlet to the railroad which we intended to board to get back to our homes. But little did we count on the counter check that awaited us at the bridge. Boldly enough we walked up to the pay window of the toll-keeper's house and deposited enough money to pay the toll. But it turned out that the bridge-keeper was something more than a mere gatherer of fees. He was also a deputy constable, and in this capacity he had assumed the responsibility of catching, holding and delivering back to the school authorities any boys attempting to run away from that institution.

He did not need to be told that here was an occasion demanding his assumption of the rôle of deputy constable. So, showing his star of authority, he announced that the whole party was under arrest and headed straight for the calaboose. Of course, we were all frightened to a light green tint for "arrest" and "calaboose" were fearsome words to our young ears.

To our great relief, the bridge man offered to compromise. He assured us that he would not take us to the calaboose if we all agreed to accompany him back to the school. We lost no time in accepting his proposal, but no doubt we would have fared better had we selected the calaboose. We were all most brutally flogged by a big, long-legged, raw-boned Irishman who was studying for the priesthood. He certainly wielded a cat-o'-nine-tails without mercy on the backs, legs and arms of all eight of us, and for days afterward every letter of the alphabet could be traced in bloody marks left by the leather thongs.

But eventually release came. While on a trip back to Leavenworth from the frontier, my father quite unexpectedly stopped over in Topeka to see how my brother and I were getting on at school. It was late in December, close to Christmas, and my brother and I managed to prevail on my father to take us along with him to Leavenworth. We had great difficulty in setting our plight before him, because the president of the school made sure to be present most of the time we were talking with our father. The president was continually interjecting remarks about what "dear children" we were and how much they all "loved" us.

But finally from our hints and winks, our father suspected all was not as roseate as the good father indicated, and to our great joy announced his desire to take us with him to Leavenworth for at least until after Christmas. We were not long in getting packed. The news of our leaving spread rapidly through the school, and the other boys from Leavenworth made us promise them that when we got home we would tell their parents just how they were being maltreated.

This promise we faithfully kept, and no sooner had the other parents heard of the woes and miseries their sons were undergoing than they sent word for them to come home. When they heard from their own sons corroboration of all that we had related, they held an indignation meeting. Some of the fathers seriously discussed going to Topeka in a body and seeking some kind of revenge, but the mothers prevailed upon them to content themselves with writing red-hot letters of denunciation.

After this experience with boarding-schools, my brother and I were sent to a private school in Leavenworth run by a Mrs. Clarke. It proved to be a most excellent school, and two of the teachers, Miss Arnold and Miss Egglestin, endeared themselves everlastingly to all of us by their kindness and consideration. We went to this school during two winters, but in the summer vacation of 1867 we were allowed to go out to Ellsworth, Kans., where my father then conducted his commission-house business. This was my introduction to the rough life of the frontier towns.

While my father and our family were in Leavenworth there sprang up a warm friendship with John Perry Sellar, bookkeeper for C. R. Morehead & Co. Finally, Mr. Sellar and my father decided to embark in the commission business for themselves and formed a co-partnership. They began business in 1867 at Fort Harker, Kans., that point being the terminus of the Kansas-Pacific Railroad.

I did not have any experience with the rough life that must have characterized Fort Harker, for during the time my father's business was located there I was attending school at Leavenworth.

Wild game, such as prairie-chickens, bob-white quail, wild pigeons, plover, wild ducks, geese, brant, jack-snipes, rabbits and red squirrels, were very abundant around Leavenworth, and my father, being very fond of hunting, would frequently return with a bag full of game. On those occasions a game dinner was in order, and all the hunters and their wives were present to enjoy the meal, which included good wine and cigars.

The summer of 1867 was spent at Ellsworth, Kans., located a little west of Fort Harker on the line of the Kansas-Pacific Railroad, and was, as I knew it at that time, a "tough little hole." It was almost wholly a town of tents and small, rough, frame buildings, but it was as busy a place as could be imagined. There were at least a hundred business houses in the town, many of them conducting their business in tents. All business appeared to be transacted on a high-pressure scale.

Unquestionably, too, Ellsworth was a lively town. It seemed as if nearly every other house in the town was a drinking place, while gambling rooms and dance halls and other questionable resorts were most common. Shooting scrapes were every-day occurrences, and the nights were frequently made hideous by drunken men firing off pistols promiscuously and shouting like bands of wild Comanches.

Of course I had seen many buffalo and antelope before reaching Ellsworth, but when I arrived there the country was fairly swarming with these animals: you could see them in all directions at no great distance from town, but it was entirely too great a risk to go out very far, as the Indians kept a close watch on all the whites.

One feature of Ellsworth that lingers in my memory is the great danger from savage Indians. They skulked about the settlement practically all the time, and frequently killed and scalped herders who went out only a mile or so to hunt buffalo or antelope. I have often seen these hunters coming back in a cloud of dust, with Indians pursuing them hotly almost into the very town.

Nearly every day the construction gangs laying the railroad toward Denver were attacked by Indians. The Indians were clever enough in these attacks to circle around the construction gang, for they knew that these men worked under the protection of either a squad of United States soldiers or guards hired by the railroad company. Though none too keen on taking chances, the Indians were able constantly to harass those laying the track, and occasionally would venture close enough to kill a man or two.

Generally, the railroad workmen kept at their work and paid no attention to the Indians. Sometimes the guards would chase a band of redskins, and, if their horses happened to be faster, would overtake a few stragglers among the Indians and kill them. But when all is said, it must be admitted that a member of a railroad construction gang in those days was engaged in what might properly be called a hazardous occupation.

Ellsworth did not long remain the headquarters of the railroad builders. Construction work went forward rapidly, and by the fall of 1867 the track had reached Hays City, Kans., and a new terminal town appeared on the map. It did not take long to build the new town, for the carpenters and mechanics worked day and night. The large forwarding and commission houses of Otero & Sellar and their rivals, W. H. Chick & Co., were soon open and ready for business. The moves from place to place had come in quick succession: first Fort Harker, then Ellsworth, and now Hays City. But everyone felt that Hays City would prove a more permanent abiding place, and settled down for a somewhat prolonged stay, as no move was contemplated until the railroad reached its next objective, Sheridan, Kans., which was scheduled for the following year, 1869.

Chapter II

HAYS CITY was, without doubt, a wild and woolly town from start to finish. Main Street was almost a solid row of saloons, dance halls, restaurants, barber shops and houses of prostitution kept by such notorious characters as "Calamity Jane," "Lousy Liz," "Stink-foot Mag," and "Steamboat."

Hundreds of freighting outfits had come to Hays City with the arrival of the railroad, and soon the surrounding country looked like a large tent city, except that covered wagons took the place of tents.

It was an impressive sight to see a thousand or more covered wagons camped around Hays City at the same time, all waiting to be loaded with freight for western Kansas, Colorado, New Mexico, Arizona and Mexico. At night the hundreds of blazing campfires made the scene look like a large illuminated city. Early in the evening, and frequently far into the night, we could hear the music of accordions, guitars, banjos and harmonicas, interspersed with songs — some sentimental, some boisterous.

On the whole, it was a collection of humanity seemingly happy, even in the face of danger. Money was plentiful; it came easy and went easy. The saloons, dance halls and gambling rooms all did a thriving business. They never closed. It was a unique phase of life, this, of such terminal towns as Hays City, and its like will never be seen again.

During those busy days, firms doing business under the general designation of "Wholesale and Retail Grocers, Forwarding and Commission Merchants," remained open both day and night. This was necessary, since it usually took all day to load a large outfit, and after that there were many odds and ends that had to be attended to. The wagon-boss had to buy all his provisions for the trip, see that his wagons and animals were in good condition, sign the bills of lading for each wagon, obtain an advance of the money needed for incidental expenses on the trip, and give drafts on the merchants owning the goods. All this had to be done in time for the train of wagons to start at daybreak. To attend to these necessary details, the commission houses utilized two full sets of bookkeepers, salesmen, clerks and porters, one set working all day and the other all night.

Shortly after our arrival in Hays City, my father met his old New Mexico friend, Adolph Mennet, who was in company with two Frenchmen, John Lawrence ("French John") and John Villepigue. All three were living in a small log cabin a short distance from town and had a few milch cows. They were soldiers of fortune, having just escaped from Mexico, where they had been engaged in fighting under the banner of the Emperor Maximilian. My father hired all three of them, and they became employees of the commission house.

Buffalo hunters had not yet begun to make Hays City their rendezvous. Because of the Indians, that means of livelihood was much too dangerous to be comfortable. But a few hunters, more venturesome than the others, took the risk, since there was good money in hides. I have seen thousands of dead buffalo on the plains, killed solely for their hides, the carcasses left to rot or become food for the grey wolves, coyotes, badgers or ravens. The freighters were always well supplied with buffalo meat, and all the camps had much the appearance of a New England wash day with the fresh buffalo meat hanging on stretched ropes to dry so as to be available as jerked meat for the homeward journey.

Frequently, while living at Hays City, I saw large herds of buffalo come within a half-mile of the town. On such occasions every man owning a horse would ride out to kill some buffalo cows, yearlings or calves. This was called, in the argot of the time, a "run," which was certainly a descriptive expression, for it was a pell-mell dash of scores of men mounted on horses. When a hunter brought down a buffalo he did not stop to claim his animal but, dropping by its side his glove or his hat or some other article to attest his ownership, he rode on after others. Of course after such a hunt every home in town would be abundantly supplied with buffalo meat — saddles, quarters, whole calf, half a yearling, humps, tongues, to say nothing of hides to be tanned and made into overcoats or robes.

With such a conglomeration of humanity, it was no wonder that almost every morning there would be an announcement: "Another man for breakfast last night." It soon became necessary to act in the interest of law and order and to act vigorously. The best citizens of the town held a meeting in a store located at the eastern corner of Main Street. The summons that went out to the better class of citizens was mandatory and forcibly worded, the notice winding up with these three words: "No excuse taken."

When the meeting had been called to order, a leader was promptly chosen, and a binding oath administered to him by the oldest man in the room. The leader promptly took the chair and made a cool and emphatic statement of the necessity for immediate action. He then asked everyone present to stand up and raise his right hand. Then he administered to all the same oath he had taken. In this fashion the Vigilance Committee of Hays City was organized.

For a while the Vigilance Committee was very active in regulating the toughest characters the frontier ever saw together at one time, and did its work well. The first task undertaken by the committee was to serve notice on the undesirables then in town, giving them so many hours in which to leave. Anyone served who failed to comply was promptly hanged. It did not take the tough element long to realize that the Vigilance Committee of Hays City meant business, and after the first few lessons in law and order the number of hangings for the good of the community became greatly reduced. Nevertheless, it was not long before Hays City boasted a good-sized graveyard, not a single grave in which was occupied by anyone who had died a natural death.

The Vigilance Committee showed discretion and sound judgment in securing as town marshal the famous "Wild Bill" Hickok. He had his hands full in keeping order in the ranks of that motley and unruly horde of humanity, but he was equal to the task and proved himself one of the most efficient peace officers the West has ever known.

It was in the year 1868 that I first met Wild Bill, and during my stay in Hays City I often came into contact with him. He dropped into the office of Otero & Sellar very frequently to talk to my father, who was a member of the Vigilance Committee. I took a great fancy to him and greatly enjoyed his company. At that time both my brother Page and myself had a stable with several fine saddle horses. No better horses could be found on the frontier, for they were trained buffalo hunters and seemed to enjoy the sport as much as the rider. You could fire off a gun between their ears without bothering them in the least. Wild Bill was very fond of good horses, and he was always welcome to any we had. Thus we became very good friends. He often took my brother and myself on buffalo hunts.

Wild Bill was one of the most perfect specimens of manhood I have ever seen. He was tall — about six feet two — and his bearing was always erect and confident, though in no wise haughty or severe. His features were regular, clean-cut and expressive. His voice was low, yet firm, and carried with it a suggestion of indomitable will power. He was strong, vigorous, agile; yet he was as gentle as a child except when in a fight, and even then he was calm and bold, without a sign of nervousness. He never became excited, always remaining as cool and deliberate as a judge passing sentence.

Beyond a shadow of doubt he was the most fearless, and

perhaps the most dangerous, man in an encounter on the frontier, but never in any instance is it recorded that he started a quarrel. There was only one Wild Bill.

He was without a peer in the use of the rifle and the six-shooter. So quick was he on the draw and so perfect was his aim that almost every time he shot it meant death to his adversary.

Previous to my acquaintance with Wild Bill, he had engaged in two of his most famous fights — that with the McCandles crowd, in which he earned his nickname "Wild Bill," and that with the noted gunman, Dave Tutt, in which in fair fight Wild Bill killed his man at the first shot. He had also been one of Buffalo Bill's scouts in the campaign against Black Kettle, in which the latter was killed.

While I knew him in Hays City, he added to his record the killing of three men in single combat. The first was a man named Sam Strawhorn, a killer of note, who came to Hays City for the sole purpose of adding Wild Bill to his list of victims. He had but recently engaged in a fight with a peace officer at Ellsworth, Kans., and would have triumphed had it not been for Wild Bill, who assisted in subduing him. Wild Bill was playing cards in one of the saloons, having been appointed town marshal only a few days before. Strawhorn, having heard of the appointment and still smarting from what he termed interference on Wild Bill's part, was headed for revenge, determined to catch his intended victim off guard and kill him. Wild Bill had been notified about Strawhorn's numerous threats to shoot him on sight, and naturally was keeping a sharp look-out. On this particular occasion, Strawhorn entered the saloon and walked carelessly toward the bar. On getting within a few feet of Wild Bill he attempted to draw his gun, but Wild Bill was too quick for him and, before he could raise his gun, he dropped dead with a bullet through his brain. Strawhorn was notoriously bad and had already been marked by the Vigilance

Committee. Wild Bill was complimented by all the best element in Hays City for getting rid of Strawhorn.

I was an eye-witness to Wild Bill's encounter with Bill Mulvey, and shall relate the details as they linger in my mind:

I was standing near Wild Bill on Main Street, when someone began "shooting up the town" at the eastern end of the street. It was Bill Mulvey, a notorious murderer from Missouri, known as a handy man with a gun. He had just enough red liquor in him to be mean and he seemed to derive great amusement from shooting holes into the mirrors, as well as the bottles of liquor behind the bars, of the saloons in that section of the street. As was usually the case with such fellows, he was looking for trouble, and when someone told him that Wild Bill was the town marshal and therefore it behooved him to behave himself, Mulvey swore that he would find Wild Bill and shoot him on sight. He further averred that the marshal was the very man he was looking for and that he had come to the "damn' town" for the express purpose of killing him.

The tenor of these remarks was somehow made known to Wild Bill. But hardly had the news reached him than Mulvey appeared on the scene, tearing toward us on his iron-grey horse, rifle in hand, full cocked. When Wild Bill saw Mulvey he walked out to meet him, apparently waving his hand to some fellows behind Mulvey and calling to them: "Don't shoot him in the back; he is drunk."

Mulvey stopped his horse and, wheeling the animal about, drew a bead on his rifle in the direction of the imaginary man he thought Wild Bill was addressing. But before he realized the ruse that had been played upon him, Wild Bill had aimed his six-shooter and fired — just once. Mulvey dropped from his horse — dead, the bullet having penetrated his temple and then passed through his head.

During this episode I had been standing about twenty-five feet from Wild Bill. My joy in the outcome was boundless, for I had been afraid that Mulvey, with his rifle trained directly on Wild Bill, would pull the trigger.

The third killing was that of a man named Bill Thompson, with whom Wild Bill had had some difficulty of slight importance. Thompson was not a bad man or tough citizen. He was regarded as cowardly; consequently Wild Bill paid but slight heed to him. One day Wild Bill entered a restaurant and, while giving his order to the waiter, was surprised to see the waiter jump back. Hastily taking cognizance of the situation, he saw Thompson not more than five paces away with a pistol pointed at him. He quickly slipped from his chair to the floor, the bullet passing harmlessly through the space where his head had been a second before. Wild Bill had drawn his pistol as he slipped from the chair, and before Thompson could take a second shot Wild Bill's pistol rang out and Thompson dropped to the floor with a bullet through his brain.

My direct acquaintance with Wild Bill was not of long duration, for in 1870 he joined Buffalo Bill's Wild West Shows and left the country. He soon grew tired of the show life and went back to Abilene, Kans., becoming town marshal for another very lawless place. Finally he drifted north and spent the latter part of his life in Deadwood, So. Dak., where he later met his death at the hands of a cowardly assassin on August 2nd, 1876, at the comparatively early age of thirty-nine.

I have a friend living in Santa Fé, Frank M. Jones, who was at Deadwood when Wild Bill was murdered. From him I have gathered a first-hand account of that regrettable affair, which runs as follows:

"Wild Bill and myself were the very best of friends and frequently played cards together. Almost every night — frequently it was early morning — we would walk home together, since we roomed just across the street from each other.

"The night before the killing Wild Bill had been playing a game of casino with Jack McCall and had won all of McCall's money and gold dust, amounting to something less than two hundred dollars. In weighing the gold dust, it was found that McCall was short some eighteen dollars and Hickok asked him if that was all he had. McCall answered 'Yes,' and started for the front door of the saloon. Bill called him back and gave him some money, remarking in a joking manner:

" 'Jack, you may need some money to provide for your lodging and breakfast, and I'll stake you.'

"McCall took the money, and they parted, apparently the best of friends.

"The following afternoon — I should say about two o'clock — Wild Bill and a few friends were playing poker. McCall entered the saloon. He was facing Bill, whom he greeted pleasantly as he passed. McCall made his way to the rear of the barroom. He at once turned and walked back toward the table where Bill was sitting. He came up directly behind Wild Bill's back while the latter was in the act of dealing the cards, quickly placed the muzzle of his pistol at the back of Bill's head — and fired, killing him instantly! At the same time he said:

" 'Damn you; take that.'

"The saloon in which this occurred belonged to Carl Mann, Jerry Lewis and Billy Nuttall, and was known as the 'No. 10 Saloon.'

"It was a well-known fact that Wild Bill had many enemies among the outlaws and bad men and was a marked man. They had even gone so far as to offer rewards for Bill's head, which would be paid to any man or group of men who would take the chance of catching Wild Bill off his guard. The probable explanation of McCall's cowardly act is that he was desirous of getting some of this money.

"He may have been specially instigated by some individual. Only a short time before, Wild Bill had incurred the enmity of a notorious gambler named Varnes. During a game of poker in which Bill, Varnes and Tim Healy participated, a dispute arose between Varnes and Healy. Varnes grabbed the pot, at the same time drawing his pistol, as Healy tried to interfere with him. Varnes had not counted on Wild Bill's interfering, since he knew that Healy and Bill were not on friendly terms.

"But he reckoned without his host, for Bill was always on the side of fair play and honest treatment, even in a game of cards. So his gun was out in a second, and, covering Varnes with it, he said:

" 'You can't get away with any such stuff in any game I'm playing in. Healy won that pot fairly, and I'll see he gets it.'

"Varnes sullenly put up his gun and Healy took the pot.

"This friendly act served to square all past differences between Bill and Healy; Varnes, however, became his mortal enemy. When McCall was tried and convicted, he admitted that Varnes had paid him a large sum of money for killing Wild Bill, and that the conspiracy between them had been arranged the very day of the killing. After this testimony had been given, Varnes left the country and was never heard of again.

"McCall, it is true, plead in his own defense at the Deadwood Miners' Court that acquitted him that Wild Bill had killed his brother near Fort Hays and that he had come to Deadwood for the sole purpose of revenge. He also claimed that he had been awaiting an opportunity and had finally killed him in the manner described, because he could not afford to take any chances with such a well-known man-killer as Wild Bill. It was discovered later that this was a fictitious story. Shortly after the trial, McCall was arrested on a warrant from the United States District Court and taken to Yankton, where he was tried before a jury, convicted of murder in the first degree, and hanged."

Mr. Jones describes Wild Bill as follows: "He was a handsome fellow, tall and well-built, about one hundred and eighty-five pounds in weight and about six feet tall, with wavy dark-brown hair and blue eyes. He was extremely quiet and seldom spoke of himself unless pressed by a friend to do so; he never cared to refer to his past life or to any of his many killings. Bill took an occasional drink, but he was not what you might call a drinking man, and I never saw him under the influence of liquor.

"Once in conversation about General George A. Custer he told me of his taking up a piece of land which was open to settlement, just outside a United States Military Reservation and putting up a building for a saloon, where the soldiers might spend their money on pay-day. A few days after he had started his business he was ordered by the commanding officer to close up and move away, because it was claimed he was on Government land belonging to the Reservation. This Wild Bill denied, and consequently refused to obey the command, claiming that the land belonged to him. A small detachment of soldiers, led by Custer, who at that time was a line officer, appeared on the scene with orders to eject Wild Bill from the premises. In the fight that followed, three of the soldiers were killed.

"Wild Bill was arrested by the military authorities, tried for and convicted of murder, and ordered shot; but his case was taken to the civil court, where he was promptly acquitted, a survey having been made in which it was ascertained that the land was off the Reservation. Since the land belonged to him, the jury felt that he had a perfect right to defend his own property. In relating this incident, Wild Bill used to say that he might have killed Custer at the time, but he deliberately kept from firing at him because he liked him and regarded him as a fine soldier."

Hays City was not free from the threat of Indian attacks, although it does not seem to me that we lived in such con-

"Don't shoot him in the back; he is drunk."

stant dread as at Ellsworth, owing largely to the fact that Fort Hays was so near.

Between the town and Fort Hays ran a beautiful stream, known as Big Creek, which was not only a favorite place for swimming and bathing, but also a popular camping ground for the freighters. The large trees growing on both banks of Big Creek yielded a density of shade that reminded one of the tropics.

On one occasion a large horse-and-mule outfit arrived from New Mexico and established camp in the vicinity of the creek. The men had barely unharnessed the tired animals and started them down to the creek for water, when a band of wild Indians dashed out of the thicket and, in plain sight of the people of the town and the soldiers at the fort, shot and killed the herders. Then by shaking tin cans and dried buffalo-skin rattles, they caused a big stampede among the 800-odd frightened animals. The leader of the Indians caught the bell mare and rushed across the creek, the entire herd following while a group of Indians forced them from the rear. In a few minutes all that could be seen of the herd was a cloud of dust. Hundreds of citizens from the town, as well as a detachment of cavalry from the fort, went in pursuit, but they never recovered the animals. Otero & Sellar had to telegraph for several cars of Missouri mules to replace those the Indians had stolen.

No account of Hays City would be complete without some mention of "Calamity Jane," one of the frontier's most notorious characters. She dressed in a buckskin suit like a man, and was regarded by the community as a camp follower, since she preferred to ply her well-known profession among the soldiers rather than among the teamsters, freighters, herders and the hunters. Calamity Jane's accomplishments as a "wild woman" were numerous: she could drink whiskey, smoke, chew tobacco and swear better than the proverbial drunken sailor.

When I used to see her about Hays City in 1868, she was a comparatively young woman, perhaps twenty years of age or thereabouts, and still extremely good-looking. She was a fearless and excellent horsewoman, and a good shot with either rifle or pistol. Money seemed to mean little to her; she spent it recklessly in saloons or at the gambling table.

After a few years she left Hays City and moved from terminal town to terminal town along the advancing Kansas-Pacific Railroad, until she eventually reached Kit Carson. Then she drifted successively to Dodge City, Granada, and La Junta, towns along the Atchison, Topeka & Santa Fé Railroad. Early in 1876 she departed from La Junta for parts farther north. All the time she kept up her connection with the dance halls and continued in her old occupation. As she grew older, she developed into a rather bright woman.

There was one redeeming feature to those unfortunate women of the frontier: that was their charity. They were entirely unlike their male associates, the bad men of the frontier who were constantly wearing a chip on their shoulders and looking for a quarrel. These women in almost every instance took the part of the weak and would spend their last dollar to aid anyone in distress. Calamity Jane was no exception to the rule.

The class to which she belonged was numerous enough in the terminal towns. The majority of such women seemed to have had some sad experience back home, and this perhaps explains why they never used their family names. As a rule, they placed little value upon money and allowed their male companions to use all of their earnings in any way they pleased. When these courtesans grew old, or when their faces and bodies began to show the effects of a hard life of licentiousness and dissipation — many were old at thirty-five — they would be placed in the discard, with the immediate prospect of filling a drunkard's grave. Sometimes they chose to end it all without more ado by the morphine or strychnine route. In those days strychnine and other poisons were sold openly by the bottle and might be purchased in any store and by any person with the price, for they were largely used by hunters for killing grey wolves, coyotes, badgers, wildcats, skunks and other animals whose skins were in great demand.

So it was no common thing to hear of the death of some unfortunate woman, driven by force of circumstances into a life of degradation, ending her unhappy existence by first stupefying her mind with large quantities of poor whiskey, and then topping it off with a dose of poison sufficient to kill fifty grey wolves. In almost every instance these unfortunates would take the whole bottle of poison, their intention being to make the job certain.

This seems an appropriate point at which to give some account of that wholesale trafficking in female human flesh, which during those frontier days was more horrible than the atrocities committed by the wildest Indians. In order to keep the dance halls filled with girls, the owners would stake some woman to go back East and bring in a fresh lot of girls. They would be induced to come West under the pretext that they could obtain work in some hotel or private family at much better wages than they were receiving in their home towns. But when they reached their destination, they would find themselves forced to accept a life of debauchery, or be thrown into the street in a strange town, there to starve to death among the riff-raff.

It was no uncommon sight to see a group of gamblers, dance-hall owners, bad men and pimps gathered at the depot to meet the train on which their victims, a cargo of fresh young girls, were coming to their inevitable ruin. They gathered on such occasions chiefly for the purpose of being on the ground and seeing with their own eyes whether their orders had been properly filled. In order to expedite delivery, assignments were generally made right on the depot platform by the smiling procuress who had conducted the party — much as a horseman would pick his horses or mules at a country fair. It was never long before the entire cargo had been initiated into the necessary accomplishments of the trade, drinking, smoking, snuff-dipping, as well as the art of roping in the improvident sucker.

Chapter III

DURING the year 1869, the firms of Otero & Sellar and W. H. Chick & Co. pulled up stakes at Hays City and moved their large warehouses to Sheridan, Kans. The freighting outfits from the West and Southwest were gathering at the new shipping point, inasmuch as it had become the temporary terminus of the Kansas-Pacific Railroad, which was making rapid strides toward Denver. Hays City was thus shorn of its glory and Sheridan came into its heyday.

When the warehouses were all ready to receive the goods which were to be brought in by the railroad, my father and his partner decided to move their families from Leavenworth. So two comfortable homes were built side by side, within a very short distance of the warehouses, and thither came the women and children of the two families.

In many ways Sheridan was like Hays City. It had much the same Main Street, much the same saloons and dance halls. The varied and manifold business activities of these concerns kept plenty of money in circulation, an atmosphere most congenial to the gambling tables, saloons, dance halls and houses of prostitution. So Sheridan fell heir to all that conglomerate and notorious gang that was drifting westward with the railroad from Ellsworth, Hays City, Abilene and other points farther east and southeast.

Sheridan seemed to have been founded for the evident purpose of outdoing Hays City in every rough-and-ready game known on the frontier, and although not as famous as the earlier town, its sins were far blacker. Sheridan seemed unable to command the services of a town marshal who could in any wise compete with Wild Bill Hickok in slamming down the lid on the lawless. In consequence, any attempt at law and order was made through the activities of the Vigilance Committee, which was organized much after the manner of that at Hays City.

Its efforts bore fruit; many times early in the morning I looked down at the trestlework bridge, a short distance east of the freight depot, and saw men hanging from the crossties. Gruesome though the sight was, the boys of the town would dress quickly and run to the bridge and look up to see if they knew any of the unlucky victims.

One particular night I recall very vividly. . . . During the earlier part of the evening there had been a shooting scrape in which a tin-horn gambler named Dick Gage had shot a young fellow in the arm over a gambling dispute. This gambler had on several occasions been cautioned by the Vigilance Committee to behave himself, and the committee had even gone so far as to notify him that they would order him to leave town if he did not mend his ways. Immediately after the shooting, he was arrested and brought before the committee, which assembled in the back room of a well-known business house. The trial began with the rope in full view on the table and the accused badly frightened. But at that moment an unforeseen occurrence changed the whole situation. . . .

It seems that after the young man had had his arm dressed and placed in a sling, he had secured a pistol and had at once started out to find the gambler who had shot him. He at last found him in the custody of the Vigilance Committee, and it so happened that at the moment he entered the room, the Committee was just at the point where it desired to hear the young man's testimony. On entering, the young man glanced quickly around and, locating his enemy sitting at the head of the table with his arms tied behind his back, deliberately walked over to him and without a word placed his pistol to the gambler's head and fired, killing him instantly.

No sooner had the young man done this than he was overpowered and disarmed. His wounded arm was jerked from the sling, and, together with his good arm, was tied behind his back with the same rope that had been used to tie the arms of the dead gambler. The rope which had been prepared with the usual hangman's knot was now placed about the neck of the young man, and without a word he was marched off to the trestlework bridge and hanged. This summary execution was certainly an object lesson to anyone who might attempt to interfere with the established procedure of the Vigilance Committee.

While the Vigilance Committee was trying to improve conditions inside the town, the Indians and the stock rustlers were making things lively for the railroad builders and the freighters on the outskirts. Frequently, dead men were brought into Sheridan, their bodies mutilated, unmistakable indications of Indian atrocity. The stock rustlers often joined with the Indians in running off horses and cattle, and were even worse than the redskins themselves, for they were more intelligent and cruel.

At this time both General Sheridan and General Custer were in the field, attempting to round up the fighting Indians and force them back onto their reservations. Frequently, the two generals would meet at Sheridan and stop over for a day and a night, while awaiting dispatches. On such occasions they would dine at our home, and my brother and I would hear wonderful tales of hunting and Indian-fighting. When it was time for us youngsters to retire, our mother would join us, leaving the men to enjoy themselves, drinking champagne and fine old whiskey, and smoking and talking until late at night.

In spite of its perils, Sheridan was a hunter's paradise. Buffalo in great abundance were to be found in every direction; they could be counted by the hundreds of thousands. As all of the hunters were splendid shots, and as they all had the latest and best rifles made, the Indians and the rustlers gave them a wide berth.

At this later day, it seems hard to believe the stories told about the large herds of buffalo on the plains in that period, but I can vouch for the accuracy of such stories, for I myself have actually seen such vast herds. Frequently, the railroad trains would be compelled to stop for several minutes in order to allow a herd of buffalo to cross the track, and on one occasion the train on which I was travelling from Fort Wallace to Sheridan was held up for several hours, while a great herd of buffalo crossed the track.

Buffalo hunters usually pitched their permanent camps on a stream or in some dry arroyo having water holes at irregular distances. Here they would establish headquarters where the hides might be stretched out and pegged down to dry, and quite often you would find acres of ground covered with "green hides." I remember on one occasion seeing hundreds of hides blowing over the prairie much like "tumble-weeds," while all the hunters in the district chased them on foot or on horseback.

As a rule the hunters were a good-natured bunch, though somewhat clannish. They had so many things in common with one another that they became much like one big family. The different hunting outfits would utilize natural landmarks, such as hills or "breaks," to set off one party's territory from another's. Each outfit recognized the rights of its neighbor, and never hunted or killed buffalo except on its own land. These separate hunting grounds varied from a width of five miles to twenty miles.

When a great number of hides were thoroughly dried and ready for shipment, the hunters would contract with some freighting teams to haul them to the railroad, where they found a quick cash sale at the commission houses. Often during the hunting season, we would have thousands of buffalo hides and wolf skins in our warehouses awaiting shipment to eastern markets. I remember distinctly that at one time we had more than thirty thousand buffalo hides and five thou-

We boys would dress quickly and run to the bridge and look up to see if we knew any of them.

sand grey-wolf skins, besides thousands of coyote, badger, skunk and antelope skins piled up in our warehouses.

We had in our employ at this time an expert buyer and seller of wool, hides, pelts and skins named Moses Friedman, formerly an employee in the house of C. R. Morehead & Co. of Leavenworth. The old man was an authority in this branch of our business and kept in close touch with the eastern markets, hence we would hold all these hides and skins in our warehouses until the prices were favorable.

During my stay in Sheridan, I met with an accident that came very near to ending my existence. One night our watch dog Bruce, who generally slept in the kitchen, began barking excitedly. When I turned him out of the back door, he made directly for the woodpile and caught by the leg a young fellow named Turner, the son of a Sheridan "dive saloon" keeper. The sudden appearance of the dog forced Turner to drop an armful of wood. He began to yell "bloody murder" loud enough to be heard all over the neighborhood. My brother and I ran out and pulled the dog from the boy, who immediately hurdled the fence and ran off in the darkness.

A few days later my brother and I and a few boy friends were shooting pistols at some prairie dogs when Turner lounged up. We were sitting down in a group, cleaning our guns. Apparently interested in what we were doing, he flopped down beside me. Our pistols were all unloaded, but two cartridge boxes were lying open on the ground, with several cartridges in each. In view of what happened, Turner must have succeeded in slipping a cartridge from one of the boxes and inserting it into my brother's pistol. Pointing the pistol directly at me, Turner said: "Here, take this," and, suspecting nothing, I at once grabbed the barrel in my hand.

Instinctively, I turned the pistol away from my stomach, and well for me that I did, for Turner pulled the trigger and the next second my right hand was literally torn to pieces. With the blood from this wound spurting in every direction, it was impossible for my companions to tell how badly I was wounded, so my brother picked me up and carried me home. My mother was almost frightened to death, of course, but she sent my brother running for the doctor and my father. At first it was feared that I would lose my hand, but the skillful doctor was finally able to save it. The work he did in shaping up my mangled hand was a splendid piece of surgery for those days. He required me to keep my hand in a basin filled with cracked ice for several days while with an acid solution he picked out all the powder grains that were imbedded in the flesh. The wound finally healed up nicely, leaving scarcely a scar.

In those days everyone, man and boy, carried some sort of weapon at all times. It made no difference what the occasion — even a wedding or a funeral was no exception — the weapon, in all likelihood a pistol, would be carried in the hip pocket or in a holster suspended from the belt. So in mere boyhood, my brother and I had become the possessors of the finest pistols and rifles that money could buy. We made great use of them in hunting. But such skill as we attained might at any time have been the means of saving our lives.

Besides all this perfect equipment of firearms, we had a stable well filled with fine saddle horses. Every year my uncle Don Manuel A. Otero of Valencia County, New Mexico, sent in his large freighting outfit consisting of many mule teams which carried his wool and pelts to the railroad, and took back merchandise and other consigned freight belonging to his neighbors on the Rio Grande. On these occasions he would send my brother and myself several fine saddle horses from his well-known herd of mares, which at that time produced the very best saddle horses in New Mexico.

The firm of Otero & Sellar had purchased three carloads of whiskey in barrels from a wholesale liquor house in St. Louis, Mo., and in addition to this supply they had received at about the same time several additional carloads for customers living in the West and the Southwest. This was at just about the time of the "Great Whiskey Ring." Scandal broke out during the first administration of President U. S. Grant, and perhaps the first investigation on the part of the Government into those frauds was made in connection with the large amount of whiskey in the warehouses of Otero & Sellar at Sheridan. A United States inspector appeared on the scene and immediately confiscated the several hundred barrels of whiskey stored in our warehouses, and as practically the same condition prevailed in the warehouses of W. H. Chick & Co., he treated their supply in the same manner, marking and taking all the barrels. He then proceeded to test each and every barrel, discovering evidence of the frauds that later stirred the entire nation.

The inspector felt it his duty to retain possession of the whole lot. The warehouses in which it was kept were built on wooden pilings or logs, four feet high, which left enough space underneath the floor for anyone to pass freely. On the inside, the flooring and the platforms on which the barrels rested were made of rough two-inch boards. Practically all of these boards had two-inch auger holes near their ends, made by the lumbermen in order to raft them together securely with ropes while bringing them down the river. Many of the whiskey barrels were placed head up directly over some of these auger holes.

One day in shifting some of the barrels, it was discovered that an apparently empty barrel could not be moved because it was held to the floor by something. An investigation disclosed that some enterprising thief had wriggled under the warehouse with a brace and bit and, aided by one of those auger holes, had bored a hole into the barrel, and then had inserted a brass faucet. Through this means he had been able to drain out every drop of whiskey in the barrel.

For some reason I always associate my stay in Sheridan with Buffalo Bill Cody. When I first met Buffalo Bill in

Hays City, he was in the employ of the United States Government as a scout, and was under the direct command of General Phil H. Sheridan at Fort Hays. Buffalo Bill would frequently come over to Hays City to see his good friend Wild Bill Hickok, and it was through Wild Bill that I first became acquainted with Buffalo Bill. Quite frequently they would borrow two of our horses and invite my brother and I to accompany them on a buffalo hunt. Our parents never refused us permission to go with these men, for they were certain no harm could come to either of us.

My personal impression of the two men is quite different in many respects:

Wild Bill was by far the more likable man: he was always kind and considerate toward others. Indeed, it was a real joy to meet him, and when we were under his care on a buffalo hunt, his entire time and attention were centered on us. In a chase he would cut out a cow and maneuver the animal so that either my brother or I could get an easy shot and down the buffalo. After we had one apiece, he seemed perfectly satisfied, no doubt feeling that he had filled his contract. He would then take us with him into the herd, killing two or three with his pistol on the run, but invariably keeping his eye on us. Wild Bill was genuinely brave; I never met his equal for courage on the frontier. I believe, if necessary, he would have tackled a buzzsaw. The word fear was not in his vocabulary. Wild Bill cared nothing for show or glamour, neither did he care for money, except so far as it paid his bills and amused him at the gambling table.

Buffalo Bill, on the other hand, was rather selfish and wanted all the pomp and grandeur for himself. I would not call him a brave man; he was much too cautious. He was smart enough to arrange matters so he would always be in the clear. On these little hunts when we were all together, he would leave us and dash off to the herd by himself, killing buffalo to the right and left of him and never once seeming to care whether we got a shot or not. He was always spectacular and in the first row on parade day. I never heard of his killing anybody or getting into any personal difficulty. He was quite a success as a Pony Express rider and no doubt was well paid for his services. As a scout and Indian fighter he had many superiors. Buffalo Bill was in no sense a bad man; he was a perfect gentleman and a good business man. He believed long hair and buckskin garments attracted attention and brought in the dollars. His greatest success in life came when he organized "Buffalo Bill's Wild West Shows," for his plans were to gather in the coin — and he succeeded. Buffalo Bill was a fine horseman and a commanding figure in the saddle. His associates were mostly officers in the United States Army. He never mingled with the common herd and was neither a gambler nor a frequenter of the saloon or dance hall. He was a good buffalo hunter and made a great business success in that line.

During the building of the Kansas-Pacific Railroad, Buffalo Bill's services were in demand in various capacities. On many occasions he would lead a party of soldiers to the end of the track to drive off some marauding band of Indians that had made a raid on the trackmen and perhaps killed a number of them. When we came into contact with him at Sheridan he had just been given a contract to furnish buffalo meat for the 1,200 men working on the railroad. It certainly took a considerable amount of meat to provide for so many, but Buffalo Bill was able to fulfill his contract. At the time it was estimated that Buffalo Bill had killed between four and five thousand buffalo by himself under contract. So there can be no doubt that his nickname "Buffalo Bill" was well deserved and fairly won.

As the railroad continued westward from Sheridan, the buffalo hunters became more numerous, and, finding competition increasing daily, Buffalo Bill decided to change his means of livelihood. Because of the serious Indian wars, scouts were in considerable demand at big pay, and so Buffalo Bill returned to his first love. He applied to the Government for a commission and was immediately ordered to report for duty at Fort Larned, Kans., where he became General Hazen's personal scout.

By early fall, 1869, the railroad had reached Fort Wallace, Kans., and my father promptly moved his family there. The chief reason for leaving Sheridan was the menace of the Indians. They were bold enough to raid the town to drive off stock and kill a number of herders. But things seemed to be going from bad to worse on the frontier in respect to Indian depredations, and even Fort Wallace did not seem safe. So my father decided to send my mother, my brother, the two girls and I to St. Louis, Mo., my mother's old home.

The train on which we went from Fort Wallace to Kansas City was attacked by a large band of Indians on horseback. They forced the train to stop by burning a trestlework bridge midway between Fort Wallace and Sheridan, and while the train was stopped, they circled around it, firing at us. Fortunately, the distance was too great for their shots to do any harm. Their plan was to circle behind the train, in an attempt to burn another bridge between that spot and Fort Wallace, thus hemming us in and making escape impossible.

The engineer and conductor thwarted their design by promptly backing the train in the direction of Fort Wallace. We had to remain at Fort Wallace for several days, while the burned bridge was being repaired, but the next time our train left we were provided with an escort of soldiers. While the Indians were firing at our train, they kept at a safe distance, for everyone on the train, including my brother and I, was armed and fired back.

We reached St. Louis in October, 1869, and my mother soon secured desirable rooms on Oliver Street, between Eleventh and Twelfth, in what was known as "Dorris Row." My brother and I were placed as boarding students in St. Louis University. We soon secured desirable rooms on Olive Street, between Washington Avenue and Green Street.

Chapter IV

AS soon as my mother and sisters were comfortably settled in St. Louis and my brother Page and I placed in St. Louis University, my father returned to the frontier, as the commission houses were already making preparations to move to the new terminal town of Kit Carson in Colorado Territory.

The president of St. Louis University at the time we entered was the Reverend Father Stuntebeck and the vice-president and prefect of discipline was the Reverend Father Zealand, both very able men. We continued at the university until the following summer, 1870. My mother decided to send us boys to the college farm just outside the city limits to spend our vacation. In September, 1870, we again entered the university for our second year as boarders.

Although our boarding-school experience at St. Louis University was a great improvement over that at the Topeka school, by the time the summer of 1871 had rolled around, my brother and I were quite eager to return to the frontier. So it was without much regret that I heard the verdict of the college physician, dear old Dr. Moses Linton, that I return to an outdoor life on the western plains for the benefit of my health. My brother begged to go along with me, and my mother finally consented, since we had never been separated before. Soon, much to my delight, we were both on our way back to the frontier.

Kit Carson, which had then become the depot of assembly for the freight going to southern Colorado and all other points in the Southwest, was different from the other towns in which we had lived, being somewhat more civilized. It had the usual Main Street, but it was a Main Street with a difference. Kit Carson presented a Main Street that was comparatively clean and decent. There were, it is true, gambling houses, dance halls and saloons, but they were of a finer type than those of the other towns.

For example, at the west corner of the principal block of business houses stood the saloon owned by my old friend Johnny Norton, who tended bar himself, ably assisted by his brother Jim. The Norton brothers were perfect gentlemen; to them it was a matter of pride to conduct a first-class saloon, catering only to the best class of people in the town. They never allowed habitual drunkards or trouble-makers to loaf around their establishment. The Nortons afterward moved to Tucson, Ariz., where John went into business with a Mr. Stewart under the firm name of "Stewart & Norton, Wholesale and Retail Merchants;" some time later they went to Los Angeles, Cal., where they became rich. It was John Norton who built the Norton Block in Los Angeles.

Continuing eastward in the same block, a visitor to Kit Carson would pass several good stores, selling drugs, dry goods and groceries, as well as restaurants and barber shops, with an occasional saloon or billiard hall in between. At the extreme east corner of the block, one would come upon the new two-story frame hotel called the "Perry House," owned and managed by Joe Perry, an old frontier character. Just across the street from the Perry House was the railroad depot, the railroad running east and west through the south side of Main Street.

One block south of the depot was the large and commodious dance hall owned and managed by Tom Kemp, which played a large part in the social life of the town. Kemp's establishment was a one-story affair occupying about a quarter of an ordinary city block. The interior consisted of a bar on the left-hand side of the main door; then the dancing floor, the orchestra being seated on a raised platform in one corner of the room. The dancing floor was terminated by a partition running the entire width of the hall, in the center of which was a door that opened into a narrow hall. On either

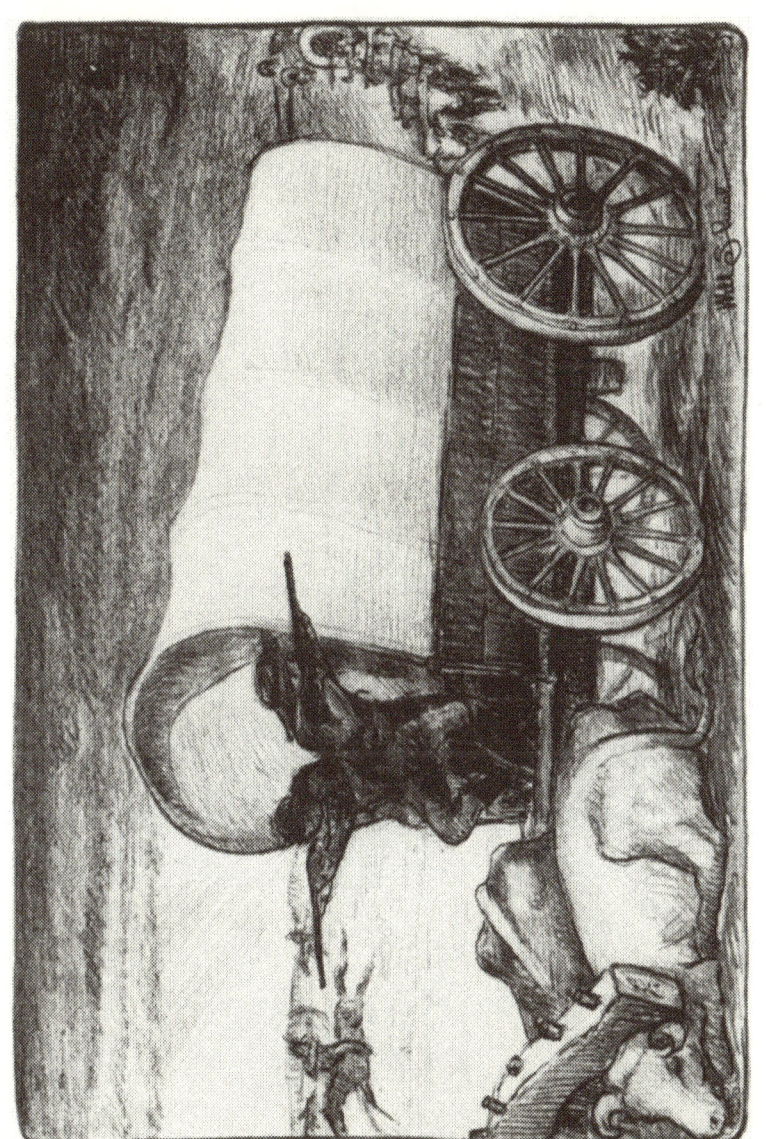
Indian attack on a covered wagon train.

side of it were numbered rooms where the dance-hall girls lived. I recall that in the orchestra, as first violin, was my old friend Chalk Beeson, who after leaving Kit Carson went to Dodge City, Kans., to become leader of the celebrated "Cowboy Brass Band" of that city, and later became mayor.

In the course of time Tom Kemp moved from Kit Carson to Leadville, Colo., where he kept a notorious dance hall which was generally styled "Kemp's Grip-bag Station." The nickname was earned in a peculiar way. Immediately after the last dance, which was usually about daybreak, the score or so of women attached to the place would come trooping down the broad staircase at the front of the building, each carrying what was in those days called a "grip-bag," in which were her toilet articles. At the foot of the stairs would be a line of men, each awaiting the opportunity to carry a "grip-bag" for some unfortunate — but willing — girl.

Occasionally, three or four admirers would seek some particular beauty and when she appeared at the foot of the stairs they would all rush for her "grip-bag." Frequently a fight would ensue between the rivals, who would be arrested and taken to jail, leaving to another, less ardent perhaps, the honor of "walking off with the bacon." In such wise would Blanche, Lillie, Hazel, Myrtle, Trix, Pearl, Stella, Cora, Margaret, Grace, Belle, Jennie and all the rest of Tom Kemp's dance-hall girls find escorts to their modest abodes.

Dance halls in those early days were a necessity. They afforded one of the principal sources of amusement and recreation. It is not easy nowadays to realize what a large proportion of the population of those western towns was made up of men — and comparatively young men at that. In a town like Kit Carson, for example, there would be connected with the two leading commission houses, Otero, Sellar & Co., and Chick, Browne & Co., about one hundred clerks, all men; then there would be the employees of the railroad, which would add perhaps thirty, likewise all men; and, in addition to these, the various stores, hotels, and other business enterprises of the town would add perhaps two- or three-score more men, not to mention the many hunters and freighters.

In fact, it seemed as if there were men on all sides, detached from home life either because they had never given hostages to fortune by establishing a home or because circumstances compelled them to come West and leave their families for the time being. On the other hand, a town such as Kit Carson would show but few unattached young women of corresponding age. This inequality between the sexes was somewhat offset by the importations of the dance halls.

During the winter months, business was naturally slack at the commission houses, and time would hang heavy on the hands of the employees. The only diversions open to them were hunting in the daytime and dancing at night. So a place like Tom Kemp's was a welcome source of diversion. To frequent the dance hall did not stigmatize a young man in the eyes of the young ladies of unblemished character living in town. The people of western towns were not inclined to concern themselves about one another's behavior; neither were they squeamish as to their choice of diversions or associates.

Therefore, the "Commission House Boys," as they were familiarly called, lost no caste by going to Tom Kemp's dance hall. Saturday night was the favorite evening, and often the dance would last until the following evening. When hunger or exhaustion would suggest the necessity of food or drink, Tom Kemp's bar stood ready to supply both. On his bar would be spread coffee, ham and eggs, fried potatoes, bread and butter, beef steaks, oysters and fish in season, and pies. Everyone helped himself until his hunger was satiated and washed it all down with such drinks as were to his liking.

The popularity of the dance hall with the clerical force of Otero, Sellar & Co. was sometimes a detriment to the business interests of the firm. I remember one such instance which was quite amusing. The firm had recently acquired a bookkeeper from St. Louis by the name of William Singleton, who came very highly recommended, both as to proficiency and character. He turned out to be a quiet fellow of circumspect conduct, who attended to his office duties faithfully. In fact, he was a little too conscious of his good behavior and often boasted that he never touched intoxicating liquors.

One day during the very busiest part of the busy season, Singleton went out to lunch as usual, but instead of returning to the office, he walked over to Tom Kemp's and began a grand spree. He ordered whiskey freely and begged to be allowed to treat everyone in the house, and when he had become sufficiently full he called for girls and music. The news spread and all who could flocked to the dance hall to see the show. And a good one it was, for Singleton was the cause of as wild a dance as the old place had ever seen.

Over at the offices of Otero, Sellar & Co. a different scene was being enacted. Many freighters were grumbling and chafing over having to wait to settle up before their departure, but there was no bookkeeper to make out the papers. All the other clerks were much surprised at the turn of events, and Mr. Sellar himself was disturbed and not a little peeved. Finally, he called one of the clerks, J. S. Garcia, and sent him to find Singleton. Garcia had not progressed far in his search when someone told him where he could locate Singleton. Forthwith, he headed for Tom Kemp's and, sure enough, there was Singleton drunk as a lord. He appeared overjoyed at seeing Garcia, and insisted upon his taking a drink and having a dance. Garcia succumbed to the temptation so completely that he forgot what he had been sent for.

In the meantime, fretting and fuming continued at the office of Otero, Sellar & Co., and in due time another clerk was sent out to find the two missing men. The same fate overtook this emissary, and the frolic at Tom Kemp's secured another recruit. This process was repeated several times, until every available clerk in the office was making merry at Tom Kemp's. Only my father and Mr. Sellar were left to run the office, and not one of the subordinates returned until the following morning.

Needless to say, the next morning the truants were lined up and raked over the coals. Singleton never returned to the office. He continued to drink for several days, winding up with a touch of delirium tremens. When he was able to travel, he departed for his old home in St. Louis without even calling to say good-bye to his employers. Meanwhile, in anticipation of such a contingency, a telegram had been sent to St. Louis for a new bookkeeper; this time the firm secured a man who did take an occasional drink, and the office once more settled down to normal routine.

In my description of the more conspicuous features of the town of Kit Carson, I must not omit mention of the Conner Hotel. This was a nice two-story building opposite the railroad tracks and directly across from Norton's saloon. The proprietor, William, or more commonly Bill, Conner ran a family hotel. This signified that it did not have such appendages as a barroom, a billard-room and a gambling-room. Bill's wife was a good, hard-working woman and she and their two grown daughters practically ran the hotel.

Just north of the Conner Hotel was a store kept by a German gunsmith named F. C. Zimmerman, who dealt in sporting goods of all kinds, especially firearms and ammunition. As he was a fine gunsmith, his store was headquarters for the buffalo hunters. Just across the street from Zimmerman was a dry-goods store owned by Jake Collar. Both Jake Collar and F. C. Zimmerman later left for Dodge City, Kans., where they carried on the same lines of business very successfully. On the north side of Collar's store was the residence of John Bell, bookkeeper for Chick, Browne & Co.

Later his sister, Miss Mattie Bell, came out to teach school, but she did not remain in this capacity for any length of time, for she soon married my old friend, Adolph Mennet, who at that time was head of the wholesale and retail departments of Otero, Sellar & Co., a position he held from 1868 at Hays City until the firm retired from business at Las Vegas, N. Mex., in the year 1881.

About a hundred yards north of Mr. Bell's home was a small frame house, the home of the carpenter Bishop, who worked as a day laborer in helping move the commission houses from Hays City to Sheridan, and then to Kit Carson. Mr. and Mrs. Bishop had a most attractive and interesting family of three comely daughters. I remember our meeting them first at Ellsworth in 1867. When the family reached Kit Carson, the three girls were reckoned as the prettiest girls on the frontier. The eldest, Flora, married Johnny McCullough, who was clerking at the Perry House. Soon afterward they left for Cimarron, N. Mex., where McCullough managed the National Hotel. Mrs. Bishop and the remaining two girls, Josie and Ida, soon followed the McCulloughs and assisted in running the little hotel. Josie married Frank Springer, a young attorney-at-law who had but recently arrived in the territory from Burlington, Iowa, and the youngest daughter, Ida, married a prominent physician and druggist of Cimarron, Dr. T. M. Michaelis. Of course, practically all the old-timers in New Mexico knew Frank Springer, who enjoyed a national reputation as a paleontologist and was one of New Mexico's most prominent citizens.

The railroad depot was on the north side of the track or rather the south side of Main Street, directly opposite the Perry House. One block west of the depot, on the south side of the railroad tracks, were the two large commission houses of Otero, Sellar & Co., and Chick, Browne & Co., the former facing east and the latter facing west. S. R. Ainslie was the railroad agent at Kit Carson, and some years later became the General Manager of the Denver & Rio Grande Railway, with headquarters at Denver, Colo.

The Kansas-Pacific Railroad continued to build west from Kit Carson toward Denver and finally reached that city during the summer of 1871. Excursion trains were provided by the railroad officials for all those residing on their line who wished to visit the great mining section of the West and to view for the first time Denver and the great Rocky Mountain range. Many people along the entire route from Kansas City west availed themselves of this opportunity, among them being our entire family.

At that time Denver was a rather small western town. The principal business streets were Blake, Larimer and Holliday, while Wazee was quite lively and brisk with gambling houses, dance halls, saloons and numerous Chinese dives and Japanese sporting houses. Champa Street was out in the country at that time, and beyond were a few scattered farms and ranches. Holliday Street was notorious because of the homes of the wealthy prostitutes, who thrived in palatial mansions in all the splendor money could buy. Denver at that time was twelve years old. The Kansas-Pacific Railroad was not the first to reach Denver, as the city had a connection with the Union-Pacific Railroad running from Cheyenne, Wyo., at that time in the form of a little branch line. We remained in Denver for several days, stopping at the old American House on Blake Street.

I shall never forget our first trip from Kansas City to Kit Carson. Of course we had been following the building of the railroad from the Missouri River to Wallace, Kans., but this was the first through trip we ever made from Kansas City to Kit Carson. More especially do I remember the last day before reaching Kit Carson. Very early in the morning we sighted an immense herd of buffalo. They were only a short distance south of the railroad track; indeed, many small bunches separated from the main herd were only about two hundred yards from our train, but as far as eye could reach toward the west were buffalo. They were scarcely moving — just grazing along slowly, while many were lying down, apparently unafraid of the train. All day long our train advanced toward the setting sun, stopping at many stations along the route for wood, water, meals and orders, and consequently we were always in sight of that same herd of buffalo. It is hard to imagine such a thing today, but it is an absolute fact.

Owing to the great danger of Indians, who were constantly burning the old wooden trestlework bridges, our train did not travel at night, stopping over at a regular station until after breakfast the next morning. We reached Kit Carson early in the day. The large herd of buffalo was no longer in sight, for it had turned south toward the Arkansas River.

We found our new residence quite comfortable and well-located, about two hundred yards west of the commission house of Otero, Sellar & Co. Frequently, very early in the morning, I have seen large herds of buffalo lethargically crossing the railroad track, grazing quietly not over three hundred yards from our back fence.

During the summer of 1871 my brother Page and I devoted much of our spare time to catching prairie-dogs and taming them. This we found was profitable business for we had little or no trouble in selling them to the tourists. Some account of how we caught these elusive little animals may be of interest. Enlisting the assistance of some of our friends among the freighters, we would borrow a wagon and team, as well as a few teamsters. We would fill the wagon with empty whiskey barrels, and then would drive to the well on Big Sandy Creek, where we filled the barrels with water. Along with the barrels we would provide ourselves with a number of gunny sacks from the store.

With this equipment we would proceed to the prairie-dog town, which was a few miles west of our home, between Kit

Carson and Wild Horse. Then we would start catching the prairie-dogs.... We would locate a hole into which we had just seen a family of young dogs scurry. It was easy enough to distinguish the young dogs from the old ones by the way they would bark. When a young dog barked, he would leap erect and merely give one bark, whereas the old dogs would first scurry back into their holes with their families and then expose merely the top of their heads and bark continuously until we got too close.

The next thing we would do was to drive the wagon to the hole we had selected and empty about two barrels of water into it, a quantity usually sufficient to fill an ordinary hole. In the course of a minute or so the little fellows would begin to come out, half-drowned, and then it was a simple matter to grab them by the back of the neck and store them in one of the gunny sacks. Very frequently they were alive enough to turn and bite our hands, and I do not know of any bite more painful. My hands today show where the prairie-dogs took nips more than fifty-five years ago.

We would carry our captives home and then proceed to tame them. After the taming process was well under way, we would allow the little animals to make homes in our back yard. We would begin the holes for them with our knives, digging to a depth of three feet and leaving it to the prairie dogs themselves to finish the job. They made nice pets, often becoming as affectionate as house dogs. At feeding hours we would go out into the yard and call them by name, and it was great fun to see them come, all in a bunch, to be fed. In their eagerness for food they would crawl all over us, poking their heads into our pockets; then when they had finished their meal they would crawl into our pockets, where they would sleep for some time, never attempting to bite, even when we happened to disturb them during their nap.

On one occasion when we were out catching prairie-dogs, I saw the largest herd of antelope that I remember having seen on the western plains; they were running very fast and it took fully half an hour for the herd to cross the railroad track. They were going south, and we judged that the herd was at least a half-mile wide — they must have numbered up into the millions. Today there are only 21,000 antelope in the United States!

Another sport we greatly enjoyed was catching buffalo calves. Mounting our horses, we would borrow two or three wagons with good fast teams and would have these follow us as we rode ahead. Each one in the party would have several pieces of quarter-inch rope, about three feet long, which would be tied to the horn of his saddle. Of course, before making these preparations we had already located a herd of buffalo, and when we were all ready away we would go.

If the herd happened to be on the move, we could with no difficulty ride up to it, or very close to it, before the buffalo would realize what was up, but once they perceived our presence the race would begin in dead earnest. Our horses were trained to their part in the game; we would run them against a calf and down it would go sprawling, the horse stopping dead in his tracks. Then we would jump down beside the fallen calf, which was so clumsy that it would need some time to get on its feet again, and would quickly tie its feet with one of the pieces of rope, leaving it where it fell for the wagon to pick up, while we continued the chase.

We found the sport the more zestful because we had to work rapidly. If a cow happened to recognize her calf among the victims, she might turn and make matters critical for us. We usually escaped such encounters by giving the mother a wide berth and going on after the herd, which was generally too busy to notice the loss of a single calf. If the solicitous mother lingered beside her offspring, the driver of the wagon would usually shoot her and take the meat to the freighters' camp. During one of these calf chases it was an easy matter to fill all of the wagons with calves, and, this done, we would turn homeward.

We would place the young buffalo in the corral belonging

to our father's firm, where we would feed them. Usually, we had a few antelope in the corral, which the herders would bring in with them, capturing them in the tall grass which impeded their escape. We did a good business of selling both our buffalo calves and young antelope to the tourists. We took orders from them, which we promptly filled and shipped by express; usually in the course of time more orders would follow from either our customers or their friends.

Large numbers of wild horses grazed around Kit Carson, but we did not participate actively in capturing any of them. Hunters, however, would go out after them, using a bunch of tame horses, which they would induce to mingle with the wild ones. Then the hunters would start a stampede of the hybrid herd in the direction of the town. The tame horses would naturally head for their accustomed corral and some of their wild mates would follow them into it. I remember on one occasion that nearly fifty head of wild horses were caught in this way, and some were really fine animals.

Chapter V

BUFFALO hunting attained large proportions at Kit Carson in the fall and winter of 1871. The Sherry brothers, Duke and William, were located on Big Sandy Creek, near the site of the present town of Chivington, Colo. This town received its name because of the Chivington massacre, which occurred on November 27, 1864, when Major J. M. Chivington of the First Colorado Regiment, surprised a large body of Indians, consisting mostly of old men, women and children, and fell upon them with the order "No quarter" to his men. It was said that in this massacre the soldiers even took Indian babies by the leg and knocked their brains out against a tree or rock. The dead Indians were not buried, but were left by Major Chivington and his soldiers simply to rot where they fell. In my visits to the vicinity, I would frequently find the skull of an Indian who had perished at the hands of this inhuman officer.

Adjoining the hunting grounds of the Sherry brothers on the west were those of Ed Grossman, who often invited my brother Page and me, together with some of our cronies, such as Louis H. Baldy and Walter Ainslie, to come out to visit him. On one such trip that I especially recall, we secured two four-mule wagons with drivers and a full equipment of bedding, provisions, guns, ammunition and the like. Early in the morning we started for the Grossman headquarters, which we reached late in the afternoon of the same day. Here we remained for two months, enjoying ourselves to the fullest extent hunting buffalo. At intervals we sent the wagons into Kit Carson with consignments of buffalo hides and wolf skins, together with large quantities of the choicer portions of buffalo meat to be distributed among our friends.

Mr. Grossman's neighbors, the Sherry brothers, were kind

enough to give us the privilege of hunting on their grounds, and this increase in range was responsible for some of our unusually large kills. The Sherry brothers' hunting grounds teemed with buffalo. One day, I remember that Duke Sherry came in with the announcement that he had just killed two hundred and fifty-nine buffalo without moving from one place, a hole he had dug in the ground about three feet square and about three feet deep. The statement seemed almost unbelievable so we all went out to verify the count, as well as see the great slaughter. Much to our amazement, we found that Duke Sherry's count was absolutely correct. The explanation was probably that buffalo will not run simply at the sound of a shot; they must see the hunter before they will flee. So if one kept them from seeing him, as Duke Sherry did by crouching in his hole, they would continue to feed quietly, unmindful of the killing of their mates.

One day while hunting on Grossman's ground, we witnessed a narrow escape from a wounded and infuriated buffalo. John Olsen, a good-natured Swede who made his living by hunting buffalo for their hides, had wounded a two-year-old bull, called a "spike" in hunter's parlance, that charged him ferociously. Seeing the danger, Olsen tried to dodge, but the bull struck him with full force on the fleshy part of the right hip, the horn going entirely through. It was fortunate for Olsen that the buffalo was almost exhausted when it struck him and dropped dead a second later.

We ran to the spot and removed Olsen from the horn, finding him unconscious and bleeding horribly. We bandaged him as best we could while one of our men hurried to the camp about two miles away, and returned with a wagon and a small flask of whiskey. We at once sent Olsen to Kit Carson for treatment; but his injury was so severe that he was a long time getting well.

On one of our most successful hunts while at Grossman's, we crawled along on our stomachs for a distance of nearly two miles, dragging our rifles by our sides, until we reached a dry arroyo about fifty feet wide and fifteen feet deep. Then we walked down it for about half a mile, keeping completely under cover, until we had reached the center of the west side of a herd of 2,000 buffalo, grazing on the east side of the arroyo. We then crawled up to where a small drain entered the arroyo, and as it was about five feet deep, we were able to push along, concealed, for perhaps a hundred yards.

A peep over the top of the drain showed us that we were practically in the midst of the herd. They had not seen us, and neither had the outlying pickets posted at intervals about the herd. Buffalo, I should explain, were much like an army of soldiers in their formations. The main herd always posted several small groups of bulls, about five or six in each group, at different points to act as a look-out. When the pickets saw anything coming in the direction of the herd they would turn and run, thereby starting a general stampede.

As I have said, we were not discovered on this occasion. We got within a very few feet of a large bunch of cows and calves. Each of us promptly picked out a cow and fired. We again and again reloaded our rifles and fired as rapidly as we could, every shot bringing down one of the animals. We continued firing until the herd, in its leisurely grazing, had moved out of range of our guns. When we stopped shooting, we could count a great many cows lying on the ground, either dead or badly wounded, and by their sides, in most instances, were the yearling calves. These we planned to shoot later, but in my case the plan was nearly thwarted by the revenge of a young two-year-old bull or "spike."

This young bull came close to one of the wounded cows, and smelling fresh blood began to paw the ground ferociously. Just at that moment I raised myself out of the hollow, and the spike, catching sight of me, began to charge in my direction. I had visions of John Olsen, and will admit I was afraid. But I held my ground long enough to fire at the animal the moment he started in my direction. This shot broke one of his hind legs, but did not halt his rush in my direction. He continued towards me as fast and furiously as his three good legs could carry him.

So finally I turned and ran for the arroyo, the bull following me at an uncomfortably close distance and coming nearer at every jump. My companions, Ed Grossman, Louis Baldy and my brother Page, were watching and were in readiness to fire a broadside into the bull the moment he came opposite their position. Luckily for me they were able to carry out their intention, and their shots dropped the bull not more than fifteen yards behind me.

Out of this herd, the four of us killed forty buffalo, including the calves. We skinned the larger ones and took the choicer parts (the hind-quarters, hump, tongue, liver and heart), leaving the remainder for the wolves and coyotes. In the case of the calves, we left the skins on and merely removed the entrails. The wagons came from headquarters and brought in everything. What remained we poisoned with strychnine, and for many days we devoted much of our time to hunting dead wolves, wild cats, coyotes, badgers and skunks, which after becoming sick from the poison would wander off to arroyos to die. Their skins were very valuable and added many dollars to our treasury.

The next day we sent two wagonloads of presents to our friends at Kit Carson. The hides and skins we sent in from time to time were sufficient to pay all the expenses of the trip. But all good times come to an end, and as Christmas approached we realized that we must keep our promise to our parents to return after two months. So, very reluctantly, we broke up camp and returned to Kit Carson.

In contrast to this, I shall now recount my experiences in the hunt for the Grand Duke Alexis of Russia, which has become famous in the annals of the West. About three or four weeks after we had returned from Grossman's, the firm of Otero, Sellar & Co. received a telegram from Denver, signed by General Phil H. Sheridan and General George A. Custer, stating that they were commanding a special escort selected by the War Department to accompany the Grand Duke and his suite through the West, one special aim being to give the royal sportsman an opportunity to enjoy a buffalo hunt. So they planned to spend two days at Kit Carson, as the buffalo were very thick in that vicinity. Hence, they were asking Otero, Sellar & Co. if they could furnish proper facilities, such as horses, wagons, ambulances, tents, provisions, for the hunt.

A few days later came another telegram, announcing that the Grand Duke's party would arrive on the following morning. Kit Carson appointed a reception committee, my father being the chairman, since he was personally acquainted with General Sheridan, General Custer, Buffalo Bill, Texas Jack (Omohundro) and many of the others who were accompanying the Grand Duke's party. Of course, the whole town turned out to witness the arrival, but as the visit was to be brief, not a moment was wasted in idle ceremonies.

Early on the morning of the arrival of the train from Denver, a scouting party had been sent out to locate a herd of buffalo and to select a suitable camping site. Shortly afterward, wagons loaded with barrels of fresh water also got under way. Behind the water wagons came other wagons carrying the tents, together with bedding and provisions.

When the train arrived the whole party started as quickly as possible for the hunting grounds, which lay between Big Sandy Creek and Rush Creek. But, before the start was made, both General Sheridan and General Custer accompanied my father to the warehouse for the purpose of "renewing assurances," while my brother and I busied ourselves with renewing acquaintances with our friends of the Hays City and Sheridan days — Buffalo Bill and Texas Jack (Omohundro).

Texas Jack (Omohundro) was a scout, of the same type as Buffalo Bill, and in the employ of the United States Government. He was constantly associated with Buffalo Bill and they were always together. Texas Jack was not a bad man; he was rather backward and seemed perfectly content to play second-fiddle to Buffalo Bill. He did not wear the regulation long hair, but in a tight hole he always managed to acquit himself with bravery and sound judgment. Later he followed Buffalo Bill into the Wild West shows.

At the camp, the two generals jointly occupied a large wall tent, while the Grand Duke was assigned one next to that of the Generals. The other tents were occupied by members of the Duke's suite, the newspaper reporters, official photographers, subaltern army officers, scouts and soldiers, as well as a considerable retinue of cooks, waiters and servants. In the entire party there must have been between one hundred and twenty-five and one hundred and fifty persons.

I was sent out to the camp in one of the last wagons to leave Kit Carson. We carried, among other things, a gallon keg of very fine whiskey, which my father was sending to General Sheridan, having previously told the General to expect it. The wagon was driven by an old buffalo hunter who, having had his feet frozen, had wrapped them in burlap. Sitting on the seat with the old fellow was another hunter, while my companion, Frank O. Kihlberg, sat on the rear seat with me. We noticed that the two men in front drank quite frequently from a small keg, but supposed that it was merely water, until the driver began to sing loudly and give clear evidence of intoxication. But still I thought little of the matter.

Our wagon was driven up to General Sheridan's tent, where an orderly informed us that the General could not see us himself as he was slightly indisposed. I therefore turned over to the orderly the keg of whiskey for the General, but I noticed that as he lifted it from the wagon he shook it and smiled a little. A minute after he had gone into the tent the General came rushing out, looking hotter than a boiled owl. In all my life I never heard one man bestow on another such curses as the General used on the poor driver. He called him every name he could think of, and I believe he would have ordered him shot on the spot if the poor fellow had not bethought himself to plead in extenuation of his misdemeanor his poor frozen feet and the pain they had given him on the journey.

The Grand Duke, hearing the shouting and the oaths, came from his tent and evidently enjoyed the rumpus. Noticing me, the Grand Duke came up to me and, taking my arms from behind, threw me high into the air, catching me as I came down — an easy performance for one of such superb physique. He seemed to take a great liking to me at once and invited me into his tent, where he gave me a drink of wine and ordered one of his servants to have another cot placed in his tent for my use.

At this juncture, General Custer rode up, accompanied by Buffalo Bill and Texas Jack, to take the Grand Duke on the hunt. They brought along for the latter's use the best trained buffalo horse they could find, and the Grand Duke, after taking his brace of pistols, bowie knife and rifle, mounted and started off with them. The four rode toward the east, over a slight rise in the prairie. After they had disappeared, a few of us followed on horseback to see the hunt.

The buffalo were grazing just behind the rise in a beautiful little valley. At sight of the party, they started to run, but the swift horses soon overtook them, and the Grand Duke killed a fine bull and two cows. None of the party, I am positive, did any shooting on that occasion except the Grand Duke. General Custer immediately sent Texas Jack back to the camp for some hunters, who quickly removed the heads and skins of the three buffalo the Grand Duke had killed and took them to camp. These were later sent to Russia as trophies. Then the party returned to camp, cases of champagne and other wet goods were opened, and everybody drank to the health, happiness and long life of Alexis, Grand Duke of Russia.

Shortly after these festivities, we noted in the distance a party of soldiers chasing a small group of buffalo. They were coming from the east, and directly in the direction of the camp. At once the Grand Duke, together with General Custer and several of the scouts, jumped into the saddle and started in the direction of the herd of ten bulls. The buffalo never deviated in their course, advancing directly toward the Grand Duke and his companions, who separated into two parties, one going to the left of the herd and the other to the right. This move apparently did not please the bulls, for they stopped short. Then one of the largest of the herd charged with head down for the Grand Duke.

It really began to look serious for the distinguished guest, but the Grand Duke was a good horseman and besides he was riding a splendidly trained buffalo horse. So the Grand Duke was soon out of danger, but he was not inclined to let the matter terminate in such fashion. Guiding his horse in a complete circle, he came back to the vicinity of the maddened bull and, waiting until the animal had turned in his direction, he dropped the big fellow dead with one rifle shot. Both the hide and the head of this animal were magnificent specimens.

On the return to camp, dinner was served and everyone enjoyed himself until bedtime. The next morning General Sheridan made his appearance, much recovered from his indisposition by a good night's sleep. The scouts who had gone out early reported a much larger herd than had been found on the first day, grazing some miles south, on the north bank of Rush Creek. This time the entire party went out, with the exception of the cooks, waiters, drivers and servants. Of course, the Grand Duke had the right of way all the time, but even so everyone in the party got his buffalo, for there were many hundreds in the herd. At noon all returned to the camp and after an excellent lunch started back to Kit Carson, arriving there in time for dinner.

On his return to the train, the Grand Duke held a general reception to which everybody in Kit Carson was invited. He shook hands and chatted with all who came, and made arrangements with the Perry House that all the guests should be served with cake and wine. All during the reception the Army band played, and the celebration went on until late in the night.

Early the next morning, the train pulled out on its way to St. Louis. The last words spoken by the Grand Duke were: "This has been the best entertainment we have received in the United States, and I shall always remember with pleasure my visit to Kit Carson, and especially the good friends I have made during my stay. I want to thank you one and all."

Around the Grand Duke's buffalo hunt has grown up a good deal of legend. Inman, for example, in his *The Old Santa Fé Trail*, adds his bit of embroidery when he writes of the old Indian chief, Two Lance, and his ability to shoot an arrow entirely through a buffalo when running on horseback, that "he accomplished this remarkable feat in the presence of the Grand Duke Alexis of Russia, who was under the care of Buffalo Bill near Fort Hays, Kans."

In another account it states: "General Sheridan called out from the carriage to Buffalo Bill: 'Cody, get in here and show the Duke how you can drive. Reed will exchange places with you and ride your horse.' Later, as they approached Medicine Lodge Creek, the General said: 'Shake them up a little, Bill, and give us some old-time stage driving.' No more was needed. On the horses bounded, faster and faster, until they came to a steep hill which led down into the Valley of the Medicine; straight down the hill they went, bounding along over the ruts, while both General and Prince were kept busy holding on to their seats. In fine old style they dashed into the camp where they were to obtain a fresh relay, but the Grand Duke begged to be excused from any more of the same kind (of driving)."

Medicine Lodge Creek is located in southern Kansas, and I am positive that the Grand Duke Alexis and his party never hunted either there or near Fort Hays, as Inman asserts.

In many other accounts of the Grand Duke's hunt I have detected an evident intention to belittle and minimize the Grand Duke's prowess, at the same time exalting those of Buffalo Bill. In one such account that comes to my mind, I remember that the statement is made that Buffalo Bill killed the Grand Duke's first buffalo. Needless to say, this is a fabrication.

In order to verify my own first-hand impressions of the Grand Duke's hunt, I secured from the Adjutant General all the information obtainable from the files of the War Department. Though meager, these data support my recollections in every respect.

Chapter VI

THE scene of my recollections now shifts, for a time at least, to New Mexico, the state with which both my father and I have been so closely connected. Early in the summer of 1872 Don Juan Maria Baca of Upper Las Vegas sent two four-mule wagons to Kit Carson, fully equipped for several days' comfortable travelling, to carry home to New Mexico some boys who had been in the East to school and who were returning for the summer vacation. Four of the boys were sons of Don Juan — Eleuterio Baca, Francisco Baca y Sandoval, Domingo Baca and Antonio Baca, the last two being twins. The other boys were Amado Baca, David Baca and Valentin C. De Baca — cousins who lived at Peña Blanca, on the Upper Rio Grande — and Anastacio Ascarate, who came from Las Cruces on the Lower Rio Grande. The remaining boy was my first cousin, Emanuel B. Otero, whose home was at La Constancia, in Valencia County.

The preparations for the return trip of the party were made with the aid of Otero, Sellar & Co., and while they were in progress, my brother Page and I conceived the idea of going along with the boys. We begged our parents to let us join the party and go at least as far as Las Vegas. When they finally granted our request we lost no time getting ready for the trip, and soon the eleven of us were on the overland journey into New Mexico.

We had a splendid outfit for our trip. There were two four-mule wagons, each with two spring seats. These were loaded with our bedding, provisions and grain for the animals. Besides these, we had a light two-horse wagon with three spring seats, which was used for conveying passengers. This wagon was added to the outfit by my father for my brother Page and me. We took along six extra horses, to be used as saddle-horses. Each of us had a good rifle and two pistols, as well as plenty of ammunition. In charge of the whole outfit was a trusted *majordomo* (wagon-boss), and he had directly under his control a considerable retinue of drivers, herders, cooks and servants, whose business it was to make life pleasant and comfortable for us.

Our first day's journey brought us to a point about midway between Kit Carson and the Arkansas River, and there we made camp. The next day we crossed the river near Fort Lyon and camped close to Las Animas, the home of Thomas Boggs, one of the very old-timers and a great friend of General Kit Carson. So strong was this friendship that when the great scout died at Fort Lyon, across the river from Las Animas, Boggs took care of Carson's children and saw to their education. We called on Boggs, who was kind enough to send over to our camp two fat lambs, which were such a welcome addition to our larder that we slaughtered one of them at once.

When I knew Carson at Leavenworth he was about fifty-six years of age and had practically retired from active life. In his latter days he had established himself on a small ranch near the mouth of the Purgatoire River in Colorado, in the vicinity of his old friend, Thomas Boggs. There he spent the short remainder of his life, which was filled with much physical suffering caused probably from an accident he had received in the San Juan country several years before. His wife died on the 27th of April, 1868, and Kit Carson himself passed away less than a month afterward, at the age of fifty-nine. During the last week of his illness he was treated by the surgeon at Fort Lyon, Colo., and assigned a room in the crude adobe building which was the post hospital. While the old scout was reclining and smoking a favorite pipe given him by General Frémont, whose guide and scout he had been, he was stricken by a severe fit of coughing, which caused the expectoration of a great quantity of blood. He suddenly reached out his hand, and, grasping that of his intimate friend, Aloys Scheurich, who was in the room, he gasped, "Good-by compadre" and died.

He was buried at Fort Lyon by the side of his wife, but as he had often expressed a desire to be buried at Taos, N. Mex., where he had lived so much of his life, his remains and those of his wife were disinterred in the latter part of 1868 and taken to Taos, where they now lie. Strangely enough, only one monument has been erected, so far as I know, to the memory of the greatest of the frontiersman. This stands in front of the Federal building at Santa Fé and was erected by Senator Stephen W. Dorsey. The rifle that Kit Carson used constantly during the last thirty-five years of his life he bequeathed just before his death to Montezuma Lodge No. 1, A. F. & A. M., at Santa Fé, of which he was a member at the time of his death.

But I cannot linger in this narrative over Fort Lyon and its associations with Kit Carson. Leaving Las Animas the next day, we went by way of what was called the Bent's Cañon Road to Trinidad, Colo., where we stopped for a day in order to rest up and make some purchases of vegetables, fresh fruits, butter, chickens and eggs. The next morning we took a very early start, for we were to cross the Raton Mountains on the toll road built by Uncle Dick Wooten, and we wanted to have time for a visit with him.

Reluctantly, we left Uncle Dick's home the next day and journeyed farther. Our camp that night was made under more exciting circumstances than our previous ones. Uncle Dick had cautioned us to be very careful of our horses and mules, explaining that he had received word that some horse thieves were in the neighborhood and were making the vicinity of Willow Springs their rendezvous. But the anticipation of a brush with horse thieves only served to give the trip an added thrill. Nevertheless, we deemed it wise to take precautions. That night we were careful to tie our animals to the wagons instead of hobbling them. We also arranged for different details to take turns at standing guard during the whole night, and we even indulged in a little practice shooting with our rifles, our purpose being not merely to see that the weapons were in good shape but also to apprise the horse thieves, if they were within hearing distance, that we were well-armed. But all this preparation was unnecessary; no horse thieves appeared on the scene during the night.

Early next morning we started for the Vermijo Ranch of Don Juan Maria Baca, where our itinerary called for us to spend the night with an elder brother of the Baca boys, Don Benito Baca, who managed all his father's business and who occasionally visited the ranches when necessary. Don Benito was a highly educated man. After leaving college he had accepted a position as bookkeeper with the firm of Otero, Sellar & Co. to study business methods. He remained with the firm for three years, during which time he lived with us as one of the family, afterward marrying my cousin Emilia, the eldest daughter of Don Manuel A. Otero of La Constancia. During the campaign of 1878 he was the candidate of the Democratic Party in New Mexico for delegate to Congress, but suffered defeat at the hands of another cousin, Don Mariano S. Otero, who was the candidate of the Republicans. Don Benito made most of his campaign on horseback and received an injury from the saddle which developed into a fistula. He was operated on immediately after the election. Blood-poisoning developed, owing, it was said, to carelessness on the part of the doctor in using unclean instruments, and he died a few days afterward at the home of Don Manuel A. Otero.

We reached the Vermijo Ranch at sundown and found everything in disorder and confusion. Don Benito and his men had just engaged in a fight with a band of Navajo Indians, who had attacked the ranch and attempted to drive off the stock. In the fight six Indians had been killed and several others wounded, but Benito's men had come out of the affray with no casualties, except one man slightly wounded.

When we started the next day on the last leg of our journey, for we proposed to reach Las Vegas on the second day out, Don Benito Baca added another wagon to our outfit. In this we took along his wounded man, José Gallegos by name, together with two wounded Indians who had been captured. Our camp at the close of the day's journey was not eventful, but the next day brought a different sort of excitement from any we had yet experienced on this trip. The driver of one of our wagons attempted to commit suicide by shooting himself through the head, which gave us the additional responsibility of a fourth wounded man to carry with us into Las Vegas.

We finally reached the town and disposed of the wounded. We turned the Indians over to the authorities, who consigned them to the county jail. José Gallegos and the man who had attempted to take his own life we took to their homes in Upper Las Vegas; Gallegos recovered in the course of time from his wound, but the driver died a few days later.

The entire party went to the home of Don Juan Maria Baca and enjoyed his hospitality. Two days later my cousin, Manuel B. Otero, Anastacio Ascarate, and the three Baca boys left for their homes on the Rio Grande. My brother and I remained in the Baca home for several weeks.

When we first arrived, our host, Don Juan, was confined to his bed with a severe cold, which later developed into pneumonia. But he recovered measurably from this and when my father and mother arrived he was sitting up and appeared in the best of spirits. A few days after our departure, however, his heart failed him and he died.

During our stay at Don Juan's home we saw some of the lawlessness that prevailed in that part of the Territory. A band of Texans had debouched into northern New Mexico and were rustling all the cattle and horses in the country. In their raids they had killed several herders who had opposed them. I saw the large herd of cattle these Texans had stolen near Las Vegas. The rustlers all wore chaps and were armed to the teeth with rifles and pistols.

The presence of this outfit was naturally a great source of excitement to Las Vegas people, and, as my father had arrived the day before, a delegation of the most prominent citizens of northern New Mexico appealed to him to do something to relieve the section from this scourge, their notion being that a man of my father's prominence might have some influence with the rustlers. My father undertook the mission, without much hope of success, and to our great delight he allowed my brother and me to accompany him.

We all rode out to their camp, located where East Las Vegas now stands. When my father asked for the leader of the band, a large, red-headed man with chin whiskers, weighing fully two hundred and twenty-five pounds, presented himself. My father urged him to have greater regard for the property of the citizens of New Mexico. When my father had finished, the leader of the Texans answered thus: "These God damn' greasers have been stealing our horses and cattle for the past fifty years, and we got together and thought we would come up this way and have a grand round-up, and that is why we are here. What is more, we intend to take all the horses and cattle we come across and drive them back to their old ranges in Texas, where they belong. My advice to you fellows is: Don't attempt to interfere with what we are doing unless you are looking for trouble."

My father did not attempt to argue the matter further, knowing that it was useless. I have never forgotten the episode, for it revealed that hostile and vengeful feeling displayed by the Texans which produced acts of lawlessness calculated to make the name "Tejano" a hated word among the New Mexicans. It is said that mothers were in the habit of censuring their children with the dire threat: "If you are not good, I'll give you to the Tejanos, who are coming back."

In this instance, as in many others, the New Mexicans were long-suffering. The people of the northern part of the Territory had suffered heavily from these pillagers and reasoned that it would cost them their lives to interfere in any way with the northern ruffians. So they stood the losses and allowed the Texans to proceed on their way. Two days after my father made his plea, the whole herd and the Tejanos had disappeared in a southeasterly direction. It was afterwards learned that the leader of this band of marauders took the proceeds of the raid and invested it in Denver, erecting one of that city's largest office buildings.

After a pleasant renewal of friendship with their many acquaintances in Las Vegas, my parents started for Santa Fé on the Barlow & Sanderson Stage, taking all of us children with them. On our arrival we took rooms in a building which stood just across the street from the old Exchange Hotel, called the "La Fonda," celebrated as being the end of the Santa Fé Trail (on the site where H. H. Dorman now has his real estate office), and here we remained until conveyances arrived to take us to my uncle's home at La Constancia.

My uncle's home was a typical haçienda, or country estate, located in the richest and most desirable part of the Territory — the valley of the Rio Grande, extending from Peña Blanca to El Paso, Texas. At such haçiendas, the life was lavish and luxurious to a degree hard to imagine nowadays; in many respects it resembled the principality of some foreign prince. The owners of these haçiendas were fittingly called "Don" and "Doña," titles of respect and honor.

Uncle Manuel and Aunt Doloritas were very fond of entertaining, and while we were there they gave several dances. The dances usually lasted until sunrise, refreshments and wines being served from midnight on. A good hot breakfast was furnished all the guests before they started for their respective homes, which might have been Peralta, Tome, Valencia, Los Lunas, Belen, or perhaps even so distant a place as Albuquerque.

The activities of such a large estate as my uncle's were numerous and required a number of out-buildings. To the rear of the main house was the country store, which my uncle operated. It was a single room, about one hundred feet long and thirty feet wide, with shelves and a counter. One side of the room was devoted to groceries, vegetables, fresh meats, chickens, milk, butter and eggs, while the other half was used for dry goods, hardware, leather goods, and the like.

Just beyond the store and bordering on the extensive vineyard was a winery, containing several immense vats. Next to the winery was a wide acequia, always full of running water, and on the other side of the acequia was a three-story flour mill, operated by water power from the acequia.

Then there were the extensive stables and corrals, as well as the slaughter-house. There were also enclosures for chickens, ducks and geese.

Around the main house of the haçienda were gardens for all sorts of flowers, vegetables and berries. In front of the house and on all sides were numerous flower beds. Separated from these was a vegetable garden and melon patch; then came the vineyard containing many acres of grapes and berries of all kinds. Next to the vineyard was an orchard containing peaches, pears, plums, apricots, cherries and apples. Beyond the orchard were extensive fields of corn, wheat, barley and oats.

The rest of the estate comprised thousands of acres on which ranged my uncle's great herds of cattle, sheep, goats and horses. These last were my uncle's chief pride since there were none better in the Territory. His stud contained a selected lot of mares together with two magnificent Arabian stallions.

Reluctantly, my parents set a day for our departure and

my uncle sent us back to Santa Fé with the same outfit that had brought us down. We reached Santa Fé the evening of the third day and, after remaining there for a few weeks, took the Barlow & Sanderson coach direct to Kit Carson.

The following spring, the news came that the Atchison, Topeka & Santa Fé Railroad was proposing to continue its line into New Mexico. It had always been my father's cherished desire to bring a railroad into New Mexico, so when this news came he lost no time in starting for Boston to discuss the matter with Thomas and Joseph Nickerson, who were the heads of the company. He urged them to prompt action and pointed out the advantages to be gained by securing the old Atlantic and Pacific right-of-way. He had previously made the same suggestion to the Kansas-Pacific Railroad, but they had not looked favorably upon it, as their primary object was to reach the mining districts of Colorado. The real truth of the matter was that the Kansas-Pacific Railroad could not raise the money. It had taken their every cent to reach Denver and when they got there they were flat broke.

The directors of the new development of the Atchison, Topeka & Santa Fé Railroad saw my father's point and decided to adopt the plan he proposed.

My father returned from his Boston trip much pleased with his success, and, foreseeing great business activity along the new line, began preparations for the removal of his business to the new town called Granada, that had been laid out where the railroad line would cross the Arkansas River.

Chapter VII

DURING the late fall and winter of 1872 and 1873, we devoted most of our time to pleasure, as the shipping season was over for 1872 and business was at a standstill. Kit Carson was not troubled with Indians, so it was perfectly safe for us to hunt. Wild ducks were plentiful in Eureka Creek and in water holes in both Big Sandy and Rush creeks. Whenever we went in the direction of these places, we would take along a shotgun or two and would usually bring back several ducks and an occasional goose or brant.

Buffalo hunting, however, continued to hold first place in our activities. We enjoyed several good buffalo hunts south of Kit Carson in the neighborhood of Kiowa, a stage station midway between Kit Carson and the Arkansas River. This locality was free from regular buffalo hunters. Although it was on the main wagon road leading into southwest Colorado and New Mexico, comparatively few freighting teams passed over it. So the buffalo and antelope in that section were unmolested and even ventured to graze around in sight of the Barlow & Sanderson stage station.

Early in the spring of 1873, after my father had returned from his consultation with the directors of the Atchison, Topeka & Santa Fé Railroad in Boston, preparations began for the move to Granada.

A farewell party was arranged by our friends among the commission houses of Otero, Sellar & Co. and Chick, Browne & Co., in the form of an old-fashioned buffalo hunt. By unanimous consent, Adolph Mennet was elected captain of the party and placed in charge of all the arrangements. A better selection could not have been made, for Mennet was an ideal frontiersman — a brave soldier and an experienced hunter. My father permitted the use of the Government ambulance that had been placed at his disposal, and this we assigned to the use of the ladies who were in the party. The men rode either on horseback or in the wagon which carried the provisions. We had no difficulty in finding many buffalo on the hunting grounds we had chosen — a location between Big Sandy Creek and Rush Creek, a short distance north of the present town of Chivington, Colo.

The men were soon in full tilt after a herd of about a hundred, which was grazing a short distance north of the road. The ladies excitedly insisted that the ambulance driver join in the chase, which he did, allowing the mules to run at break-neck speed over the prairie. But suddenly there came a change in the program. An old bull stopped, looked back for an instant, and then started to charge directly for the ambulance. The driver endeavored to escape by turning the mules in another direction, but that did not deter the old bull. He dashed after the ambulance, and the race became quite desperate.

Adolph Mennet, realizing the danger the ladies were in, had turned his horse and was galloping toward the bull as fast as his mount could carry him. The ladies by this time had become frantic, for the bull was gaining at every bound. But Mennet's splendid horse brought him close enough to the infuriated animal to fire two shots into the buffalo, which dropped in its tracks, not more than fifty yards behind the ambulance. In the ambulance were my mother and Mrs. Mennet.

The mules were as badly frightened as the ladies, and the driver had great difficulty in getting them under control. But as soon as he had stopped them, the ladies piled out of the rear door, eager to see the animal that had caused their fright. They had had all the chase they wanted for that day, and so they brought the hunt to an end by serving a good meal in camp style. In the afternoon we started back for Kit Carson, loaded with buffalo meat and tongues. I recall that on this hunt we had killed an even dozen of cows and yearlings, and a few young bulls. The trip back was slow, as everyone, including the mules, was tired. We did not reach home until late at night.

A few days later I had the good luck to bring down one of the most interesting specimens among the many buffalo I killed. Some herders happened to drop into the commission house with the report that on their way into town they had seen a lone buffalo bull crossing the railroad track about a mile east of the town. They added that he seemed to be headed toward Big Sandy Creek. One of the clerks in the railroad office, Sol Smith by name, and a nephew of the actor, Sol Smith Russell, felt the same interest in this news as I did. So we both got our rifles and a handful of cartridges and started afoot toward Big Sandy. Reaching the creek, we got down under the bank and walked in a southeast direction for about a mile, then concealed ourselves on the north bank in an old deserted dug-out.

Since the dug-out was roofless, we could make observations over the back, and we discovered that the lone buffalo was going north in a direction opposite to that which we had expected. The situation looked hopeless so far as reaching him was concerned, and being tired from our slow trot, we gave over the chase for the time being. Down we sat on the dirt floor to rest for a few moments before starting home. Sol lit his pipe and puffed away, while I told a story. Several minutes later, we had an impulse to take another look over the rear end of the dug-out. To our great surprise, there was the buffalo coming directly towards us — and not fifty yards away! He had evidently heard us, for he stopped and turned west, presenting his full left side.

My gun was in my hand, while Sol's was standing in the corner against the wall. Not a moment could be lost; so I fired straight for the old fellow's heart. He ran for about a hundred yards, then dropped. We were not long in getting

The old bull buffalo charged the ambulance.

to him and discovered that I had killed a unique specimen. He certainly was an old-timer, for he showed the marks of many a hard-fought battle with the younger bulls, who had finally sent him adrift on the lonesome trail. His hide had hardly any hair upon it, his body being as hairless as that of an elephant, but he had a magnificent head. This I sent to Denver, where it was properly mounted. For years it hung in the office of Otero, Sellar & Co., and today it occupies a similar place in the office of Gross, Kelly & Co., at East Las Vegas, N. Mex.

The day of our departure from Kit Carson finally came. Pat Shanley was back for the second round of loads, and all that remained was placed on the wagons. Instead of going with the rest of the family in the government ambulance, I chose to go along with the wagons. Shanley took a route that followed Big Sandy Creek until its junction with the Arkansas River; then the road turned east until it reached Granada. I enjoyed the trip immensely, as the game was plentiful and the hunting good. We were never out of sight of buffalo from the time we left Kit Carson until we reached Granada. Antelope, geese and duck were plentiful during the entire journey, and occasionally we would run across a band of wild horses. After getting within ten miles of the Arkansas River we were constantly on the look-out for hostile Indians, who at that time had gone on the war path and were beginning to be troublesome on the line of the Atchison, Topeka & Santa Fé Railroad in western Kansas.

We arrived at Granada about the middle of August, 1873, and found it a bustling place. The railroad had just been completed to that point, but the bridge across the Arkansas River was not yet finished. Rails were down so the train could pass over, but much remained to be done before it would be a finished job. Hundreds of carpenters, plasterers, painters and other workmen were busy building the new town. The large commission houses of Otero, Sellar & Co.

and Chick, Browne & Co., the railroad depots, and practically all the other buildings in the town were in process of construction, there being very few buildings of any sort that were really completed. The Perry House joined the commission houses, and moved to Granada, occupying the same place as it had in Kit Carson, the east end of the main block opposite to the depot.

Until a home could be built, our family occupied rooms in the second story of the commission house which were intended for the clerks. This compelled the clerks to sleep on the floor downstairs, with their trunks beside their sleeping places. We all took our meals at the new hotel just across the street from the warehouse. John Windram and his wife ran it, and served really excellent meals. So, on the whole, we managed to live comfortably and contentedly for the time being, although we sometimes yearned for the greater comforts we had enjoyed at Kit Carson.

We had not been in the town long before we began to grow acquainted with the wildness of Granada. Just after finishing supper the evening after my arrival — my father with the balance of the family having arrived with the Government ambulance two or three days ahead of the Pat Shanley wagons — we were crossing the street between the Windram Hotel and the warehouse when we heard shooting behind us — so close that on turning we could see the flashes of pistol-fire a few yards from us.

This shooting scrape had been started by a man named Oliver, who had recently been a prisoner at Fort Lyon. While he had been standing on the corner just back of the Windram Hotel, an Army lieutenant happened to approach the hotel intending to get his supper. Oliver, who had a particular grudge against the young officer, claiming that he had kicked him while he was in jail, opened fire. The lieutenant quickly pulled his gun, and, backing away from the hotel, returned the fire vigorously.

This was the duel we were witnessing with some danger to ourselves, for Oliver was firing toward our warehouse. Neither of the men was ever arrested; in fact, the community rather favored Oliver. The consensus of opinion was that an Army officer who would treat a prisoner as Oliver alleged he had been treated, deserved what Oliver had intended to mete out to him.

But Granada was not really a wild town from the standpoint of bad men and gun-play. Though we did have some killings, they were nothing in comparison with those that had taken place in the earlier towns along the Kansas-Pacific Railroad. The town marshal was "High" Davis, and the nickname was appropriate, for he was about six feet eight inches tall. He had a brother serving as deputy who was almost as tall as "High." The brothers owned a small farm between the town and the river and ran a dairy, besides selling chickens and eggs, butter and vegetables. Both were good men and made capable officers, but they were not as handy with a gun or as quick on the trigger as the marshals of some of the other towns I had lived in.

Granada, of course, had its dance hall, which figured largely in the life of the town. It was at the east end of Main Street, in the block just east of the Perry House, and was owned and managed by Ham Bell, who had come to Granada from Dodge City, Kans. Like Chalk Beeson, whom I have mentioned in a previous chapter, he returned to Dodge City and in the course of time became its mayor. Ham Bell was a fine fellow and ran what was rarely known in those days, a very quiet and orderly resort. The girls in his place were what were called "hand-picked," and were not like those I have described in earlier chapters. I cannot remember any difficulties occurring there during the careful management of Ham Bell, and I was frequently there. In fact, I took numerous lessons in dancing there, and many an evening I frequented the place in company with such of the commission-house boys as Jacob Gross, A. M. Blackwell, C. N. Blackwell, Thomas B. McNair, Harry W. Kelly and J. S. Garcia.

I shall never forget an amusing incident connected with Ham Bell's Dance Hall. Among the girls attached to it was one who went by the name of "Dolly Varden." She was quite a character and a conspicuous member of the entourage. She was a rather large woman, pleasant and good-natured always, and the sort that never seemed to grow old. In fact, she was more like a child than a grown woman, and seemed to act the part as well. Her dresses were loud, displaying violently colored flowers and striking figures, and above all she liked to be noticed and admired. Somehow the name "Dolly Varden" had been fixed upon her by the frequenters of the dance hall, because in those days a style of dress with a loud pattern of bright colors and flowers was called "Dolly Varden" after the young lady in Dickens' *Barnaby Rudge,* described as a coquettish girl who always dressed in extremes of bright-colored flowered material. And ever thereafter she went by that name.

One night her little one-room house caught fire, and the volunteer fire company was called out. As the commission-house boys composed the major part of the fire company, they did the best they could to save their friend Dolly Varden and most of her belongings. After taking an inventory, it was found that Dolly's losses were small. What amused us most was that one of the commission-house boys had been devoting his attentions to the young lady on that particular evening, and having imbibed too many old-fashioned toddies, had accidently dropped his lighted cigarette on his own clothing, which caught fire, destroying the house as well as all of his belongings. So when he was rescued by his companions, he was a sorry sight to behold. There was no insurance on the property, but the next morning Dolly received a neat sum in full payment for all her losses and the name of the culprit was never divulged by his comrades.

While in Granada I had a pleasant group of associates among the commission-house boys. Harry W. Kelly, now president of Gross, Kelly & Co., East Las Vegas, and I were clerks together in the retail department of Otero, Sellar & Co., and we were also roommates and side-partners generally. It was perhaps natural that a close friendship should spring up between us, for our fathers had been good friends in Leavenworth, Kans., during the closing years of the Civil War, and it was as a favor to him that my father had taken Harry into his store to secure business experience. Harry and I were about the same age and there were precious few things we ever overlooked in the way of available amusements.

Among the commission-house boys were a number of good musicians, a few having excellent voices. In Ham Bell's orchestra was a man by the name of Kelly, who played the banjo to perfection, and during pleasant weather he would come over to the commission houses with his banjo in the afternoons, and the singing would commence. Thomas Benton McNair and Arthur M. Blackwell, clerks of Chick, Browne & Co., and Henry W. Gibbons and my brother Page, representing Otero, Sellar & Co., were acknowledged to be the best singers in the crowd. Kelly's favorite song was one composed by himself and named *Fort Dodge*. As it is no doubt long out of print, if indeed it ever attained such distinction, I give it from memory:

FORT DODGE

I

It was bright shown the sun on that morning,
When four men from Fort Dodge marched away,
With food and supplies for their comrades
They were to reach Big Coon station that day.
It's a day we shall all well remember;
That gallant and brave little band,
Who against odds would never surrender,
But bravely to their arms they would stand.

CHORUS

Then let us give three cheers for our comrades,
That gallant and brave little band,
Who against odds would never surrender,
But bravely to their arms they would stand.

II

Fifty Indians surprised them while marching,
Their scalps tried to take, but in vain,
The boys repulsed them at every endeavor,
For they were boys who were up to that game.
"Let the redskins be ten times our number,
Be cool when you aim," was the cry
Of the corporal in charge of our party,
"We will conquer the foe or we'll die."

CHORUS

III

They fought with a will and persistence,
Till assistance at last came to hand,
Two mail carriers appearing on the action
To strengthen that brave little band.
Paddy Boyle charged the lines of the redskins,
To the fort for help he did go,
While the balance, they still kept on a-fighting
And gallantly they beat off the foe.

CHORUS

IV

A company of cavalry then mounted,
Our comrades to rescue and save;
General Sully, he issued an order,
Applauding their conduct as brave.
And when from their wounds they recover,
May they live many years to relate,
Of the fight which occurred in September
In the year Eighteen Hundred Sixty-eight.

CHORUS

The members of the quartet had their favorite songs. Mack Blackwell, as A. M. Blackwell was called, was partial to *Old Black Joe, The Poor Old Slave, Nellie was a Lady, I Miss You, Nettie Moore, 'Way Down Upon the Suwanee River, Take Me Back to Old Virginia, Dixie Land,* and many other negro melodies. Thomas Benton McNair would sing *con amore Tenting on the Old Camp Ground, Marching Through Georgia, My Old Kentucky Home, Speak to me, Love, Only Speak, Down the Ohio.* My brother Page had a beautiful baritone voice and played his accompaniment on the guitar. His favorite songs were *The Old Sexton, In Days of Old when Knights were Bold, Muldoon's Picnic, The Man who Attended O'Reilly's Bar,* and several beautiful duets with Henry W. Gibbons.

Hunting continued to be a favorite diversion of mine, and the vicinity of Granada abounded in game with which I was, at that time, unfamiliar. Near a small station on the Atchison, Topeka & Santa Fé Railroad called Holly, not far from Granada, were numerous water holes and sloughs. During the proper seasons these were alive with wild geese, brant, duck, snipe and other water fowl. Harry Kelly and I were both passionately devoted to hunting, and in addition to the pleasure we had from the sport we bettered our incomes by selling game. There was a steady demand along the line of the railroad for whatever we might offer, and with ducks and cottontail rabbits bringing $3.00 a dozen, and the other game selling readily at a proportionately good price per pound, we were well paid for our time and effort. Very often when we had a whole day at our disposal, a Sunday or a holiday, we would return with a wagon well filled with various kinds of game.

Antelope were numerous in that section, and we had much sport hunting them on horseback with greyhounds. With a gun they were hard to get, but when we used greyhounds it was not so difficult. The antelope is very timid and easily frightened; one bite of the dog seems to kill them easily. I remember that once when I was hunting with Adolph Mennet, he shot an antelope with a 50-caliber Sharp's rifle, the bullet entering at one flank and coming out at the opposite shoulder, and tearing a frightful hole through which the poor creature's entrails were dragging on the ground. Yet the antelope had enough stamina to run at least two miles in such condition and would doubtless have escaped, had not a dog run out from a camp it was passing and caught it after a short chase. The antelope succumbed to one bite of the dog. The dog quite naturally thought the antelope belonged to him, and was sitting by it when I came up. Foolishly, I took hold of the dead antelope, but had no sooner done so, than the dog jumped at me viciously and bit me very severely on the left leg. As I review the circumstances today, I think the dog was right, but my reasoning at that time was far from being calm, and the dog paid the penalty for his interference.

Shortly after moving to Granada, a special train carrying the principal officials of the Atchison, Topeka & Santa Fé Railroad came out for the purpose of securing the services of my father to act as their agent in acquiring the needed right-of-way in New Mexico. They were anxious to have this settled before any of the rival roads might enter the Territory.

The officials in the party were Thomas Nickerson, Joseph Nickerson, George H. Nettleton, M. L. Sargent, A. A. Robinson, George R. Peck and Edward Wilder. Many ladies accompanied the party.

At this meeting my father was invited to become identified with the company. This he consented to do, whereupon it was arranged that A. A. Robinson, chief engineer, and George R. Peck, general counsel, should immediately accompany him to New Mexico to secure the right-of-way through the Territory before either the Kansas-Pacific Railroad or the Denver and Rio Grande Railroad could possibly get there.

A. A. Robinson and his wife, and George R. Peck were guests at our home for several days while the arrangements were being made for the overland trip. After the party had departed, Mrs. Robinson remained at our home in Granada until Mr. Robinson returned several weeks later.

Afterwards when William B. Strong became vice-president and general manager of the Atchison, Topeka & Santa Fé Railroad, a warm friendship grew up between him and my father. Mr. Strong made his first trip to Santa Fé with my father for the purpose of organizing the New Mexico & Southern Pacific Railroad (the New Mexico branch of the Atchison, Topeka & Santa Fé Railroad), at which time my father was elected a director and vice-president of the new railroad company. The duty of naming the additional New Mexico directors, to conform to the New Mexico statutes, was left entirely to him.

My father introduced Judge Henry L. Waldo of Santa Fé, who had been his attorney for many years, to Messrs. Strong, Peck and Robinson, who appointed him legal representative of the Atchison, Topeka & Santa Fé Railroad in New Mexico. Aside from business, Judge Waldo and my father were warm personal friends, and each held the other in the very highest esteem. Many years of valuable service proved that a better selection could not have been made. Judge Waldo was not only one of the foremost lawyers in the Territory, but he was a capable, honorable and distinguished citizen as well. I only wish that New Mexico could boast of more like him at the present time.

Chapter VIII

AS I have indicated before, I had a great fondness for horses and dogs. It was at Granada that I acquired Kiowa, the horse that among all those I have owned stands preëminent for equine excellence. Just a week after our arrival at Granada, a party of New Mexicans, headed by Pablo Medina, returned from a successful buffalo hunt in northwestern Kansas. With them they brought some wild horses they had captured, and out of the bunch I bought a two-year-old blue-roan pony, which I named Kiowa. In all my experience on the frontier I have never known a horse his equal for intelligence, speed and endurance. He remained in my possession for thirty years, until he finally died of old age.

One of the diversions most popular with the men and boys of the frontier towns was horse-racing, and Kiowa helped me to win many a contest of this kind. Some three miles down the Arkansas River was a large island called Newell's Island after a man named Charlie Newell, who lived on it. Charlie was a fine fellow who liked a horse race just a little better than any other kind of sport. One day a party of race-horse men arrived in Granada from Kansas and let it be known that they were looking for a race. Charlie Newell had seen Kiowa perform, and was confident of my horse's ability to beat almost any horse in a quarter. When he learned that the race-horse men were in town, he asked me if I would not let him arrange a race between the horse those men had and my pony.

As this was going a little more deeply into the racing game than hitherto, I thought it best to consult my father. At first he vetoed the whole thing, but finally I got his consent on the conditions that I would not ride in the race. This was a disappointment, but I had to submit to it with the best possible grace. I had a young friend working in our store who was a good rider and quite light in weight, as well. So I went to Mike Harkins and asked him if he would ride Kiowa. He literally jumped at the chance, and I knew that with him in the saddle my pony would be well handled in the race.

The Kansas horse turned out to be a large stallion nearly twice the size of Kiowa. In reality he was a well-known race horse from the eastern circuit, and he looked like a thoroughbred. The details of the race were quickly arranged. The distance was to be 440 yards. Kiowa was allowed a handicap of fifteen feet at the finish. The start was to be made by one of the judges firing a pistol and each side was to put up as stakes $1000 deposited with some responsible person. Of course, a race of this kind encouraged any number of side-bets, and practically every male resident of Granada made his wager on the outcome. If he had money, he bet it, but if he had none, he put up a wagon, a horse, a mule, a saddle, a pistol, or some other desirable kind of personal property.

Mike chose to ride Kiowa without saddle or bridle. All that he wanted, he said, was a leather halter. His dress was far from what is usually *de rigeur* for a jockey. He was barefooted and bareheaded, all that he had on being a white shirt and dark blue pants. He did not even carry a whip. At the signal to start, Kiowa jumped into the lead and held it all the way, never giving an inch and finishing twenty feet ahead of the stallion.

It was a great day in Granada. The whole town turned out to see the race, and after Kiowa had won I had a hard time staving off offers to buy him. Charlie Newell was unquestionably the happiest man in town, and he took great delight in saying to me and everyone else, "I told you so." He had staked about everything he had in the world on the race, and Kiowa's victory was very profitable to him. He gave Mike a hundred dollars and made me a very handsome present.

The dogs I owned during our stay at Granada deserve mention. One was a fine English bulldog named Duke, who became a real comrade of my pony, Kiowa. Duke would never leave Kiowa day or night, except when I was riding Kiowa, and even then he would have gone along if I had not chained him in the stable. In the spring and summer, Kiowa was generally picketed with about 125 feet of rope in the grass near our house. On all such occasions Duke would stay with Kiowa, never leaving him and permitting no one to approach unless it was one of our family. To Duke's faithfulness I am greatly beholden, for it kept me from losing Kiowa.

One day the iron pin to which Kiowa's rope was tied came out of the ground. A herd of horses happened to be passing the house that day, and Kiowa naturally followed in their wake, thus exposing himself to every chance in the world of being conducted into the Indian territory, whence the herd was bound. Not until late in the afternoon did any of us notice Kiowa's absence, and when we did, we discovered that Duke was likewise absent. Not a trace of either could we find during the next few days, although we made a diligent search.

I was forced to the conclusion that I had lost forever both my beloved horse and my beloved dog, when some freighters, returning from the Canadian River, passed and in answer to my inquiries told me that they had seen that herd a few days before and had noticed a horse following it, some distance behind and dragging a long rope with a bulldog pulling at the end. This was the first information I had regarding the direction Kiowa and Duke had taken, for I was sure it was they. It was a stroke of luck, for the road from Granada to the Canadian River was hardly better than a cattle-trail and little travelled.

I did not stop to reflect on the matter, but immediately began making preparations to hunt for Kiowa and Duke. But before I was able to get my plans under way, in walked

Duke leading Kiowa by the long picket rope! Duke was tired and haggard, clearly showing that he had suffered terribly on the trip, which had taken ten days. I doubt very much whether he had had anything substantial to eat since he left home. The pony, on the other hand, looked as fine as usual, for he had found plenty of grass and water.

I think there has never been a better example of a dumb animal's love and affection, and, I might add, of determination. There is no doubt in my mind that when those freighters saw Duke tugging at Kiowa's picket rope, he was trying to turn the pony in the direction of Granada, and I am sure he never gave up until he had accomplished his purpose. When he had finally induced Kiowa to accept his views, he took the end of the rope and led Kiowa back to Granada. I learned later from reliable sources that dog and pony had followed the herd of horses for more than 150 miles before Duke could change Kiowa's mind.

With careful feeding and nursing, Duke soon regained his usual good condition, only to be poisoned a few weeks later by some inhuman brute. We did all in our power to save him by pouring melted lard and sweet oil down his throat, but the poison had already done its work. The poor dog seemed to know we were doing all we could for him. I shall always remember his pitiful and pleading look and the way his eyes said thanks for all we were doing. We buried Duke in the yard close to the stable, where he had loved to play in company with his companion, Kiowa.

As part of the equipment for the hunting I enjoyed so much, I kept a pack of sixteen greyhounds, but I sometimes used them in other ways, as witness the following incident: Kiowa's winning the race with the Kansas stallion was noised abroad throughout the country, and I gained some little renown as a sportsman. The fact that I had this pack of sixteen greyhounds also became known. So into the town one day came a saloon-man from Dodge City, called "Dog" Kelly from the fact that he was willing to run his pack of greyhounds against any dogs in the country and for any kind of stake. He was itching for a race with my dogs and boasted much of the speed of his prize dog, a bitch named Modoc, entirely black and a perfect beauty, whom he had brought along with him. He looked me up and proposed a race, saying that he would put $1,000 on the result. As I did not care to go extensively into that sort of thing, I refused his offer, but told him I was perfectly willing to run one of my dogs against his Modoc for fun. That did not appeal to him at all, for, as he said, it was always money that talked in his case.

When Charlie Newell and others of the sporting group in Granada heard that these negotiations were in progress, they scented a good race, and at once took a hand in the affair. Through their interest the race was arranged. We were to match the fastest hound in my pack, a large black dog with a full white face named Fleet, against Kelly's Modoc. Kelly was confident that his bitch would win, and he piled side-bet upon side-bet. Charlie Newell and his crowd took every bet that came their way. So Granada was once more thrown into a ferment of excitement over a race.

The day of the race was perfect for such an affair. The two dogs were placed in a wagon under the sole care of the judges we had selected, whose horses were tied to the back of the wagon and led in this fashion until they were needed for the race. Behind the wagon followed about fifty of the residents of Granada and vicinity, who wanted to see the race and who, in nearly every instance, had money on the result. Our party crossed the Arkansas River two or three miles west of Granada and continued north for a short distance until the level plains were reached. After we had gone about a mile farther, one of the judges, who had been looking through a pair of field-glasses, called a halt and announced that he had discovered an antelope about a mile away. We all knew that this meant that the race would start at once.

The judges cautioned all the followers on horseback

against scattering and interfering with the chase. They also forbade any of them atempting to pass the judges or to yell at the dogs. One of the judges took the dogs from the wagon and examined the double slips that leashed them, in order to see if they worked properly. The design of these double slips made it possible, by pulling a heavy cord, to drop the collars from the necks of both dogs simultaneously, to insure an even start.

The dogs were pointed in the direction of the antelope, for greyhounds run altogether by sight and must see what they are after before they will start. As soon as the dogs caught sight of the antelope they became wild with excitement, tugging hard at the slips. The judge braced himself, which threw the dogs upon their hind legs ready to spring. While the dogs were in this position, he pulled the cord of the slip and away they went.

The antelope, to our surprise, never moved from his position but stood as though looking in admiration of the approaching dogs. And a beautiful sight it was: the dogs running neck and neck with the graceful motion peculiar to their breed. In the meantime, the judges had mounted their horses and were riding full speed in the wake of the dogs, while the rest of the crowd galloped forward in the rear of the judges.

By this time the dogs were within about half a mile of the antelope, and the latter, scenting trouble, started away at full speed. The race was on, and we of the "gallery" could see every jump made by the antelope and the dogs. The dogs were running side by side; to all apearances, they were one dog, so evenly did they keep the pace. But as the race went on, my dog, Fleet, began to gain the lead and gradually increased it to a full length by the time he had come within twenty feet of the antelope. In another moment, Fleet had grabbed the antelope's hind leg, swinging him completely off his feet. Modoc was so close that she grabbed the animal's neck as it swung around.

When the judges and the rest of us rode up, the buck was dead, and both dogs were lying down, panting in complete exhaustion. First of all, the dogs were looked after; their mouths were washed out with sponges and they were made to drink from canteens; then they were placed in the wagons and covered with blankets. By this time the judges had made their decision, and announced that Fleet was the winner. Everybody was satisfied, even Dog Kelly, who said that it was the greatest race he had ever seen and that it was worth a thousand dollars of any man's money to see one like it.

Like all towns of that section, Granada lived under the constant shadow of danger from the Indians. In the fall of 1873, in particular, there was great excitement in the town on this score, and as I remember the circumstances well I shall relate them. A band of about two hundred Cheyenne and Arapahoe Indians passed through Granada, going west, ostensibly on a visit to John D. Prowers, who lived near Fort Lyon. Prowers was a wealthy stockman who had married into one of the tribes, and, as it was no unusual thing for his wife's relatives to visit him, the visit by this band of Indians excited no particular suspicion. But for some cause, the redskins on their return began to attack the isolated ranches, killing a number of people, as well as driving off the cattle and horses. The news of their outrages had reached Granada before they arrived; so when they appeared the citizens of the town were prepared for them.

It happened that the day of their arrival I was out chasing jackrabbits with my greyhounds about two miles west of town in company with Frank A. Manzanares and Tom Nolan. The dogs had just started after a jackrabbit, when we noticed a man on horseback riding at break-neck speed toward Granada. Guessing that he was a courier with some important news about Indians, we at once gave up hunting and hurried back to the town. There we found everyone busy organizing a volunteer military company. Every man who had a rifle and pistol and every available horse were being

Duke brings Kiowa home.

pressed into service. Captain Payne, who afterward became the great Oklahoma boomer, had just been elected captain of the company, and he was making a speech to a large group of armed men collected in front of a dry-goods box, upon which he was standing. In no uncertain terms, he told them what to expect and what was expected of them.

Three hours later the Indians appeared. Some were evidently intending to come into the town, while the rest had been instructed to drive the large herd of cattle and horses south of the town, in the very locality where we had been chasing jackrabbits a few hours before. Captain Payne, at the head of about one hundred of the best men available, started west to meet the Indians coming toward the town. The Captain demanded that they proceed around the town, in the same direction taken by the band with the cattle and horses. This they proceeded to do without debate, but the head chief asked permission to be allowed to enter the town with ten of the other chiefs in order to buy enough supplies to last them on the journey to the Indian Territory.

Captain Payne saw no objection to this, and the old chief and his lieutenants rode back to Granada. They hitched their horses in front of our retail department, walked in, and soon were busy making their purchases, which consisted entirely of foodstuffs and tobacco. I watched them carefully, and detected no sign of fear or suspicion on their part, and no indication that they were premeditating a dastardly outrage on their subsequent journey. When they had packed their goods on their horses, they said good-bye in the most friendly manner, and headed down the river towards Newell's Island, where they expected to meet the rest of the band.

That night guards were placed around the town, and the precaution was taken for more than a month. The town continued in a fever of excitement and terror, for dead bodies were brought in for burial almost every day. I was one who stood guard, usually with my old friend Adolph Mennet, on the hills south of the town. I never missed a single night when Mennet was on duty, winning from him the compliment, "I would rather have Miguelito with me on guard duty than any man in town, for he is always awake and listening."

That same band of Indians, after leaving Granada, met one of our young men, John Dietz, as he was returning on horseback from a hunting trip that had taken him about twelve miles east and south of Granada into the vicinity of a small town named Aubrey. They not only killed him but mutilated his body and then scalped him. His naked body was found the next day and brought to Granada for burial. The Indians also attacked the ranch of an old man named Rogers, living near Twin Buttes, some ten or twelve miles south and east of Granada.

I was one in the party that went down to the ranch after the news of the attack came. We found that every man, woman and child had been killed and that the bodies of all had been horribly mutilated. The Indians had seemingly built a fire on the chest of Mr. Rogers while he was still alive, for the indications were that he had attempted to scratch the burning wood and rags from his body just before he breathed his last. His right hand was elevated over his chest, with burnt flesh hanging from the finger nails. We placed the bodies, six in all, in a wagon and carried them to Granada for burial. All the woodwork of the buildings and out-houses was burnt or destroyed. Even the chickens, dogs and cats were killed, while the cows and horses had evidently been added to the Indian herd. Within the following ten days more than twenty additional bodies were brought in, all found within a radius of fifteen miles of Granada.

The seriousness of the situation lead to troops being called from Fort Union, N. Mex., to protect the section. We had at Granada a troop of the Eighth Cavalry, commanded by Captain McClave, that took entire charge of the guard duty which had formerly been attended to by the citizens' committee. I became well acquainted with both Captain Mc-

Clave and the young surgeon accompanying the troops, Louis A. La Garde, and as both of them were very fond of hunting, we enjoyed many expeditions together. Finally the Indians were driven back to the reservation, and things became quiet and orderly once more. The soldiers stationed at Granada returned to their post, and I lost the two boon companions.

About this time my uncle, Ambrosio Armijo, sent his large mule train to Granada, loaded with wool, which was to be reloaded with freight for New Mexico. The outfit was in charge of his son, Mariano Armijo, who was as "wild as a March hare" and whose only thought was to spend money and have a good time. He soon talked my brother Page and Mike Harkins, the young man who had ridden my pony, Kiowa, in the race, to return with him to Las Cruces, N. Mex. Poor Mike Harkins was killed soon after his arrival in the Territory during an altercation with a drunken soldier. Page remained in New Mexico until ordered back by my father on his return to Granada.

The great herds of buffalo were moving north, and buffalo meat and hides were becoming scarce around Granada, although there were still many herds to be found in the Canadian country, south of Dodge City, Kans., and, as late as 1874, many small herds were grazing around the railroad station at Lakin, Kans. The building of railroads and the incoming of settlers soon solved the buffalo question; very few were seen south of the Arkansas River after 1873, and the following year scarcely a buffalo could be found south of the Kansas-Pacific Railroad.

Otero, Sellar & Co., in addition to their regular line of business, were also large Government contractors, receiving and forwarding supplies to the different military posts and Indian reservations throughout the southwest. One of the many routes extended from Dodge City, south into the Indian Territory. "Routes," as designated by the Government, means simply an established wagon road. For instance, the

Fort Bascom route went to Fort Bascom; the Silver City route went to Silver City; the Camp Supply route went to Camp Supply; the Canadian River route was the route going by way of the Canadian River. All intermediate points were billed Via certain "routes," etc. A "time contract," as designated by the Government, meant that you were given so many days in which to deliver the freight. For instance, under our contract with the Government, we would pay the freighting teams, let us say, eight cents a pound for hauling the freight from the end of the railroad to Fort Bayard, N. Mex., via the Silver City route, the said freight to be delivered at Fort Bayard in forty-five days. Should the freighter fail to delived the goods within the specified time, he would be subject to a demurrage charge for every day he took over the forty-five, in accordance with a provision printed in the bill of lading. In all such cases a board of survey would be called by the commanding officer at the point of delivery and the cause of the delay would be submitted to the board. If it was found to be unavoidable and not the result of neglect, the board would waive the penalties. After the Atchison, Topeka and Santa Fé Railroad reached Dodge City, the Canadian River route and the Camp Supply route, both in the Indian Territory, were started from Dodge City, rather than from Granada, Colo., where Otero, Sellar & Co., the Government contractors, had located. This made it necessary either to establish a branch house at Dodge City to handle our Government contracts for those routes or to have some representatives at the point designated by the Government. We chose the latter alternative and appointed Charles Rath and Robert Wright of Dodge City to represent our interests at that point. As a consequence, it became necessary at times for some member of the firm of Otero, Sellar & Co. to visit Dodge City and confer with Charles Rath and Robert Wright. Very frequently it became a matter of considerable importance to hasten large outfits of freighting wagons from Granada to Dodge City, in order to meet the requirements of the Government. Many of these shipments were *time-contracts,* and in case of demurrage the penalties were heavy. On most of these trips to Dodge City, I accompanied my father, as I was anxious to renew my acquaintance with some of my old Kit Carson friends — Jake Collar, Chalk Beeson, F. C. Zimmerman among others. On one of these trips I first met Bat Masterson and Dave Mathers, known as "Mysterious Dave."

In the spring of 1874 my father went on a trip to New Mexico for the Atchison, Topeka and Santa Fé Railroad, leaving my mother, two sisters and myself in Granada. On his way back, he was taken down with an attack of pneumonia at Cimarron, N. Mex., and the family was notified by telegraph of his serious condition. My mother decided to go at once and to take all of the children along, excepting my brother Page, who was away with our cousin, Mariano Armijo, in southern New Mexico. So, having secured a Government ambulance from Fort Lyon and with Frank Davenport as driver, we started for Cimarron. Although the plains Indians were again troublesome and the Navajos were on the warpath in the vicinity of Bent's Cañon, we were fortunate in making the trip to Cimarron without misadventure.

During our stay at Cimarron, we stopped at the National Hotel, kept by John McCullough, formerly of Kit Carson. My father was rooming there, and we found that he had been a very sick man. After several more weeks in bed he recovered sufficiently under Doctor J. M. Cunningham's treatment to be allowed to return to Granada.

At this time the Utes and Apaches were located near Cimarron, and I well remember a little trouble that occurred between them while I was there. One night they came into Cimarron and shot up the town with bows and arrows. It was simply a case of poor whiskey and a friendly drunk winding up into a rumpus among the two Indian tribes, but some of the arrows they exchanged at one another happened to go through windows of certain houses in Cimarron. One instance was very amusing. The bookkeeper at the large Aztec Flour Mill, located in the center of Cimarron, was hard at work that night and, being almost totally deaf, he did not become aware of the excitement, until he saw two arrows sticking in the wall just above his head. He did not linger long at his work, but jumped from his high stool and made a hasty escape from the building.

After things had quieted down, I went with Doctor Cunningham and a party of citizens, including Indian Agent Rinehart, to see what damages had been done. A little distance from the flour mill we came across a dead Indian, a fine looking Ute, about twenty-five years of age. He had been shot in the left side, the arrow having passed through his heart. While we were taking the body to a vacant room his mother and several other Utes came up, and we allowed them to take the body with them to their camp.

On our return trip to Granada after my father's recovery we were not so fortunate as to escape trouble with Indians. Some Navajos chased us into a stage station at Bent's Cañon, where we were compelled to stay for several days until the scouts reported the country clear of Indians. We had no further trouble until we reached the Arkansas valley, where we saw a band of plains Indians near Caddoa, who gave us a lively chase until we reached the protection of a sheep ranch belonging to some Englishmen, where we stayed for the night. The Indians were afraid to come too near us during the chase, for we had a couple of 50-caliber Sharp rifles, and had taken a few ineffectual shots at them merely to show them what we had in the way of arms.

The next morning we started before daylight with an escort of four men heavily armed, travelling as rapidly as possible, and reached Granada before dark. Our friends seemed surprised to see us alive, as they had concluded from information they had received that the Indians would probably attack and kill us as they had done with quite a number of herders in the section we had come through.

Chapter IX

IT was about this time, 1874, that I received an appointment to Annapolis, and left with my mother for Washington, D. C., to prepare to enter the Naval Academy. After the necessary papers were made out, she took me to Annapolis and placed me in charge of Professor Thompson, who was to tutor me for the next regular examination for entrance to the Academy. I did not relish the idea of entering the Naval Academy and sought an excuse to get away. It came sooner than I had expected.

One afternoon while Professor and Mrs. Thompson were attending an official reception, I learned that a steamer was leaving for Baltimore. I lost no time in packing my trunk and getting it down to the steamer. Then I wrote a letter to Professor Thompson, placed it on his desk, and made my departure. I had sufficient money to get to St. Louis, but when I got there I had to apply to the agents of Otero, Sellar & Co. for extra funds. They telegraphed my father to learn his wishes in the matter, and his reply instructed them to buy me a ticket to Granada and give me a sufficient sum for expenses on the way. Immediately I started back to the country that was much more suited to my tastes and inclinations than the United States Naval Academy.

On my return, I returned to my old pursuits. I recall an antelope hunt at about this time, which brought with it a brush with horse-thieves. In the fall of 1874, a party of us arranged a hunt in the Twin Buttes region, south of Granada. Bill Ponties, Eli Babb, Henry W. Gibbons and my brother Page rode in the wagon, while my cousin Charles H. Armijo and I went on horseback. Charlie rode a fine racing mare, which he had but recently bought, and I rode my favorite pony, Kiowa. Shortly after we passed the sand hills south of town we noticed four suspicious-looking men on horseback, who seemed to be following us, but, as we were well armed with rifles and pistols, we felt secure enough. Nevertheless, when we found that they continued to keep at the same distance behind us, we decided to keep our eyes on them.

After reaching Twin Butte Creek, we camped on the high slope just above the bank near a water hole. We discovered a little later that the four men who had been following us had left the main road and had made themselves a camp about a mile down the creek. From what we had seen, we decided it would be wise to take precautions. The wagon horses were picketed a short distance in front of the wagon, while Kiowa and the mare were allowed to graze immediately behind the wagon. We arranged among ourselves to keep a guard posted all night. Hardly had we made everything ship-shape in the camp and eaten supper than there came one of the hardest rainstorms I have ever experienced. It was a genuine cloudburst. Twin Butte Creek, ordinarily a shallow stream, became a roaring torrent that overflowed its fifteen-foot banks. We were all wet to the skin and all of our camp equipment was thoroughly water-soaked, except our guns and ammunition.

When the rain was over, the sky cleared and the moon came out. It happened to be my turn to stand guard, my companion being Eli Babb. The other four in our party were sleeping in the wagon, while Babb and I sat under the rear part of the wagon with our rifles across our laps. Everything was quiet, when suddenly Kiowa snorted and turned his head in the direction of the swollen creek. I looked in the same direction, and distinctly saw a man crawling towards the two saddle horses with a knife in his hand. I touched Babb's arm and pointed toward the man, who was not more than fifty steps from where we were sitting.

Both of us raised our guns, aimed and fired. The man

jumped up with a loud yell and disappeared. Our four companions came running from the wagon, with their guns ready for action, and, seeing some objects moving in the distance, we all began to fire, scattering ourselves as we did so, because the other crowd had begun to fire at us. The firing continued until daylight, when it suddenly ceased. But ours was a highly indignant group and far from willing to call the affair over. So when daylight came, four of us rode down to the camp we had seen below us, determined upon summary action, but to our chagrin we found the camp deserted. The men's tracks were fresh in the mud and easy to follow, so we kept hot on their trail for several miles, but finally had to give up the pursuit.

Some weeks afterward the body of a man was found on one of the small islands in the Arkansas River, below the junction with Twin Butte Creek. It was generally believed to be the body of "Dirty Dick," alias "Unclean Richard," a horse-thief. However that may be, one thing is certain: Dirty Dick was never seen around Granada again. Babb and I never claimed that we killed the man whose body had been found, but of this I am sure: if we did not kill the fellow we shot at that night, we did manage to give him a good scare.

News soon reached us that the Kansas-Pacific Railroad had determined to run a branch line into New Mexico, and had already started to build south from Kit Carson toward Las Animas. Immediately, the Atchison, Topeka & Santa Fé Railroad put on pressure so that both roads reached La Junta about the same time, the Santa Fé continuing on to Pueblo.

A short time before leaving Granada, while I was hunting with my pack of greyhounds, Kiowa stepped into a mole-hole and fell, rolling over on me and breaking both bones of my left arm at the wrist. It was a painful fracture and for several weeks I was unable to hunt or to do much of anything else.

In the summer of 1875 we moved to La Junta, Colo. There the commission houses were located on the north side of the railroad tracks, and Main Street faced the two depots, which were between the warehouses and the street. On the east corner of the principal block on Main Street was Billy Patterson's first-class saloon, and just across the street to the east was Joe Perry's restaurant, where most of the commission boys took their meals. West of Patterson's saloon were several shops and saloon and Rufe Edwards' dance hall.

Harry Kelly and myelf had a room in the warehouse. The only door to the room was on the inside; however, there was one convenient window on the outside. The night watchman was Captain York, who had been an old sea captain, and certainly looked the part. He had received strict orders about that outside window — the blinds were to be locked every night. Harry and I had to use considerable tact with the old sea captain in order to use the window as a door on those special occasions when we were out late "sitting up with a sick friend."

We did not stay in La Junta long. The Denver and Rio Grande Railroad was actively building south from Pueblo and had reached El Moro, six miles north of Trinidad. As El Moro seemed the more promising place commercially, the commission houses built their main establishments at El Moro in the spring of 1876 and used the La Junta houses simply as branch offices until they finally disposed of them to the Atchison, Topeka and Santa Fé Railroad. La Junta, however, was a lively place, and I recall several exciting experiences.

One night George Mitchell, the popular bartender at Billy Patterson's saloon, was called to the side-door of the saloon and shot dead. As this happened early in the evening, nearly everyone in town went over to see "Curly," as George was familiarly called because of his curly black hair. His body had been left where it fell until the sheriff arrived from Las Animas, the county seat. No one was ever apprehended for this murder. The supposition was that some drunken driver or herder from one of the many camps in the neighborhood had gone into the saloon for a drink and had been refused it by George on the ground that he had already had enough. This treatment must have angered the fellow, who had thereupon gone around to the side-door and knocked. When George answered, he had poked his pistol into his face and fired, making his escape in the darkness.

Occasionally I became involved in some attempt to keep lawless citizens within bounds. One night just after we commission-house boys had eaten our supper we heard a call for help from Andy Ruder's butcher shop, just two doors east of Joe Perry's restaurant. We rushed over and learned from Andy that some horse-thieves were in his stable after his mules. We surrounded the stable, and, after getting some guns, went in and found one man. He begged for his life and we decided not to lynch him, as we had originally intended doing.

After we had satisfied ourselves that he was not on theft-bent, we tied about ten feet of one-inch rope to each of his wrists, and "conducted" him to the railroad water tank. We dragged him directly under the spout of the tank and held him there. Another one of our crowd climbed up to the tank and turned the water on. We let it strike the fellow full in the face, holding him there until he was nearly drowned. Then we took him to the west end of town and turned him loose, ordering him to run and keep running, and never to show his face in La Junta again. When he started to run we fired a few shots over his head to add emphasis to what we had said.

On another occasion I was called in to help in a little domestic trouble. Just back of Ruder's butcher shop was the house occupied by a carpenter named Green Thompson, who had a good-looking wife and two attractive step-daughters.

Thompson was a brute, who treated his family little better than animals. They were in constant fear of him, especially when he was drunk. Many times Mrs. Thompson was forced to call the police on account of his brutality. Mrs. Thompson and the girls were great friends of the commission-house boys and, knowing the conditions in her home, they were all sympathetic. She kept us informed of her troubles, for whenever she delivered our washing to us she would give a recital. Harry Kelly and I had rather constituted ourselves guardians for Mrs. Thompson and the girls, and were much concerned over the state of affairs.

One evening after supper we dropped in at the house and found that just a few minutes before Thompson had been horribly abusing his wife because she did not have any money to give him for whiskey. He had also grossly insulted one of his daughters, Vinez, a child of sixteen, by telling her that she was old enough to begin making money and suggesting a repulsive means of doing so. When I saw them all in tears and had heard their pitiful story, I became quite indignant, and said, "Why don't you get a gun, and the next time he abuses you just shoot the brute?"

I meant every word I said, but little did I think that Thompson would overhear me. Yet, as I afterward learned, he was standing at the front door listening, with an ax helve in his hand ready for me. Luckily, I happened to leave by the back door, followed by Harry Kelly, who had been in the house with me, although he had not suggested such violent action as I had. As we were going out of the yard Harry saw Thompson coming toward us with the ax helve in his hand. He yelled, "Miguel, look out, here comes Thompson!"

We lost little time in getting back to the commission house, but Thompson followed us even inside the office and with blood in his eye he pointed at me, saying, "I'll thank you, young Mr. Otero, to keep your advice to yourself and not be telling my wife to shoot me." He knew he could not attack me there, so he walked out of the office. But everyone in the place had a good laugh at my expense.

To tell the truth, it was hard to escape being drawn into the numerous affrays that developed in La Junta. Harry Kelly and I were star witnesses in the justice-of-the-peace hearing in connection with the killing of Tim Shea by Rufe Edwards. Rufe Edwards, the dance-hall owner, was a very quiet and gentlemanly gambler who never drank to excess and never molested anyone. His mistress was Lee Edwards, quite a pretty woman and rather quiet and exclusive. In La Junta at the same time lived a noted gambler named Tim Shea. For some reason, the latter's mistress had been barred from Edwards' dance hall. Therefore she felt aggrieved at Edwards, and told Shea of the indignity. Gallantly enough, Tim assured his lady-love that no man could wound her sensitive feelings and get away with it.

So he walked over to the store of Otero, Sellar & Co., and purchased a Colt .45 caliber and a box of cartridges, which he opened at once, thrusting six bullets into the chambers of the revolver. That was at nine o'clock in the morning. At about half past eleven Tim again entered the store and requested that he be allowed to return the pistol and the box of cartridges, explaining that he wanted the money in order to go west to Pueblo on the noon train. His request was granted, and as he put the money into his pocket and started for the door he turned and said: "Good-bye, boys. I'll be leaving you in half an hour, but before I go I intend to kill one damn' son of a bitch."

Tim seemed so positive that Harry Kelly and I followed him. He crossed Main Street and entered Billy Patterson's saloon. In a few minutes he again appeared outside and started up the street toward Rufe Edwards' dance hall. He passed the open door where Rufe was standing; then he took three or four steps forward, and, turning quickly, attempted to draw a pistol.

But Rufe was too quick for him. He reached for a shotgun

by the door, and, as Shea was drawing his pistol, fired a charge of buckshot into his chest, which made a hole big as a man's hand. Tim jumped about four feet into the air, and then fell to the sidewalk stone dead. Harry Kelly and I had not only seen it all, but were actually examining the body almost as soon as it struck the boards of the sidewalk.

Everything was new in El Moro, the commission houses and all the other houses as well. This condition was emphasized even in the names of some of the town's institutions. Colorado, moreover, had just been admitted to statehood, and this fact, too, was recorded in some of the names of establishments in the town. There was a New State Hotel and a New State Saloon, the former run by Mr. Winkfield and the latter by Rufe Harrington. The two buildings stood next to each other on Main Street, while on a side street, facing the railroad tracks, was George Close's dance hall.

One night a number of us were returning from a dance at Mrs. McDowell's "Log Cabin," as her boarding house was called. Though it was after midnight, the fun was in full swing at George Close's dance hall. So we stopped in for a while. During a dance, a half-breed Indian known as "Navajo Frank" came in and tried to trade his rifle to George Close for a bottle of whiskey. George refused to make any sort of trade, for the Indian already had swilled down too much, and besides it was against the law to sell or give liquor to an Indian.

This refusal made the Indian very angry and out the front door he walked, cursing like a trooper. He stalked across the street until he reached the railroad tracks; there he sat down on the end of one of the cross-ties facing the dance hall, and, pointing his rifle towards the glass of the front door, fired into the hall while the dance was going on. An unusually pretty girl, Jennie Lawrence, who had only recently come from Pueblo, was dancing with Jimmie Russell of Trinidad. The Indian's bullet struck her in the left side, passing

My Life on the Frontier 99

through her heart. She must have been killed instantly. The bullet then passed through Russell's coat sleeve, and on over to one of the fiddlers in the orchestra. After passing through his arm, it buried itself in the wall. The poor dead girl was covered with a sheet just where she fell.

Navajo Frank escaped, but he was captured some years later in East Las Vegas and hanged by a mob in broad daylight in front of my home. An account of this I shall give in a later chapter.

In El Moro was a large livery stable owned by Governor Albert C. Hunt, formerly territorial governor of Colorado. It was managed by a man named William Greenstreet and was well stocked with fine horses and good Concord buggies. The livery stable also operated a line of busses, which ran to Trinidad and met all the trains. The commission-house boys were liberal patrons of Greenstreet, and usually would have everything engaged for Sundays and holidays for all the girls lived at Trinidad, and it became our Mecca on such occasions.

Between El Moro and Trinidad was a small settlement known as Chilili, which was a great place for dances, for many pretty girls lived there. Two of these in particular, Donaciana Trujillo and Gertrudes Gallegos, used to come to El Moro to trade and became acquainted with several of the commission-house boys. They used to invite us to the dances, and very frequently we would go over. One night Harry W. Kelly and I went to Chilili, and narrowly got back with our lives.

It happened to be a fiesta day of the Catholic Church and considerable "rot-gut" whiskey and cheap wine were in evidence everywhere in the settlement. As the dance progressed Kelly and I became aware of a growing hostility toward us on the part of some of the men, owing to the marked preference shown us by the girls. We overheard some ugly remarks, and shortly after became aware of loud talking on the outside near the front door. Finally came two or three pistol shots, accompanied by a loud demand to be allowed to enter.

The constable, however, refused to allow this excited crowd to come in, and managed to lock the door, but, knowing the cause of the row, he came over to us and advised us to get away if we could without being discovered by the mob. One of the girls conducted us through the other rooms to a door on the side of the house opposite the dance hall, thus making it possible for us to slip away unseen. As she was conducting us we could hear that crowd cursing and firing an occasional shot, apparently to frighten us. I am entirely willing to admit that their efforts were successful.

When we got out of the house our troubles were not at an end. For one thing, it was a bright moonlight night, and, for another, El Moro lay in the direction of the door where that group of angry and intoxicated men were standing. It seemed that they could not help but discover us. All we could do was to dodge around another house, which took us a little farther away from them, and then cautiously and swiftly make a run for El Moro, which was about three miles distant. No sooner was the plan formulated than we put it into execution. As we started from the corner of the house some of the mob caught sight of us and called to the others to follow.

Then began the chase, Kelly and I in the lead, with the mob in pursuit, firing down the road in our direction. We were careful not to follow the travelled road, and as the ground was level on each side we made good time in spite of the fact that we were zigzagging, while they were firing straight down the road. We could plainly hear the whiz of the bullets as they passed between us, but since the pursuers were too drunk to aim accurately, we escaped unharmed. I think, however, our escape was really due to the fact that we were good runners. The men in the crowd were too

Otero, Sellar & Co. at El Moro, Colorado.

drunk to run fast, but both Kelly and I were splendid sprinters even under ordinary circumstances, and under such compelling circumstances we were next to invincible.

The crowd kept after us as though they were determined to have us dead or alive, firing at every jump. When we reached Grey's Creek, a stream about sixteen feet wide, Kelly and I leaped the whole distance without the slightest trouble. The pursuit flagged after we passed Grey's Creek, but Kelly and I were not long in getting on the opposite side of the Purgatoire River and into El Moro. The next day a delegation from Chilili, composed of some of the girls and several of the men, came over to explain and apologize for the inhospitable treatment we had received.

When we reached the warehouse we ran into more trouble, for we noticed a student's lamp burning in Mr. Sellar's bedroom, and realized that he must be awake and reading. Mr. Sellar's rooms were directly over the office, while our rooms adjoined his with a door entering Mr. Sellar's apartments.

We had left one of the warehouse doors unlocked so that we could enter without making any noise. Consequently, all we had to do was wait until the watchman was on the opposite side of the warehouse and then slip in. But there were no flashlights in those days, so we had to feel our way through the warehouse. It was customary when a large outfit came into town to be loaded for the owner or wagon-boss to bring his bed over and sleep in the warehouse, and that evening Jack Chandler, a well-known freighter, had arrived and made his bed in the main aisle of our warehouse. Harry was in the lead, and the first thing I knew I heard a low cry coming from his direction. It seemed that Harry had stepped on Jack Chandler's neck and, being a powerful man, he had grabbed Harry's leg in such a manner that the latter thought he had stepped into a bear's trap. We quickly explained to Jack, and then all three of us enjoyed a brief interval of suppressed laughter over the accident. Then Harry and I continued on our way, finally reaching the retail department. Here we had to proceed more carefully, because we could see, through the upper window, Mr. Sellar reading in his bed, with the student's lamp on a table at the head of the bed, while an extra large lemonade glass filled with choice brandy and imported ginger ale stood near the lamp.

We felt our way slowly to the staircase. After reaching the second floor, we were groping along as best we could when suddenly Harry walked right into a stepladder which stood opened in the main aisle. Of course it closed and fell with a crash. Harry and I ran to our room and had hardly jumped into bed, still dressed, when our door swung open and Mr. Sellar, in his night-dress, entered. Feigning to have been awakened out of a deep sleep, I mumbled: "Who's there; who's there?" Mr. Sellar merely asked: "Boys, did you hear a noise out here like something falling?" We both quickly answered: "No, sir!" He left us, and we could hear him going to each room asking the same question and getting the same reply. When he had made the rounds and returned to his bed we got up and undressed and were soon dreaming of our very adventurous evening. Of course, many questions were asked the next day, but Harry and I were silent as the two twin Sphinxes.

Chapter X

AT Trinidad the principal hotel bore the high-sounding name of the United States Hotel. It was kept by a man named Grant Rifenberg, whose staff included George W. Ward, chief cook; Charlie Tamme, head waiter in the dining-room, and George Curry, then a young boy, who was porter and general roustabout.

I had much association with this trio later, and I shall here give a short account of them.

Charlie Tamme was a typical Dutchman and one of the finest men I ever knew. He was as gentle and kind as a woman and as honest as the day is long. In his Trinidad days when he was but a young man he spoke very broken English. I remember his telling an interesting story of an encounter with a bear on Fisher's Peak, just back of Trinidad. He was out hunting deer and had followed a trail which took him to the circular park below the high rim of the peak, where there was quite an attractive little lake. As Charlie pushed through some bushes he suddenly ran into a large cinnamon bear busy eating wild raspberries. At the intrusion, the bear started for Charlie, and Charlie, dropping his rifle, made for the nearest tree, a rather small sapling, which he climbed as quickly as possible. But so slender was the tree that as Charlie climbed higher and higher toward the top it bent groundward, ever nearer and nearer the enraged beast at its foot.

But a kindly Providence stayed its curving at a distance just a foot or two beyond the bear's reach. Every time Charlie moved the tree would shake and shiver and bring him a few inches nearer the bear, while the bear would slap at Charlie with his paws, missing him by just a few inches. Finally, the bear seemed to tire of the sport, and, much to Charlie's joy, took his departure. Charlie remained aloft until he was fully satisfied the bear was gone for good, and then, descending to solid earth, he never stopped running until he reached Trinidad. To hear Charlie tell of this experience in his droll, broken English was enough to double anyone with laughter.

When the railroad progressed to Las Vegas, Charlie Tamme progressed with it and opened the first saloon and billiard parlor in the town. It was a popular place and Charlie and his partner, Ward, made a great deal of money. Afterward they sold out, and Charlie built the Tamme Opera House in East Las Vegas, now the Duncan Opera House, a venture which broke him. In later years he became city clerk of East Las Vegas and held the office until his death. George W. Ward built what was known as the Ward Block and, like Charlie Tamme, eventually went broke. Later he became superintendent of the New Mexico Insane Asylum, at Las Vegas, in which position he remained until his death several years later.

Before running across George Curry at Trinidad, I had known him back in the Granada days of 1873. He was then only ten or eleven years old and was living with an uncle, John Riney, who ran a small dairy. Mrs. Riney conducted a boarding train for the railroad men building the line of the Atchison, Topeka & Santa Fé Railroad, which was just then coming into Granada. George Curry and his brothers left their uncle as soon as they were able to earn a living, and George drifted down to the old United States Hotel at Trinidad. In the course of time he moved from Trinidad to Raton and began his New Mexico career as a helper in a gambling resort. In Whitlock's saloon he ran the chuck-a-luck table, a well-known gambling device and as much an adjunct of every gambling saloon on the frontier as faro, roulette, keno, monte or stud-poker. It was while he was working for Whitlock that he became involved in the lawlessness that ran rampant in Colfax County at that time.

My Life on the Frontier

This man Whitlock was bitterly opposed to the Maxwell Land Grant Company, which dominated Colfax County, and openly urged the settlers to contest every claim of ownership that the Maxwell Company made. He was also at loggerheads with the Hixenbaugh family, well-known as peace officers, one of whom was sheriff at the time. Whitlock's dislike for the Hixenbaughs led him to send to Texas for a notorious killer by the name of Thomas Rogers, generally known as "Red River Tom," Whitlock's intention being to run Red River Tom for sheriff of Colfax County. If he were elected, Whitlock would be rid of the Maxwell Land Grant Company and of all the officials who were inclined to side with the company.

Just about this time one of Whitlock's chief henchmen was arrested and taken to Springer, the county seat, where there was a strong jail, presided over by a fearless jailor named Jesse Lee. Whitlock was indignant over this arrest and took it as an excuse for asserting his power. He charged certain of the officials of the Maxwell Company of being at the bottom of the arrest, and he even went so far as to notify such prominent residents of the county as Harry Whigham, his son-in-law, T. M. Schomberg, Melvin W. Mills, the District Attorney, and several others, that they should not only leave Colfax County but also the Territory of New Mexico. The situation became so acute that these men felt it necessary to comply with Whitlock's orders to remain alive. They all went to Trinidad, Colo., for fear of being murdered.

One of the leading agitators in Colfax County at this time was O. P. McManes, who was elected a member of the House to the twenty-sixth Legislative Assembly. The Governor, Lionel A. Sheldon, ordered the militia to proceed to the town of Cimarron, at which point they were to be held in readiness for any eventuality in Colfax County. The Raton gang soon learned of the appearance of the militia, and one night a party of men headed by George Curry proceeded to

Cimarron under cover of night. A dance, especially arranged by the Raton gang, was in progress, with all the militiamen as patrons, and while they were enjoying the dance George Curry and his followers captured all the arms, ammunition and equipment belonging to the soldiers, which they took to Raton.

It began to look as though Whitlock and his gang were going to have things their own way in Colfax County. But at this moment another man stepped into the picture — Jesse Lee, the intrepid jailor at Springer. Whitlock together with Red River Tom, George Curry and his brother, Jimmy Curry, went over to Springer determined to release their imprisoned associate. When the Whitlock gang appeared at the jail door, or rather the front entrance to the court-house, Jesse Lee was standing at a window on the second floor directly over the front door.

After they had made their demand for him to open the door, he not only refused but very firmly advised them all to leave the court-house premises at once. This they refused to do, and shooting commenced, resulting in the death of Whitlock, Red River Tom and Jimmy Curry. George Curry was the only man of Whitlock's party to escape, and this was because he took refuge behind a small brick house and remained there until United States troops arrived from Fort Union under command of Captain Kirkman of the 10th U. S. Infantry. Then he placed himself under their protection. This general purging of the leaders of the Whitlock gang had a calming effect upon Colfax County.

Shortly afterward, George Curry left for Lincoln County, then another extremely lawless part of the state, and became clerk for J. C. DeLaney, post-trader at Fort Stanton, where he remained until 1884. Then he moved to Lincoln, the county seat of Lincoln County, working for James J. Dolan of Lincoln County War fame, who by that time was on the road to becoming a respected citizen. He was the county

My Life on the Frontier

treasurer. George Curry became his chief deputy, and in this manner got his start in politics. After holding several county offices, he was elected by the Democrats of Lincoln, Chaves, Eddy, Doña Ana and Grant Counties as territorial senator from that district, and when the Legislature convened was duly elected President of the Senate.

While I was Governor of New Mexico the Spanish-American War broke out, and I sent for George Curry and commissioned him Captain of Troop "H," First U. S. Volunteer Cavalry, which afterward became known as "Roosevelt's Rough Riders." When a few years later I was requested to name some qualified men from New Mexico as officers for the 11th U. S. Cavalry, about to sail for the Philippine Islands, I named George Curry as first lieutenant. He was promptly mustered into the service and took a prominent part in the military operations in the Philippines.

When President Roosevelt forced the resignation of Governor H. J. Hagerman, he appointed George Curry his successor. He served in this capacity from 1907 to 1910, when he resigned. George Curry had been a life-long Democrat until his association with Theodore Roosevelt. Then he decided to leave the Democratic Party for good and aligned himself with the Republicans. When New Mexico became a state, George Curry was elected Representative to Congress on the Republican ticket. After Holm O. Bursum succeeded Albert B. Fall as a United States Senator in 1921, he appointed George Curry his private secretary, a position he held until President Warren G. Harding appointed him a member of the boundary commission to settle some disputed land claimed by both the United States and Mexico. He held this position until the summer of 1927, when he handed in his resignation at the request of the Department of State and retired to private life at Socorro, N. Mex.

George Curry is in many ways a remarkable character and typical of the rapid metamorphis of the democratic West.

He is essentially a self-made man. He has used to great advantage the considerable natural ability with which he was endowed. He is a very likable man, always loyal to his friends. I am pleased to number George Curry among my earliest friends and wish for him every success in the future.

After this long digression, I must return to details of my life at El Moro and Trinidad.

On New Year's Day, 1877, I was out deer-hunting with Sam Dennison in Chicosa Cañon, about five miles northwest of El Moro. Dennison and myself had been walking on the south side of the cañon. While eating our lunch we saw quite a number of white-tailed deer on the opposite side. We crawled back a short distance, then crossed the cañon behind them. Before we knew it, we were on top of the herd. The deer that were lying down jumped up not more than twenty steps from us, but we failed to get one. They all bunched together and ran around the south side of the mountain. Dennison followed them, while I continued on to the top. Looking over, I saw the leader entering a path between two cedar trees at the foot of the mountain, a distance of more than six hundred yards. I fired as quickly as possible without taking particular aim and then started down the mountain toward the two cedar trees to catch the trail. Dennison joined me just as we reached the trees. Twenty feet ahead was the body of a big buck! My bullet had entered the left flank, passing under the ribs and lodging in the heart.

A few days later while hunting I spotted a fine black-tail buck on a rise about three hundred yards from where I was standing. I fired quickly, breaking both of his hind legs at the joint. I ran over to where he fell and in my excitement went close to the wounded buck, which turned over backwards, almost striking me with his horns. I jumped to one side in time to save myself, but fell down the side of the mountain, dropping my gun. I quickly recovered my balance and, picking up my gun, shot the deer through the head, killing him instantly.

Wild ducks and geese were very plentiful around El Moro, in several large lakes northwest of the town. On one occasion J. R. DeRemer, Harry Kelly, Tom Parker and I pumped a hand car loaded with bedding, rubber boots, guns, ammunition and provisions for more than twenty miles in a terrific rainstorm. But we were amply repaid for the hardship, for we killed nearly two hundred wild ducks, which we took home and divided among our friends.

One day the firm of Otero, Sellar & Co. sent me up the Apishapa River with Charlie Carr of Trinidad to receive fifty head of cattle. After receiving, branding and starting the cattle toward El Moro in charge of two reliable herders, we felt that as we were so near the Spanish Peaks we would go there and visit an old friend named Henry Schultz. We did so and received a royal welcome, Schultz killing the fatted turkey and putting before us an abundance of good things to eat, as well as his best wines and liquors. After a few days' visit we started back for El Moro.

As we were going along we passed two men driving a wagon en route to Trinidad, with a load of deer for sale. They had six fine black-tailed deer, and, as they were evidently destined for the market, we offered to buy them. I was short of money and gave the men a due-bill, telling them that if they would call at the store the next day and ask for Mr. Otero I would take up the due-bill. When Charlie Carr and I reached El Moro early in the afternoon we drove up in front of the store and unloaded the deer in the presence of a number of our acquaintances.

We called my father and Mr. Sellar out to the front of the store and presented each of them with a deer. My father suggested that I send one to his friend, Bela M. Hughes, who lived in Denver, which I agreed to do. All the while Carr and I were telling how we had killed each deer and boasting how many others we might have killed. I must confess that we allowed our friends to get the impression that we were great hunters.

But the next day fate pricked our bubble. The two men from whom we had bought the deer came to the store with my due-bill and carried out to the letter my instruction to ask for Mr. Otero. Naturally, they were ushered into the private office of my father. With looks of dismayed surprise they said, "You are not the Mr. Otero we are looking for. We want to see the man who bought our deer. Here is his note." The evidence was too incriminating, and my father grasped the significance at once. He conducted the men into the general office, where I had my desk, and remarked, "This, I think, must be the Mr. Otero you want to see." I recognized the men and paid the due-bill, but not before everyone in the establishment caught on. I had to stand all the roasting myself, because Charlie Carr had returned to his home in Trinidad.

As I recall those El Moro days, it seems to me that dancing played a particularly large rôle in our social life. One dance would lead to another and even to a whole series, as in the following instance: The merchants of Trinidad gave a large dance for the farmers and stockmen of Las Animas County, and of course a good number of the commission-house boys were in evidence, including Jacob Gross and me. Jake was paying very marked attention to the daughter of one of the farmers living in the Purgatoire River section. Jersey Moore was the girl's name. She was a very attractive young woman, remarkably pretty and a splendid dancer. Jake monopolized every moment of her time, there was no doubt of that.

Her brothers — old man Moore had three or four sons all very husky and inclined to be rough and boisterous — were also at the dance, and one of them who had been drinking heavily took exception to Jake's marked attention to Jersey. He went after Jake with blood in the eye, and for a few minutes it looked as if there might be a fight. But the row was smoothed over and apologies were tendered and accepted by all the interested parties, the outward seal of amity being that Jake ordered a few more bottles of champagne to the entire approval of the Moore family.

Thinking that he ought to make himself as solid as possible with the Moores, Jake announced a dance for the following evening in honor of Miss Jersey, and invited the Moores to come over to El Moro to attend it. The Moore family arrived the next day *en masse* and put up at the New State Hotel. At the proper time Jake called for the belle of the ball and conducted her to the ballroom, which was at the schoolhouse. The dance was a howling success. We danced until daylight, the supper was delicious, and champagne flowed freely.

During the dance I decided to add another dance to the series. So I suggested to Jake that we join forces and give another dance at Uncle Dick Wooten's on Raton Pass. When we broached the matter to our guests, all agreed it was the thing to do. We planned to dispatch a messenger early the next morning to tell Uncle Dick to have everything in readiness for the dance, but when morning came (we were of course up to greet the sun) we found we could not obtain a messenger. As negotiations must proceed without delay, Jake and I went over to Greenstreet's stable and hired what we used to call a "pole buggy" and a good team of horses and started for Uncle Dick's.

We had already been two whole nights without sleep, but we did not hesitate before the prospect of another — but that is youth. Nevertheless, nature will assert herself. As we drove along, Jake dropped off to sleep, leaving me to keep the horses going toward Uncle Dick's. I thought I could hold out until we reached the toll-gate, but I was too confident. Soon I was asleep sitting upright in the seat and holding the lines in my hands. Fortunately for us, the horses were gentle and imbued with the homing instinct. Finding that no one was guiding them, they turned around and went straight back to El Moro. They actually went through the Main Street of Trinidad, and when they drew near to El Moro they took a short-cut from the regular road and reached Greenstreet's stable by the most direct route. Here they stopped, and we were awakened by Mr. Greenstreet with much laughter. We immediately made negotiations with Mr. Greenstreet for him to take a fresh team and go at once to Uncle Dick's and make all arrangements, and this he did to our entire satisfaction.

Realizing that we were "all in," Jake and I got a room at the New State Hotel, and devoted the rest of the day to making up for lost sleep under more normal conditions. Late in the afternoon we drove out to Uncle Dick's, where we were joined by our guests. We had a good time at the dance, which as a matter of course lasted all night. The next day Jake and I took a room at Uncle Dick's and stayed there all day and the following night. When we returned to El Moro, after having not seen the inside of the office for three whole days, we expected my father and Mr. Sellar to rake us over the coals. But to our surprise nothing was said.

Trinidad was growing wilder and more lawless day by day. It was by now much on the order of the old railroad towns of Kansas. Many saloons and dance halls sprang into existence, chief among them being Merrill & Conkie's.

About this time an old man named Shaw came to Trinidad from somewhere in Kansas, accompanied by his pretty twenty-year-old daughter. The father rented a small adobe house with two rooms and established himself and his daughter in it. The town marshal at the time was Brigido Cordova. He was a fine-looking fellow, very popular with his friends and always ready for a quarrel.

In passing the Shaw home he had discovered the attractive girl living there, and at once began an effort to ingratiate himself with both father and daughter. He would stop on every possible occasion apparently to talk to the old man, but in reality to see the young woman. Finally he became bolder, and attempted one day to force his attentions on the daughter. Both the father and girl resented this, for they had learned that Cordova was a married man. They felt that his visits were for no good purpose and decided that they must end.

So when Cordova called one afternoon and insisted that the young woman accompany him to a dance in the vicinity of Trinidad, the old man promptly told him that his daughter could not go. He went further, saying that he did not like to have Cordova come around his premises at all.

Cordova became very angry and threatened the old man. With great bragadocio, he said that he would come around to see the girl whenever he pleased and would like to see the man who could stop him. That night he tried to get into the house, but the old man shut the door in his face and locked it. This served to make Cordova desperately mad, and he pounded loudly on the door, cursing and threatening to break down the door. When Shaw repeated his refusal to open the door, Cordova started to tear down the barrier.

While this was going on, Shaw stepped to the door with his Spencer rifle full-cocked in his hands and ordered Cordova to stop damaging his house. But Cordova's only reply was a curse. Thereupon the old man raised his rifle and fired through the door, the bullet striking Cordova in the center of his chest and tearing a hole through his body a full inch in diameter. Of course he was killed instantly.

The dead man's friends soon gathered around the house, and after they had taken the corpse to Cordova's home returned with a rope and began to threaten to take the old man out and hang him. But Shaw had no notion of surrendering himself to them. He opened the door and, standing behind the wall with his Spencer rifle poking out through the door, he held the crowd at bay. Then some of Cordova's friends procured some turpentine balls, ignited them and threw them into the room. To halt this method of attack, the old fellow had to close his door. This was what the mob wanted. As soon as the rifle barrel disappeared, they climbed up to the top of the house and began an attack from that quarter. They poured coal oil down the chimney and began to dig into the roof.

The noise and excitement drew a large number of spectators, but they all seemed afraid to do anything to stop the would-be lynchers. Finally, Mart Arbuckle, a young man from Houghton & Swan's hardware store, volunteered to rescue the old man and girl, if another man would go with him. Frank Wallace said he would go. So, arming themselves with a new Winchester rifle apiece, they barged through the mob and reached the door.

First they ordered the men on the roof to come down. Then Arbuckle told the mob that he and Wallace intended to save the old man and his daughter, and that if anyone attempted to interfere he would certainly get killed for his trouble.

With the mob cowed by his determined stand, Arbuckle persuaded the old man to come out, accompanied by his daughter. Then with Mart Arbuckle in front, the old man and the girl next, and Frank Wallace bringing up the rear, with his back to the old man and his face toward the mob, they marched to the Stevens Block and entered one of the buildings. But even then it did not look as though the lives of the father and daughter could be saved.

The mob was apparently getting ready to attack the Stevens Block, when someone thought of appealing to Clay Allison, the noted killer, for aid. The rumor was started that Clay Allison and a company of a hundred or so cowboys were coming. At the same time a messenger was dispatched to Allison. This move had the desired effect, and soon the mob quieted down and finally broke up. Clay Allison and the cowboys arrived the following day, but by that time the trouble had blown over.

The old man was tried before the district court under Judge Hallett of Pueblo and duly acquitted. He and his daughter immediately returned to their Kansas home. A party of friends on horseback accompanied them for several miles and saw them safely out of Trinidad. Mart Arbuckle afterward went to Leadville, Colo., during the great mining excitement. He was killed by a man named Bush in a mining-claim dispute.

While we were in El Moro in 1877, my old room-mate, Harry W. Kelly, came down with a very severe attack of typhoid fever. We had him removed to our home at once, where he hovered between life and death for many long weeks. Our family physician said: "Had it not been for the promptness in removing him from the warehouse to your home where he could receive every care and comfort and the splendid nursing given him by Mrs. Otero, who watched over him day and night the same as she would have done for her own son, it would have been exceedingly doubtful if he would ever have recovered."

At the crisis, the doctor gave out very little hope of his recovery, so my father telegraphed for Harry's mother to come out at once. My mother, however, never relaxed her care.

Mrs. Kelly arrived just after Harry had passed the turning point and remained with us until Harry had sufficiently recovered to leave for Leavenworth.

Chapter XI

EARLY in the spring of 1877, Nels Newell and I took a one-horse buggy and started on a fishing trip in the Stonewall country west of Trinidad. We had heard that speckled trout were plentiful there, and wanted to try our luck. We left Trinidad in the evening, shortly after supper, and traveled slowly all night. During the latter part of the night we camped to secure some needed rest and slept late into the forenoon. Imagine our surprise when we finally woke up to find that we had made our camp within a hundred yards of a large band of Ute Indians who were on a deer hunt.

Fortunately, they were not on the warpath. Indeed, they were in a most friendly mood, and several of the party came over to our camp while we were cooking breakfast. One of them even brought a nice piece of venison, which we added to the breakfast menu and ate with much relish. In return, we gave them some sugar and some canned goods together with a few fishing hooks and about twenty-five feet of fishing line, some smoking tobacco and cigarette paper. After breakfast we went down to the stream and began to fish. I cannot remember ever having more fishing luck, for as fast as we threw in our lines, we would pull out a fine large trout. We fished the rest of the afternoon, and then returned to our camp with fully one hundred and fifty good-sized beauties, not one of them weighing less than half a pound. After a hearty meal, we hitched up and started home.

While we were in El Moro an amusing incident occurred. The night-watchman of Otero, Sellar & Co. was William Henry Harrison Allison — no relation of Clay Allison. He was a cripple and walked with a cane, one leg having been badly broken when he was a boy. He was very religious and

Clay Allison

seemed to regard it a duty to lecture the younger fellows whenever he thought they were too exuberant, and especially if he thought that any of us had "looked too long upon the wine when it was red," as he used to say, or had remained away from quarters too late at night.

Of course, we were inclined to resent his self-appointed paternalism, and one day Gillies, Kelly, Nichols and I entered into a conspiracy. We decided to give Allison the benefit of a fake duel. According to prearrangement, Nichols and I got into a serious row, figuratively, under Allison's nose, and as we had expected, Allison tried to act the rôle of peacemaker. The more he tried to dissuade us, the more convulsed with rage we apparently became.

Finally, we parted with dire threats against each other, and each of us secured a pistol. Allison was fully aware of our having armed ourselves. In fact, we circulated the rumor that we were going to fight a duel, and named as our seconds Kelly and Gillies. When Allison learned of this, he appealed to them to bring matters to a peaceable halt, but they were obdurate and insisted on the duel. Poor Allison became almost frantic in his anxiety to prevent the encounter, and, finally, went to Messrs. Gross and Mennet, but we had let both of them into the secret, and they carried off their part exceedingly well. On the ground that it was none of their business, they flatly declined to interfere.

Seeing no other recourse, Allison came back to Nichols and me and pleaded with us more earnestly than before, but to no avail. Then he turned again to the two seconds, Kelly and Gillies, but with a like result. Nichols in particular carried off his part well; he managed to be drinking and flourishing a pistol every time he and Allison met. After we had kept up the fun for several hours, with Allison becoming almost crazy, we staged the climax.

While Nichols and Allison were talking, the two seconds appeared on the scene. Allison, so excited that he was almost crying, begged them "for God's sake" to stop it all before there was bloodshed. While this was going on, I arrived and without ceremony fired a shot at Nichols, who staggered and fell. Gillies managed to reach him quickly and spilled a bottle of red ink over his white shirt bosom. Nichols breathed very hard, as if he were growing weaker and weaker. Kelly turned to me and congratulated me on the outcome. Gillies, still bending over Nichols, finally shouted, "Get a doctor quick." Allison started as fast as he could for the nearest medico, and I am sure he ran every step of the three blocks at top speed.

Before he returned, Nichols had put on clean clothes, and when Allison reappeared with the doctor, he found us sitting in the main office laughing over our successful plot. From that day on we were never bothered with his advice.

Our fun continued. One night Kelly and I learned that John Collier, one of the clerks, was out later than Mr. Sellar would permit. We discovered that he had a key which enabled him to come in without being detected. None of us had been accorded this privilege save Collier and that fact rankled in our bosoms. As the door Collier entered was directly under Mr. Sellar's rooms, we decided to make the latter aware of what Collier was up to. We had recently secured one of the contrivances known at that time as "burglar pistols," a device that screwed into the door frame and, by the means of a stiff spring, held a pistol in such a position that anyone opening the door would find the barrel pointing directly at his face. There was also a lever that would cause the pistol hammer to fall and fire the load.

We loaded the old pistol with plenty of powder and paper wads and hid ourselves near the door to see the fun. Shortly after midnight, Collier entered the office and tiptoed to the door. As he quietly opened the door, the spring flew back, and off went the pistol with a report loud enough to wake the dead. Before the others came to see what it was all about,

Kelly and I removed the pistol and no one could discover how it all happened.

The commission-house boys were like one big family, and as clannish as the Celts of the Scottish Highlands. They stuck to each other through thick and thin in any kind of difficulty. They were constantly thinking up some new joke to play on one of the clan, or would all combine to worry some unsuspecting tenderfoot. Whenever a new clerk appeared and catered to the bosses to secure special favors, the word would be passed around. Then, God help him.

Those boys of the early frontier included: Jacob Gross, Adolph Mennet, Benito Baca, Reginald Finley, Frank O. Kihlberg, Walter Ainslie, Frank A. Blake, Charles O. Cole, George M. Gillies, Thomas Henry Parker, Harry W. Kelly, Robert K. L. M. Cullen, Page B. Otero, Henry W. Gibbons, Frank B. Nichols, William Hamilton, J. S. Garcia, John Collier, Alfred Rossier, Mike Harkins, Meliton S. Otero, Charles H. Armijo, Moses Friedman, John Laurence, John Villepigue, W. H. H. Allison, A. J. Crawford, William S. Crawford, Pierce J. Murphy, William Ring, Manuel Sosaya, George Slocum, Benjamin Johnson, Charles Humes, Cliff W. Able, Prof. Charles Longuemare and myself. All of the above were employees of Otero, Sellar & Co.

The W. H. Chick & Co. gang consisted of Francisco A. Manzanares, Thomas B. McNair, Arthur M. Blackwell, C. N. Blackwell, Millard W. Browne, Cecil W. Browne, Ernest L. Browne, Cassius C. Gise, Peter Simpson, Henry Chick, Lee Chick, John Bell, Thomas D. Bell, Thomas Nolan, D. A. Clouthier, Placido Sandoval, Maurice J. Walsh, Alec Stockton and Miss Belle Jennings. Nearly all have passed into history; few are living today.

As soon as they knew that the Denver and Rio Grande Railroad would not build to Trinidad, many of the merchants moved over to El Moro. Among them was Oliver L. Houghton, one of my dearest and best friends. He erected a fine two-story pressed-brick building, known as the "Houghton Block," where he conducted his large wholesale and retail hardware, guns and ammunition business. Like ninety per cent of the commission-house boys, Houghton was a bachelor and at once became a member of the clan. His hobby was trotting horses, and he usually had the best that money could buy. One day while he and I were out duck hunting and I happened to wing a couple of geese, they both fell into the lake and floated to the center. We found a small skiff tied to the bank, and got into it, Houghton doing the rowing. The wind was blowing hard, and Houghton accidentally let one of the oars slip from his hand. In reaching for it, we came within an ace of upsetting. The little boat was half filled with water and we had to use our hats to bail and prevent our sinking. Then we paddled back to shore with the remaining oar, never thinking of the geese, for it had been a narrow squeak.

Trinidad in 1876 was a comparatively old town, the headquarters of many wealthy stockmen. When the commission-house boys arrived on the scene, they proceeded to "wedge-in" with all the Trinidad girls. I must say, a finer set of young women never lived. I always want to remember Marion Bloom, Belle Hardy, Rose and Mamie Beattie, May, Maggie and Laura Hastings, Nettie Baird, Jennie Saunders, and Julia and Louise McKay. The young men included Caldwell Yeaman, James M. John, David C. Winters, Julius Clark, C. E. Lull, Harry Mulnix, and a great many others whose names I do not recall at this time.

My stay in the vicinity of La Junta, El Moro and Trinidad brought me into contact with Clay Allison, who deserves to rank with the famous killers of the period. He was born in Tennessee in 1835 or thereabouts, and as a young man had moved to Texas to enter the cattle business. He was well on the road to becoming one of the cattle kings of the Texas Panhandle, when he became involved in a terrible fight with an old friend and neighbor. The trouble was so deep-rooted that it could not be settled amicably. So the two men agreed to fight it out — and here appears that grim humor that characterized Clay Allison.

It was agreed that a grave should be dug, six feet deep, six and a half feet long, and two feet wide. They were to strip themselves to the waist, sit down at the two ends of the grave with a bowie knife in the right hand of each. At a given signal they were to begin fighting and were not to stop till one or the other was dead. Finally, the survivor was to cover the victim with the earth removed in digging the grave. The story went that Allison killed his man but was himself so severely wounded in one of the legs that he was thereafter lame. It was also averred that Allison kept to the agreement and buried his dead enemy.

Then, to get away forever from the scene of the trouble, Allison disposed of all his interests and moved to Colfax County, New Mexico, where he again started in the cattle business. When sober, Clay Allison was well mannered and extremely likable, but under the influence of liquor he was a terror to the whole neighborhood and a good man to avoid. Gradually, his name became dreaded in the whole section. He had actually killed so many and was so keenly aware of the readiness of friends and relatives to "get even," that he never stood or sat in a room with his back to a door or a window.

One day in Cimarron, while drinking in one of the saloons, Allison was approached by a noted desperado known as "Pancho," who invited him to have a drink. Allison started to drink with him. Pancho, seeking to get the drop, began to fan himself with his wide-brimmed hat. It all appeared casual but in reality it was to distract Allison's well-known "quick" eye. Allison suspected immediately. Noticing that Pancho was stealthily trying to draw his pistol, Allison suddenly pulled his gun and fired, killing Pancho instantly. Allison insisted on going before a Justice of the Peace. He was easily acquitted on the plea of self-defense.

Another famous story concerns Clay Allison's killing of

the desperado "Chunk." One day at a horse race meeting, Chunk and Allison met. They bore a mutual dislike for each other, so it was not long before they quarrelled and arranged a death duel.

Allison, with his flair for the bizarre, was contending that they mount horses, face each other at a distance of a hundred yards, and at a given signal run their horses toward each other, firing at pleasure, until one or both had dropped to the ground. But before an agreement could be reached the dinner bell rang, and Chunk suggested that they eat first and fight afterwards, saying that it would be better for the dead man to go to hell with a full belly. Allison agreed, and the two men went into the dining-room together taking seats at opposite ends of the long table, around the sides of which were seated several other guests. Allison placed his pistol beside his soup plate; Chunk laid his in his lap. As Allison was lifting his spoon to his mouth, Chunk quickly raised his pistol from his lap and fired. Allison, who had detected the move, dropped his spoon and dodged to one side, thus getting out of the line of fire. At the same time, he grabbed his pistol and fired. Chunk was hit in the center of the forehead, his head fell forward into his dish of soup.

Allison coolly replaced his pistol in its scabbard and resumed eating his soup. He then ate a full dinner leisurely and when he had finished arose and, taking the dinner bell from the shelf, went to the door and began to ring it vigorously, announcing: "Gentlemen, the proposed horse duel is now declared off, owing to an accident to one of the principals." All this time Chunk's body remained where it had fallen, and all who sat at the table were forced to go on with the meal as though nothing unusual had taken place.

During the spring of 1876 Clay Allison and his brother John were at Las Animas, Colo. Allison always traded at our store, because he liked my father. He also seemed to be very fond of me.

In Las Animas, Clay Allison became involved in a rather

amusing episode. He and his brother had had so much to drink on this occasion that the wise saloon-keepers had closed their doors to them and the people on the streets were avoiding them as they would two mad dogs. That afternoon a whiskey drummer named Frank Riggs arrived in the town, and as he was proceeding to the hotel, valise in hand, he met Clay Allison riding on horseback.

Riggs greeted him and remarked casually on the merits of the horse. "Yes," replied Allison, "you can bet your life this horse is a fine one, and if I say the word, he will kick your hat off. Come over and see." At this point Riggs realized how drunk Allison was, and began to think of a way of avoiding trouble. He remembered that the saloon-keepers of the town were in the habit of closing their places to Clay Allison when he was on one of his thorough-going sprees, and reasoned that it being more than likely that all the "ginmills" were closed to him, Allison would be most desirous of a drink.

So Riggs said: "I'll take your word about the horse kicking my hat off, but I know something better than that stunt. You come and join me in a good drink. I think I know where we can wet our whistles."

Allison's mind brought to the fore of his consciousness the situation in the town. He said incredulously: "You are not going to break into one of the saloons and commit a burglary, are you?"

"I know a much better way than that," answered Riggs. "You tie up your horse and come with me. I'll leave my valise in this drug store until we come back."

Allison agreed, and Riggs took him to the back door of a saloon belonging to one of his regular customers. A loud knock on the door brought no response, but as the clink of glasses could be distinctly heard inside, Riggs knew the proprietor and several customers were drinking. He called out, "Hey, Bill, let me in. It's your friend Riggs, the whiskey drummer." Thereupon the proprietor threw open the door, and in walked Riggs and Clay Allison.

"I just met my friend Allison," said Riggs, "and have invited him to have a drink with me. It's my treat, boys, so let every man in the room take a drink with me to the health, happiness and long life of my friend, Clay Allison."

Then Riggs handed the bartender a five-dollar bill, saying as he did so, "You can hand me the change when I come back with my valise. I left it at the drug store at the corner."

With that he slipped out of the door, secured his valise and made a mad rush for the depot, reaching it just in time to catch a freight train.

The sequel to the story is that from that day on Riggs cut Las Animas from his visiting list. There was always the possibility that he might meet Clay Allion again, as well as the chance that he would receive a cold reception from certain citizens who had found themselves in the same saloon with a drunken Clay Allison.

I think it was on this same visit that Clay Allison and his brother John made things so lively at the dance hall that the affair is remembered to this day. In the midst of a dance, both men took off every stitch of clothing and then forced everyone to continue dancing, enforcing their orders with their six-shooters. Sheriff John Spear summoned his chief deputy, Charlie Faber, gathered a posse of about fifteen to twenty men and proceeded to the dance-hall.

Faber, who was in the lead, opened the front door, and at once commenced firing at the two naked men. At the outset, he wounded John Allison, who fell to the floor, but his bullets did not touch Clay, who used his six-shooter vigorously and effectively. His very first shot apparently killed Faber, and the rest of the posse, including John Spear, made a hasty retreat. Clay walked to the door where the body of Faber lay and, taking the dead man by the hair, dragged him to where his brother John was lying wounded on the floor, remarking, "John, this is the damn' son of a bitch who shot you. I got him all right; so don't worry. You'll get well soon."

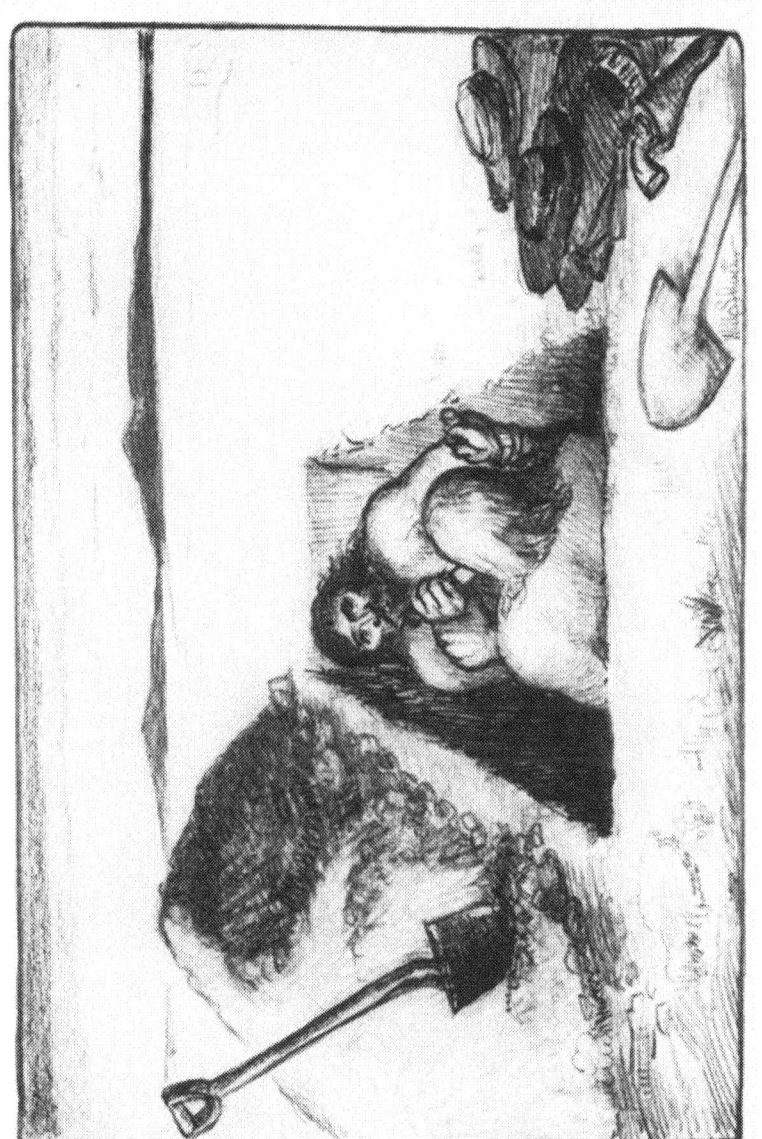

The duel in the grave.

And while he was making this gesture of bravado and *diablerie*, Clay was crying like a baby and attempting to dress himself and John at the same time. John soon recovered, and Clay was duly acquitted, since the deputy sheriff had opened fire without warning of any kind, making it a clear case of self-defense.

Clay Allison frequently added to the gayety of life in El Moro. Once while on one of his big drunks, he met a hunter known as "Buckskin Charlie" and began to drink with him in Rufe Harrington's New State Saloon, adjoining the New State Hotel. Eventually, Clay and Charlie quarreled. The upshot was that they agreed to a fight without pistols or knives. Allison managed to get Charlie down and pounded him so unmercifully that he had to be removed to the Trinidad hospital.

That same day Allison pulled another exciting stunt. Somehow he secured a sawed-off shotgun and loaded it with bird shot. Allison was a man with strong likes and dislikes. One of his pet aversions was Dr. Menger's stove-pipe hat. As Dr. Menger passed the saloon wearing his stove-pipe hat, Allion stepped out of the saloon to the sidewalk and, poking the shot gun against the top of the hat, shot it off the doctor's head. Then he took the doctor by the arm, led him into a store, and bought him a fine Stetson hat. Next he made the doctor come into Harrington's saloon and take a drink. The doctor and the town as well took the episode good-humoredly, calling it just another piece of Clay Allison's foolishness.

But when Clay Allison got on one of his sprees it was generally productive of fun a-plenty, as I sometimes had occasion to know from personal experience. On that same day, it being a holiday, Jacob Gross, A. M. Blackwell, Frank B. Nichols, Pete Simpson and I were playing cards in the second-story room of Harrington's New State Saloon, directly above the bar. Allison entered the saloon below and in his excess of spirits began shooting through the ceiling. The bullets came up close to the card table around which we were gathered. Looking about for a place of safety, we saw a large Charter Oak cooking stove which happened to be part of the equipment of the room. We made a run for the stove and all five of us jumped on top and watched the splinters fly up from the floor each time one of Allison's bullets came through.

Allison continued this drunk for more than a week. During that time he had a room at the New State Hotel, to which he would retire at an early hour, after putting up his famous black horse at a livery stable. That horse was the pride of Allison's heart. It was a beauty and as well trained as a circus horse. Allison never tied him when he went into a saloon, but simply turned him loose to graze. When he wanted the horse to come to him, he would whistle through his fingers and the horse would come at full speed.

Frequently when on these periodical sprees, Allison would bring out a bucket full of beer for the horse, but the wise animal would take only a swallow or two and then upset the bucket with his nose. Sometimes Allison would call for a bucket of fresh water and then pour a quart of whiskey into it and ask the horse to drink. But as soon as the horse smelled the whiskey he would shake his head and upset the bucket.

One day during an epochal spree in El Moro he met me in front of the saloon and asked me to take a drink with him. Of course I did so, whether I wanted to or not. Then Allison asked me to take dinner with him at the hotel. Again I accepted and had a devilish poor time, as Allison was excessively drunk and added to my disquietude by laying his pistol by his plate. I was on pins and needles all through the meal, but fortunately there was no one else in the dining-room besides ourselves and the waiter, who was a great friend of Allison's. I was not uneasy about my own safety, for there had always been a strong friendship between Allison and I.

It was after this drunk that Allison came over to the store, and in an excess of generosity, presented his horse to my father, saying: "Don Miguel, you are the only man living that I would give this horse to." Of course my father declined to accept the present, with many, many thanks.

Some years later, Clay Allison went back to his old home and married his childhood sweetheart. He returned to his western home via Las Vegas and I had the pleasure of meeting him and his bride at the St. Nicholas Hotel, where they were stopping during their visit in Las Vegas. They were en route to their ranch home in the lower Pecos Valley, where he was again successfully operating a cattle ranch. On another occasion he came back through Las Vegas with his wife and little daughter to consult a physician about the child's health.

Allison became a greatly changed man after his marriage. He was never again guilty of drinking to excess nor becoming involved in shooting scrapes. He realized, however, that as a hangover from the old days there were many men who would shoot him on the least provocation. He was especially suspicious of the town marshal of East Las Vegas, Arthur Jilson, who had always been unfriendly toward him. So Allison would on these visits come over to the San Miguel National Bank of Las Vegas, of which I was at the time cashier, and ask me to accompany him about the town as a bodyguard. This I was always glad to do.

Allison met his death in a paradoxical manner. Returning from one of his trips for ranch supplies, he was driving his heavily loaded wagon down the steep incline leading into a dry arroyo, when his crippled leg slipped from the brake and the wagon shot down to the bottom of the arroyo. Allison fell off the seat, struck the ground and the heavily loaded wagon passed over his body, killing him instantly.

Mrs. Allison, together with her two young daughters, continued to manage the cattle ranch. Some time later she was married to J. L. Johnson, a merchant doing business in Pecos City, Texas. They moved to Fort Worth, where Mrs. Johnson died quite recently. Both of her daughters by Clay Allison grew to womanhood, and, I understand, have married very happily.

Chapter XII

IN the fall of 1877 my father decided to send my brother and me to Notre Dame University. So we started, accompanied by our mother, and in due time arrived at South Bend, Ind., two days before the beginning of the term. My brother was assigned to the senior yard and I to the junior yard, as the playgrounds for the older and the younger boys were respectively designated. Both of us were good baseball players. My brother, who had developed quite a reputation in the West as a pitcher, became the moundsman of the senior nine; my skill earned the place of third baseman on the junior nine, though I also served as substitute pitcher.

The active life we had led in the West qualified us for the different field sports. I recall that in October after our entrance there was a field day. This was on St. Edward's day, that being the patron saint of Rev. Father Edward Sorin, the founder of the order, who was still alive. My brother won first prize in both running and throwing in the senior yard, while I won first prize in the same events in the junior yard.

My stay in college terminated a few weeks later. In November I was taken with a severe cold which developed into pneumonia, and, after my recovery, the doctor advised my parents to get me into a drier climate. Upon receiving this advice, they summoned both my brother and me to St. Louis, where they were located at the time, and put me through a thorough examination by a noted specialist in that city. His advice was directly contradictory to that of the Notre Dame physician, for, as he found nothing seriously the matter with my lungs, he did not see why I could not remain in St. Louis, should my father desire to carry out his intention of putting me into school at St. Louis University.

I had been hoping that the St. Louis doctor would confirm

the advice of the other physician, for I wished to get back to the frontier. But my father was influenced by the St. Louis doctor's verdict, and placed my brother and me in St. Louis University again. As our parents were to remain in the city for a week or so longer, we appealed to them to allow us to remain with them at the boarding-house until their departure for the West. The day they left, we went to the depot to say good-bye, and were expected afterward to go straight back to the University.

But instead, we took matters into our own hands and simply returned to the boarding-house at which we had been staying with our parents and engaged one of the best rooms for ourselves. We did not go near the University, but rather gave ourselves a good time in the city. Of course in time our parents were somehow apprized of the situation, and then came a telegram from my father instructing us to come home forthwith, sending enough money for all our expenses up to date and for the trip. This was exactly what we had been maneuvering for, and we lost little time in complying with our father's wish. We got back to El Moro in January, 1878, and there was no further attempt to send my brother and me to school.

It was delightful to again become part of the excitement of those early towns. One of the first happenings after our return was the war over right-of-way that the Atchison, Topeka & Santa Fé Railroad and the Denver and Rio Grande Railroad were engaged in. Both roads wanted to obtain possession of the route by way of Chicken Creek in the Raton Mountains. The Atchison, Topeka & Santa Fé claimed and had possession of the Raton Pass and built its line just where it is today.

The trouble began when the Denver and Rio Grande Railroad discovered another pass running up Chicken Creek which ran west from the Raton Pass. They were apparently in peaceful possession, with their engineers busily running the survey. But the Atchison, Topeka & Santa Fé claimed everything in the Raton Pass and at once attempted to run off the Denver & Rio Grande engineers by force of arms.

Possession being nine points of the law, breastworks were quickly thrown up and the Denver & Rio Grande Railroad engineers dispatched some of their men to Trinidad and El Moro to purchase rifles, pistols and ammunition. The Atchison, Topeka & Santa Fé had not been sleeping on their rights, for as soon as the word was passed out that the Denver & Rio Grande engineers were resisting the court orders, they started purchasing every available gun, pistol and shooting iron, and soon there was not a single firearm for sale in either Trinidad or El Moro, and for a time it looked like real war.

The Atchison, Topeka & Santa Fé forces proved themselves much too strong for the little narrow gauge railroad and soon had them completely routed, taking possession of Chicken Creek. Then the Denver & Rio Grande engineers pulled up stakes and left everything in the hands of the victorious warriors. No one was killed or wounded; in fact, as I remember, not a shot was fired. The Atchison, Topeka & Santa Fé did not want the Chicken Creek Pass for the purpose of using it. They simply did not want their rivals to get into New Mexico. The success of the Atchison, Topeka & Santa Fé Railroad naturally pleased me, for, as I have stated in a previous chapter, my father was much interested in the progress of this railroad into New Mexico. His services in securing a right-of-way were exceedingly valuable to the railroad, and it was glad to recognize them by electing him a director.

I well remember the impressive celebration that took place when the first railroad rail was laid on New Mexico soil. The spot was just over the line between Colorado and New Mexico at a point on the old switchback. My father had been honored by being selected to drive the golden spike that would fasten this first rail, and this he did amid cheers and flag-waving. Immediately afterward, the officials of the road and the guests on the occasion repaired to a private car and enjoyed an elaborate dinner which closed with toasts, my father responding to "New Mexico."

In recognition of the part my father had played in this railroad development, the first railroad town and station to be built in New Mexico was named Otero. It was about five miles south of Raton, and the commission houses thought it a good policy to establish branches at Otero. I was among the clerks transferred from El Moro to Otero, for, as I seemed a hopeless case so far as going to school was concerned, my father had decided to put more responsibility upon me in the business. So I was designated bookkeeper and cashier for the branch house at Otero, although I was then only eighteen years old.

Otero was a booming town for the next few months, or, to be exact, until the railroad reached Las Vegas. It was here in the spring of 1879 that Russ A. Kistler made his first appearance in New Mexico. He called at the office one day and asked for Mr. Otero. As my father was not in town, I asked if I could serve him. That led Mr. Kistler to tell me of his trouble. His press had arrived and was on one of the freight cars in the railroad yards, but that he was unable to obtain it until he could pay the freight charges.

He very frankly said that he was terribly hard up just then and had not enough money for his next meal. He had hoped to negotiate a small loan with my father. I inquired how much he needed and he replied, "Twenty dollars," adding at the same time that if I would let him have this amount he would either return it in a few days or allow my father to take it out in advertising in the paper he was going to start. I thought the case was a meritorious one and agreed to let him have the amount he needed, accepting his proposal to take it out in advertising.

The first issue of the Otero *Optic* came out on May 22,

1879, and it ran successfully until, with the general exodus from Otero, Kistler transferred his establishment to Las Vegas and renamed the paper *The Daily Optic.*

I remember a humorous incident that happened at Otero during the summer of 1879. One of the large stockholders of the Santa Fé Railroad living in Boston sent his son to Otero to learn the railroad business, under the special care of the railroad agent, requesting him to give the young man some kind of light work in the office and at the same time see that he took daily horseback rides so that he might regain his failing health. He was a student at Harvard and was somewhat run down physically. We wanted to make his visit pleasant for him, but failed utterly, for he was one of those knowing youths, perfectly well satisfied with himself in every way, who thought he knew a little more than the average westerner. He held himself aloof from the common herd and particularly shunned the "vulgar commission-house boys."

The railroad agent who had the responsibility of caring for the young man was, as is usually the case, looking out for his own advancement with the company. So he agreed with all the bombastic utterances, and humored the visitor in every way, to our great disgust.

One evening we held a meeting in our office for the purpose of laying plans to take the young Bostonian out on a real "snipe hunt." Certain members of our clan were appointed to "feel him out" gradually, and at last he became greatly interested. We told him that many of the boys objected to his joining the party, owing to his attitude in the past in avoiding our company. This seemed to soften him, and he intimated that in the future he would try to tolerate us. So we finally consented to allow him to accompany us merely as a looker-on, but if he liked it, we might get up another party while he was here.

The night was settled on, and we all met at the agreed-

Steamboat landed on her ample frontage, high and dry and squarely on top of the wriggling heap of men and women.

upon place. At once we started east, crossing Red River and then going southeast for about four miles to the sand hills and brush. Every detail had been carefully prepared, and every man knew his part perfectly. The Harvard student was being entertained regarding the peculiarities of this particular kind of snipe, the methods we would have to use to capture them, and the hard work involved in driving them. This last fact became the ground for a lively controversy as to who should hold the bag, which seemed the easiest part of the whole performance.

Many of the party had scattered and soon the whistling commenced. The word was passed about that a large flock had been seen running south. Soon we all started to whistle and the Eastern lad was asked to join with us, as this was done to hold the birds together.

At this point a general dispute arose as to who should hold the bag, several insisting that it was their turn. No one would give in. Finally, one of them threw the bag on the ground saying: "Well, take it. I am through." Then the young man from good old Boston came to the rescue and volunteered to hold the bag himself, saying that he felt quite sure he could do much better at that part than he could in chasing the birds. Some further discussion ensued, and, after considerable wrangling, it was agreed that inasmuch as he was a stranger and an invited guest, it would be only proper to allow him the privilege of holding the bag. So each one became alert in showing him the easiest way to hold the bag and impressing upon him the necessity of whistling all the time.

After getting him into proper position, we left him holding the bag. We circled all around him once, and then started briskly for home, leaving the young man all alone. When we had reached the outskirts of the town, we heard a bunch of coyotes and grey wolves howling loudly near the place where we had left the young Bostonian, and many in the party became alarmed and suggested that we go back. But just then something passed us like a flash of greased lightning; it was the young man speeding for dear life, pale and nearly dead with fright. It was a good lesson and from that night on until he returned to his eastern home, he was a changed individual, and really enjoyed our company.

Before concluding my recollections of Otero, I must relate a good story connected with our old Brobdingnagian denizen of the dance halls referred to in a preceding chapter as Steamboat. She had been a familiar figure on the old frontier for many years, and as the years passed her shadow grew not less but greater. Everyone knew her beaming, good-natured face, and her tenderheartedness was proverbial.

She deserves a page in the history of the old frontier, for casually speaking the greatest old specimen dangling on memory's string, was the fair, fat, and forty Steamboat, whom I mentioned in my second chapter as being at Hays City, Kans., in 1868. She was really an adjunct to the commission houses, starting with them from the first and continuing at every move until reaching Las Vegas in 1879.

She really was a fragile old girl and would not have weighed more than three hundred and fifty pounds on the platform scales. Her name was Dolores Martinez and she was an exceptionally bright native woman or she could not have remained so long in the dance-hall business and its subsidiary attachments.

It was in the fall of 1878 that she managed to get her three hundred and fifty pounds avoirdupois over Raton Pass from Trinidad and into the new town of Otero, and there she established a dance hall. It was not long before her place of amusement was the most popular resort in the lively little place. All the tough characters on the border camped there that winter and enjoyed the rough-and-tumble amusements at Steamboat's *sala de baile* on Main Street. The usual run of promiscuous shootings and gun plays occurred among the trigger-conscious citizens who frequented the joint, although I do not recall that anybody was ever killed there, which seems passing strange, considering the greater part of the owl-eyed strangers and frequenters who danced attendance at Steamboat's art gallery.

One bright afternoon in spring a gayly attired dude strayed in, fresh from the East, and took a seat just as any well-behaved wall-flower would have done. He amused himself by rubbering around with his legs crossed and minding his own business in the orthodox fashion as became a refined young man of good breeding. The hammer-clawers saw at a glance that he was an inoffensive tenderfoot, and the dance went on with joy unconfined.

A big lub of a cow-puncher came in just as an overgrown horsefly alighted on the tip of the patent-leather shoe, which was sticking out in everybody's road. The cow-puncher saw a streak of sunlight fall softly upon the insect. Immediately, the degenerate son of the range pulled his trusty six-shooter and took a hasty crack at the harmless fly, remarking that he bet that he would get it. Mr. Cow-puncher got more than he wagered for, because in an instant, he had stampeded the whole congregation of brave men and fair women. The single door at the rear was the only way out. They made a dash for it like a flock of scared sheep on a mad race for their lives. The second old buck out stumbled and fell in the narrow doorway, and the others rushing behind tumbled over his prostrate form until he was buried six or eight deep under the squirming, excited humanity — men and women all piled up in a heap like the dead in the sunken road at Waterloo. As for poor Steamboat — where, oh, where was she in all her sadness?

She was near the front door when the rumpus started, and having neither time nor desire to linger longer in such tight quarters, she let out an awful squeal — much like a hungry coyote when scenting a dead horse — gave way to the terror of the instant, and made a dash for the rear exit as the other frantic inmates had done. She was off to such a late start, however, that the gangway was choked. She saw a slight opening at the top, and made a flying leap for it. Steamboat was pretty nimble on her feet for such a big chunk of a woman, and it was remarkable how gracefully she sailed through the air. It seemed as though the flight of time had passed for one brief instant, and then the "sylph-like" form of Steamboat landed on her ample frontage squarely on top of the wriggling heap of men and women. For an awful moment she poised there, balanced in mid-air, half in and half out. The louts yelled like so many hyenas, but it was to no avail. Just then the villain, who was still following her, took deliberate aim and creased her anatomy with a speedy bullet. With a display of feminine agility that was really astonishing under such trying circumstances, the old girl lost her toe-hold and fell backward with a crashing thump on the hard floor.

The cavaliers who were not injured in the wild charge, picked her up tenderly, and lifting her elephantine body with much care they packed her into Doctor Robbins' field hospital next door, which was always on tap for such emergencies. Cock-eyed Charlie Hall, the head nurse, when no one else was around, patched up the shattered old Steamboat, so as to get her safely out of drydock and back to port in an hour or so, a little the worse for the wear and tear of a hard trip, but, if I may change the figure, like the ambitious prize fighter "slightly disfigured but still in the ring." The town gave the "old landmark" a great reception that night. As for the tenderfoot, the cow-puncher and the horse-fly, they all got away and were seen no more.

Steamboat followed the advance of the railroad and was soon afterward located in Las Vegas along with her old friends and associates of the early days on the frontier, the commission-house boys. From Las Vegas she went back to her mountain home near Mora, taking with her quite a neat little sum of hard-earned shekels, enough to keep her comfortably for her few remaining years.

My stay at Otero was of only a few months' duration. Early in 1879 a dispute arose between William Hamilton, the head salesman of the store at Otero, and me. Mr. Hamilton carried the matter to Mr. Sellar. Mr. Sellar decided in favor of Mr. Hamilton, although my father was away at that time in southern New Mexico and I was not given a fair hearing. Feeling wronged and humiliated, I immediately resigned, took what money was coming to me, and left on the first train for Denver, where I joined my brother who had gone there soon after our return from St. Louis.

While in Denver, we secured a nice room with Mrs. Perry, an old friend of our family, and were very comfortably situated, whenever we occupied the room. Our chums were numerous, and the gay life of Denver kept us busy keeping dates, so it was not at all unusual for us to sleep out with different friends every night for a week or ten days at a time, which at first alarmed Mrs. Perry. We had sufficient money for all purposes, besides having an excellent credit which we never abused. Estabrook's stable was one place we patronized very regularly, for he had the finest outfits in the city, and we both loved good horses. Frequently elaborate dances were given at Central Park, and all the beautiful women living on Holliday Street were there. We never missed these occasions and drove out in splendor, each behind a span of fast trotters. I can never forget the Denver of fifty-odd years ago, for in those days it had no equal; it was in a class alone.

On this same trip, I became anxious to make a run up to Leadville, which was then attracting a great deal of attention throughout the west. I made up a party, including John A. McBeth, Al. G. Hood, George Hauser, William Hauser, Charlie Keimle, Nels Newell and my brother Page. We went via the South Park Railroad, occupying one entire narrow-gauge Pullman car.

Our arrival at Leadville was in the midst of a severe blizzard, and I shall never forget the experience. At that time the principal street was Harrison Avenue, and, after a big supper at Watson's restaurant for which we ordered almost everything he had on the bill-of-fare, including cocktails and wine, some one suggested that we go over to see our old friend of the Kit Carson days, Tom Kemp, who was then running his celebrated "Grip Sack Station."

The suggestion met with hearty approval, and we all had an enjoyable renewal of acquaintance. Tom Kemp was so pleased to see us that he practically turned the house over to our party. We danced until midnight, paying little attention to the blizzard outside. When we finally left the hall, we were almost bowled over by the wind. Whirlwinds of snow were so strong that we could hardly make our way up Harrison Avenue, and when we finally reached the hotel, we were almost frozen. The next day one of our friends who had been with us at the supper and dance was stricken with pneumonia and two days later was dead.

While at Leadville I was almost inducted into the mining game. An old friend, Charlie Watkins, whom I had not seen since leaving El Moro, insisted upon my buying a quarter interest in the La Plata Mine, which adjoined the Iron Mine belonging to Leiter of Chicago, and which he had for sale for $1,500.00. He offered to give up his commission which would ordinarily have been $75.00, and let me have the interest in the mine for a net price of $1,425.00. Thinking I would like to make the investment, I telegraphed my friend Jacob Gross, the cashier and manager of Otero, Sellar & Co., asking him to let me draw upon my father's account for that amount, offering to put up as security the interest in the mine I proposed buying. But Mr. Gross was canny in the matter. He telegraphed his refusal without direct instructions from my father, who was then absent and could not be reached by telegram, and strongly advised me to be careful in speculating in mining property, closing with a suggestion that I had better come back to New Mexico. So, not being able to command the money, I had to drop the idea of purchasing an interest in the mine. A short time afterwards the mine became one of the greatest producers in Leadville, the output running into many millions.

After a few days more in Leadville, we returned to Denver agreeing that we had had a good time in spite of the weather. All of our party were, with one exception, members of the Chaffee Light Artillery of Colorado, with headquarters at Denver. The company was equipped with two old twelve-pounder brass muzzle-loaders. My brother usually worked as No. 1 on one of the guns, and I worked as No. 3 on the same gun, while the Hauser brothers worked the same positions on the other gun.

Soon after our return to Denver this company was ordered to proceed to Pueblo fully equipped. There was a railroad strike on at that time and we were expected to retake the roundhouse from the strikers. This we did without firing a shot. The Indians were also troublesome in western Colorado. In addition to these outbreaks there was lawlessness of a general character. About the same time the lieutenant-governor of Colorado, a prominent mining man by the name of Robinson, was killed, and I was detailed as one of the military guards while his body was lying in state.

Early in the summer we were ordered to the state encampment at Camp Pitkin near Denver. Albert H. Jones, who was later United States marshal of Colorado, was captain of our company in those days; the first sergeant was Willard S. Hopewell, who later came to New Mexico and settled in Sierra County, where he became one of the prominent cattlemen of the Territory, as well as a leader in the Democratic party.

I recall an amusing incident that occurred while at Camp Pitkin, which will bear relating. I was on guard duty one night at the tent which was used as a calaboose, and among the prisoners were my brother Page and his old chum, Nels Newell. Just across the road was a canteen. Newell and my brother left the camp and went over there without permission, and being caught off limits, were arrested and placed in the calaboose.

As they had been drinking freely at the canteen, they no sooner were established in the calaboose, than they fell asleep. When they awoke after awhile, they found their whistles very dry and wanted a bracer of some sort. Lifting the side of the tent and peeping under it, they discovered that I was on guard duty, and they at once began begging me to have a heart. Furthermore, they gave their word of honor that if I would let them go to the canteen they would come back after just one drink. I finally said: "If you fellows are pretty good runners, slip out when I am going up to the end of my beat, and I will try hard not to see you. But mind you, get back the same way without delay!"

This they did, and furthermore they were back on time. But it so happened that a tale-bearing soldier was at the canteen when they came in, and knowing that they had been taken to the calaboose, he took it upon himself to go to the tent of the first sergeant and report what he had seen. The sergeant called the corporal of the guard, and they lost no time in coming over to my beat and relieving me of further duty. In fact, they consigned me to the calaboose myself.

About twenty-five years after this event, I had the pleasure, when I was Governor of New Mexico, of appointing my friend Hopewell captain of cavalry in the New Mexico National Guard. Many a good laugh did we have in later years over the incident at Camp Pitkin, for our friendship grew stronger with the passing years. Colonel Hopewell was prominent in the development of New Mexico. He devoted much of his time to mining and railroad-building, being president of the Santa Fé Central Railroad which built a line from Torrance, N. Mex., to Santa Fé.

Chapter XIII

IT would seem more than strange for an old-timer like myself, who practically grew up on the frontier, to write of other early frontiersmen in the western country and then to ignore Uncle Dick Wooten, whom, as I have already indicated, I knew personally for many years and in whose company I have spent days at a time. In fact, I think I knew Uncle Dick better than I did any of those I have been at pains to mention in this book, Wild Bill Hickok, Buffalo Bill, Kit Carson, Clay Allison, and the rest.

As I have already related, my first actual meeting with Uncle Dick took place during the summer of 1872, when I stopped at the toll-gate near where he lived in the Raton Pass. But even before that I had heard my father and mother speak of him so frequently that he seemed to have been always an acquaintance. Then during my El Moro and Otero days I lived for three years within a radius of fifteen miles of his home, first on the north side and then on the south side of Raton Pass. During these three years I was frequently at his place.

Uncle Dick was a fine old man, always kind and gentle, and as hospitable as a Southern colonel. When dances were given at his home, and the fun was over, which meant either broad daylight or at least sun-up, we would have a good breakfast before starting home, and the last words of Uncle Dick to us would invariably be, "Now, boys and girls, come out here whenever you like. Just send me word and I'll arrange everything, even the music. All you have to do is to get your conveyance and land right here with me. I'll do the rest."

On these parties we were always careful to observe the conventions, and would have several married couples along to act as chaperons. The atmosphere at Uncle Dick's parties was always wholesome and above criticism, for he was a stickler for the proprieties.

His place was an attractive spot for picnics and camping parties, and many were the groups that resorted thither for that sort of pleasure. Uncle Dick took an especial interest in such outings, and enjoyed himself as much as any member of the party. He was always a most welcome addition to the crowd, and he contributed greatly to the pleasure by his tales of early life on the frontier.

Uncle Dick, whose full name was Richens Lacy Wooten, was born, so he told me, in Mecklenberg County, Virginia, on May 6th, 1816. As a young man he came out to Independence Mo. — it was about his twentieth birthday, I believe he said — and there attached himself to a wagon train of Bent & St. Vrain which was loaded and ready to start west for Bent's Fort on the Arkansas River, near the present site of Old Las Animas, Colo. All the rest of his life was spent in the Far West.

Uncle Dick was in no sense a bad man, as the term was understood in the West. He had killed a number of men in his life, but I think that every one was either an Indian or an outlaw and the killing had been in self-defense. As a frontiersman, Uncle Dick was much on the order of Kit Carson. Both of them stood in the highest esteem with the Indians and were regarded by them always as good friends, but both had their eyes well opened to the Indian character and could not be taken in. They knew how little reliance could be placed upon the word of an Indian, especially when mischief was lurking in the back of his head, and they seemed to know almost intuitively how far to trust their red friends.

There was, however, a difference between the two men in their means of livelihood. Kit Carson was a noted scout, Indian fighter, guide, and trail-blazer, in addition to being a soldier. Uncle Dick followed the less exciting and more pacific activities of trapping, hunting, stock-raising, farming, and conducting a trading station for the Indians. One of the leading qualities of the frontiersman, however, is discernible in both men; that is, versatility. Both were illustrations of how readily a man of that time could change from occupation to occupation as circumstances directed.

Uncle Dick was probably more successful as an Indian trader than at any other vocation. He knew to a T the trick of taking beads, trinkets, bullets, guns, pistols, knives, blankets, hats, tin pans, iron kettles and the like to the villages of the Indians and exchanging them for buffalo robes, hides, buckskin, furs and ponies, at the same time satisfying the Indians and enriching his own pocket. During the many years that he was engaged in this business, he travelled over practically all the western country.

From all this experience, Uncle Dick came to have pronounced ideas regarding the different tribes of Indians, and I have frequently heard him say that if the white man had adopted a hands-off policy, the Indians would have settled the Indian question themselves by killing off one another. He argued that in all the fighting comparatively few Indians were killed by white men or even by the soldiers, and that the wars between the different tribes were responsible for the great destruction of Indian life.

He knew the habits of the Indians so thoroughly and intimately that he could tell many interesting and little-known facts concerning their customs and procedures. I recall his once describing to me how the Indians, or rather certain tribes of them, poisoned their arrowheads. I give it approximately in his own words: "They would take a piece of fresh liver from an animal recently killed, and place it on the end of a long stick. Then, having located a rattlesnake, they would keep poking it at the snake which would of course become very angry and would bite the liver several times. After this had been done, the liver would be placed in the sun and allowed to decompose. Then the arrow points would be dipped into this mass of poison until they were entirely coated with the vile stuff. A very slight wound from such an arrow meant certain death and but few of the Indian tribes would use them, because of their fear that some of the poison might get into their systems through a cut finger or hand, and this they well knew would mean death to them."

From Uncle Dick I learned many interesting particulars regarding his own varied and rather migratory life. He was in the Battle of Fernandez de Taos, which took place two weeks after the cowardly murder of Governor Charles Bent on January 19th, 1847. Uncle Dick was a member of the volunteers and fought through the entire engagement. Soon after the Taos battle, he received a letter from Col. A. W. Doniphan asking him to join his campaign into Old Mexico, and, as Uncle Dick had promised the Colonel on another occasion to serve him as guide, he felt in duty bound to go. So, taking a fast horse, he overtook Col. Doniphan's command, which had already started, and remained with it until it reached a point almost within sight of Chihuahua, when the Colonel sent him back to Santa Fé with important dispatches for military headquarters. The return trip was without accident, and Uncle Dick delivered the dispatches entrusted to his care, but he decided to go back to Taos and make that his future home. Shortly afterward he went into business at Taos, married, and settled down to a life of merchandising.

Uncle Dick was at Taos in the winter of 1848-49 when Frémont's fourth expedition reached the town after a most trying experience in crossing the Uncompahgre Mountains. Uncle Dick it was who chanced upon the half-starved and half-frozen men and brought them into town. He conducted Frémont to the home of Kit Carson and saw to it that the other members of the party were lodged at other homes in Taos. About the same time Uncle Dick accompanied Col.

Newby's force in a campaign against the Navajos. On this expedition he was not only of great assistance as a guide, but what is more, was able to make peace with the Indians after the military officer had failed.

About the time that California was being settled because of the gold rush, Uncle Dick decided to try his luck in the new country. Having heard of several persons who had made fortunes by driving cattle and sheep to California and selling them in the mining sections, he bought in the neighborhood of Watrous, N. Mex., some nine thousand head of sheep, and then had them driven over the mountains to his home at Taos.

There he provided himself with everything he thought necessary for the fifteen-hundred-mile journey over mountain ranges and across barren deserts. Uncle Dick was not daunted by the dangers to be encountered and reasoned that he had always been taking chances.

At the same time, however, Uncle Dick made his preparations shrewdly and carefully. Finally, in the spring of 1852 he pushed forward with his well-equipped outfit, and though he met with many hardships during the trip and had encounters with Indians several times, he got through to Sacramento with his herd. Here he disposed of his sheep at good prices. As his losses were comparatively small, being but about one per cent, Uncle Dick was able to bring back to Taos in gold and drafts nearly $50,000.00. This money, I have heard him say, he carried concealed in his saddle bags.

On his return to Taos, Uncle Dick closed up his business there and moved to the valley of the Arkansas River, his intention being to try his luck at farming. This he did for about three years, but growing tired of this he determined to try something else. An opportunity presenting itself, he formed a partnership with an old neighbor, Joseph Doyle, in the freighting business between Fort Union and Kansas City. But soon after the arrangements were made, Uncle

Dick's wife died, leaving him with four small children to care for, a circumstance that almost necessitated Uncle Dick's retiring from the freighting venture. But his wife's father, a French-Canadian, Manuel Le Fevre, who still lived at Taos, took care of the children until Uncle Dick married again.

Uncle Dick continued in the freighting business for some years, but then began to feel the old urge to try his hand at something else. He went to Denver when that place was just becoming a town, built a large log store, two stories high, and went into the general merchandising business. But Denver was having a hard struggle and money was scarce, so Uncle Dick had to conduct his business largely on credit. In the course of about three years, he realized that he was losing money rather than making it — so he decided to turn to something else.

The Civil War being in progress, grain was in great demand, so Uncle Dick went back to farming, returning to his old place on the Huerfano, below the present site of Pueblo. But fortune no longer cared to smile on him. Hail storms destroyed his crops, heavy floods ruined his land, and, on top of all this, Indians were a constant menace to his stock. Uncle Dick promptly gave up farming, never to try it again.

He then conceived the idea of going farther south to Trinidad and building a much-needed wagon road through Raton Pass down to the Red River on the New Mexico side. The Colorado Legislature readily gave him a charter permitting him to build the road from Trinidad to the New Mexico line and to charge toll, and the New Mexico Legislature gave him a similar charter from the Colorado line south to Red River. In the spring of 1868, Uncle Dick moved down with all his family, livestock and belongings, and located at the point where he proposed to build the tollgate.

Even while his home was under construction, he began work on the road through the Pass, which when completed became famous far and wide as the best mountain road in the western country. The work took immense time and patience, and Uncle Dick deserved every dollar he made out of it. Barlow and Sanderson's Stage Line used the new road. The Government made considerable use of it in the movement of troops and supplies southward. All the freighting outfits travelling between New Mexico points and the end of the railroad tracks in Kansas and Colorado went by Uncle Dick's toll road.

His pride in his achievement was certainly pardonable, for, to use his own words as reported in Conard's *Uncle Dick Wooten*, "I had undertaken no light task, I can assure you. There were hillsides to cut down, rocks to blast and remove, and bridges to build by the score. I built the road, however, and made it a good one, too. That was what brought the Santa Fé Trail through this way, and as the same trail extended to Chihuahua, in Mexico, my twenty-seven miles of turnpike constituted a portion of an international thoroughfare."

All this patronage made the operation of the road profitable. Uncle Dick told me the only trouble he ever had in collecting toll was occasionally with some Mexican freighter who disputed his right to collect toll. The Indians, he admitted, sometimes tried to dodge paying it, but he made a point of never quarreling with them about it, for he was only too glad to have them go on their way. But every once in a while some of the Indians would present him with a nicely tanned piece of buckskin or a buffalo robe; so he felt that they were not without some appreciation for his indulgence toward them.

The advent of the railroad of course put an end to the toll-road. The Atchison, Topeka & Santa Fé Railroad built through Raton Pass in 1878, and that meant that the days of the old road were numbered. But Uncle Dick was able to dispose of all his property to the railroad and the coal-mining companies that were coming in, retaining only the use of his home.

The last years of Uncle Dick's life were spent in peaceful retirement in his home at the foot of Raton Pass. He remained to the end amid the mountains he had loved and in sight of the road he had made his monument to posterity. He died on August 22, 1893, at the ripe old age of seventy-seven years.

At the time the switch-back was in use during the building of the tunnel, the Santa Fé Railroad Company brought out what was at that time thought to be a mammoth locomotive. It specially was built to haul trains over the switch-back, from the last station in Colorado, Wooten, to Willow Springs, N. Mex., now Raton. The engine was named "Uncle Dick," as an additional compliment to the old pioneer who discovered Raton Pass.

R. L. Wooten, Jr., Uncle Dick's eldest son, was a prominent citizen of Las Animas County, Colorado. He was elected to the office of State Senator of Colorado, and later was chosen sheriff of the county, both of which offices he held with great credit. Later he moved to El Paso, Texas, and more recently to Albuquerque, N. Mex., where he was appointed Chief Deputy Sheriff of Bernalillo County. On January 20th, 1925, while waiting for a street car in front of the County Court House, he was accidentally struck by the car and knocked unconscious. He died a few days later, on January 26th, 1925. He was buried in Fairview Cemetery at Albuquerque.

As soon as the military encampment at Camp Pitkin was disbanded and we were relieved from further duty, I left Denver for El Moro, Colo., which I reached the same afternoon, finding everything in confusion. The whole town was busy migrating to Las Vegas, which was to be the next extension of the railroad. The town looked like a circus pulling up stakes and preparing to move to the next stand. Many houses

Uncle Dick Wooten

had already been torn down, and the lumber was being loaded on flat cars.

That same evening I drove to Trinidad to call on old friends. Two days later I took the train for Otero, where I found conditions much the same as at El Moro. There was not, however, quite so complete a determination to move, as many of the residents of Otero were inclined to remain until the railroad had built farther south to the new town of Albuquerque. When I learned that the construction trains were only a few miles north of Las Vegas, I became a victim of the current fever to get to that point.

The commission houses were still doing business at Otero, but at the same time they were making preparations to leave for Las Vegas on a moment's notice. Finally the news came — the railroad had reached the Las Vegas yards and the construction train was going through that day. So a number of us secured permission to ride down on it.

For our accommodation an old dilapidated day coach was attached to the rear end of the construction train, but we had no thought for the discomforts of the ride. We had come prepared to make a picnic out of it and had along plenty to eat and drink, the last including several cases of Phil Best's Milwaukee beer and many quarts of fine old Bourbon, Rye and Scotch whiskey.

Just about the time we were preparing to leave Otero for Las Vegas, Lieut.-Gen. Phil H. Sheridan was visiting New Mexico, and was given a great ovation by the citizens of Santa Fé on June 14th, 1879. In the evening a grand reception took place in the Palace of the Governors, followed by a gorgeous military ball. All the élite of Santa Fé and the surrounding country were there to do honor to the distinguished hero of Shenandoah Valley.

About this same time, June 21st, 1879, New Mexico lost one of her most prominent citizens, Hon. Benito Baca, who died at the residence of his father-in-law, Hon. Manuel A.

Otero, my uncle. Don Benito had been the nominee of the Democratic party in New Mexico for delegate to Congress in the fall campaign of 1878. He had made a most strenuous and ardent campaign almost entirely on horseback. Campaigning in those days was not as pleasant as it is today, with comfortable automobiles and fine hotels. Days and nights in the saddle together with other hardships caused a fistula to form in his rectum. A doctor residing at Belen operated on him with a dirty, rusty knife. Blood poisoning set in causing death.

Benito Baca was a highly educated man. On leaving college he entered the employ of Otero, Sellar & Co., at Hays City, as bookkeeper, remaining with the firm for five years. During all that time he lived at our home as one of the family. He married my cousin Emilia, and left two children — Ofelia Baca, now Mrs. Frank A. Manzanares, residing at East Las Vegas, N. Mex., with her two daughters, Emilia and Rebecca; and Benito Baca, living at Santa Fé with his wife, Ethel, and an only son, Eugene.

Benito was like one of our immediate family and his untimely death was a great shock to us all.

Chapter XIV

OUR excursion to Las Vegas was a wonderful success. We pulled into the Las Vegas yards early in the afternoon and found the new town a busy place, indeed. Everywhere buildings were going up, while tents and hastily built shacks of all kinds were being used as restaurants, saloons and living quarters.

From the yards our party walked over to the Old Town, for we expected to stay at the Grand View Hotel kept by Doctor Sutfin and his wife. On reaching the hotel, I was informed that rooms had been reserved for my father, who was expected in Las Vegas on the next stage coach, as well as for my mother and sister, who would be down from Denver, whither they had gone after the break-up of the home in El Moro.

This information was none too pleasing to me, for not having seen my father since I had so suddenly resigned my position with Otero, Sellar & Co., I was not altogether certain what his reaction would be. Sure enough, he reached Las Vegas the next day, and after hearing my side of the trouble, he said little except to direct me to report for duty at the office of the commission house the next morning.

When I went over, I found that rapid progress had been made in getting the main office into shape. My old friend Jacob Gross was at his desk as cashier and manager, while Frank A. Blake was holding down my old position of head bookkeeper. I told Mr. Gross that my father had said I was to resume my old position; so he informed Mr. Blake of the situation, and the latter cheerfully turned over the books to me.

My supplanting him in that position was not so cold-blooded as it may seem, for a few days later there came the announcement that my father and Mr. Gross were about to start a National Bank on the plaza in the Old Town, and that they were to hold the respective offices of president and cashier of the new institution. This removed Mr. Gross from Otero, Sellar & Co., and I automatically became manager, while Mr. Blake again became head bookkeeper.

As Mr. Gross was very busy with the organization of the new bank, he tendered his resignation to Otero, Sellar & Co., the same to take effect immediately, for, besides the labor of starting the bank, he wished to take a trip to St. Louis, to rest up for a while before assuming his new duties with the bank.

While on this trip he met Miss Caroline Linton, youngest daughter of my old physician, Doctor Moses Linton of Saint Louis University, whom he married about a year later.

Six months later, the San Miguel National Bank of Las Vegas was opened on the plaza in the Old Town, where Rosenwald Brothers store building now stands. The first meeting of the stockholders was held on January 27th, 1880, and the following directors and officers were elected: Miguel A. Otero, president; Thomas B. McNair, vice-president; Jacob Gross, cashier; Louis Sulzbacher, attorney; Joseph Rosenwald, Lorenzo Lopez and C. N. Blackwell, directors.

Shortly after my arrival in Las Vegas preparations began for the arrival of the first regular through passenger train. The officials of the road planned a great excursion, which was to reach Las Vegas on July 4th, 1879.

I decided this was a good opportunity for a frolic, so I set about getting up a party of young fellows to go back on the railroad to Trinidad, where we would join the excursion train and come on to Las Vegas, accompanied by some of our young lady friends.

The idea took with my associates, and our mission was entirely successful. We all arrived on what has always been regarded as the first regular through passenger train to enter

Las Vegas. The train with Charlie Brooks as conductor and Dan Daley at the throttle was handsomely decorated with bunting, ribbons and evergreens. Naturally, every man, woman and child in Las Vegas was on hand to see it come in, and the crowd was increased by the presence of most of the farmers and ranch owners for miles around. A brass band was on hand, and a reception committee, of which my father was the chairman, welcomed the visitors. That night a grand ball was given by the Citizens' Committee at the old Exchange Hotel in Old Town, while over in the new town those with inclinations to more hilarious and indecorous surroundings found what they wanted at Close & Patterson's Dance Hall, which as usual was open and ready for business at all hours of the day and night.

All who knew Las Vegas in those days will understand how very important was Close & Patterson's place. It was located on the vacant lots now opposite the present Harvey House, The Castaneda, and was a very large dance hall. In those days it was always crowded from sundown to sunup. The personnel consisted of about twenty-five regular girls, whose solicitude for the patrons of the house was of a kind to support the large sign hanging over the bar and bearing the inscription, "Everybody entertained in the best possible manner."

As I write of Close & Patterson's dance hall I am reminded of an amusing incident in connection with it. In the issue of the *Daily Optic* for February 7th, 1880, there appeared these startling headlines:

ALL THE DANCE HALL GIRLS TO BE BAPTIZED SUNDAY
THE MILLENNIUM HAS COME!

The town was for awhile electrified, and when it read the story underneath the headlines it discovered that an enterprising reporter had taken up a casual remark by

George Close and had embroidered it into this startling announcement.

In those days the new towns were visited by missionaries from different denominations who in their evangelistic efforts liked to concentrate upon the dance-hall girls. George Close was enjoying such a visitation at his establishment when a friend of his dropped in. In their conversation George blurted out, "Say, Jack, I am going to shut up shop and turn missionary." When Jack in astonishment inquired, "What's the matter now?" Close replied, "Well, those missionaries are trying to take all the girls away and get them to join the church. A dance hall can't run without girls, can it?" Then George added, "They are back there holding services now. Come on, let's go back and I'll show you."

The two started back through the dance hall, and the reporter, desiring to see what was going on, accompanied them. Entering one of the rooms, the trio found all of the girls rounded up and corralled, so to speak, in one corner, and entirely at the mercy of two clerical-looking gentlemen and a group of lady satellites who were assisting in conducting the services. The dance-hall flock looked as demure and innocent as so many lambs and seemed much affected by the earnest words they had just been hearing. Sadie was noticeably demure; Big Hattie looked as sorrowful as though she had lost her "man;" Careless Ida had penitence written all over her countenance; while Lazy Liz, and Nervous Jessie were wiping their weeping eyes. The scene was indeed a touching one, and had the reporter stayed there much longer he, too, would have been numbered among the converted. Even French Pete, the notorious gambler, was there, and he was overheard to say, "I guess I will have to quit rolling high-ball and turn missionary, too."

George Close was unable to face a scene like that long, and he conducted his friend back into the dance hall, saying to the crowd of men gathered there, "Boys, I guess Saturday night will be my last show, as all of the girls propose to be baptized Sunday. What I dislike about it is on account of the musicians and rustlers, for they will surely have to rustle now in dead earnest." It was this remark that the enterprising reporter caught and blazoned to the community in the headlines of the *Daily Optic* for Saturday, February 7th, 1880. The town caught on and thought it a good joke, but George Close, for the time being, felt that the reporter had gone rather far in manufacturing all this out of a remark uttered in private conversation. I don't think, however, that the patronage of his establishment fell off on account of the fun.

One of the important events of the early part of the year 1880 was the opening of the new saloon managed by Locke and Brooks. The evening of January 17th was set for the occasion, and cards were sent to almost every man in the community. Fred Locke was a fine old gentleman, who looked like either a banker or a wealthy minister, for he dressed in a Prince Albert and high hat, occasionally changing to a cutaway, with white shirt and neat tie. As might be expected from a man so fastidious, everything about his bar was as neat as a pin. As a mixer of all kinds of palatable drinks, he had no equal in the West and no superior in the East, *me judice*. By his friends and steady patrons he was dubbed "Lord Locke," and everyone treated him with the greatest respect.

His partner, Charlie Brooks, was an old passenger conductor on the Atchison, Topeka and Santa Fé Railroad, who counted his friends by the hundreds. The partnership of these two was a happy combination. When they announced their grand opening and sent forth their invitations, everybody made a point of showing up, unless he was sick a-bed. I had received a private tip from Rush J. Holmes, a wholesale liquor merchant, that he had sent over to the new saloon a barrel of the finest Old Kentucky whiskey that ever reached New Mexico, and I made up my mind not to miss the occasion. So I was there all right, and, what is more, I enjoyed the evening immensely, as did all the others, for we had plenty of good things to eat and drink, and a fine orchestra playing choice selections.

From that night on Locke & Brooks had the most popular resort in Las Vegas. Not long afterwards Charlie Brooks died at the Las Vegas Hot Springs from inflammatory rheumatism, and his interest in the saloon was purchased by William G. Lockwood. In the course of a few years they had changed their location to the Houghton Building, next to the corner, where they continued to do a large and profitable business. When the railroad reached San Marcial, in the lower Rio Grande valley, the firm broke up. "Lord Locke" went back East to his old home and was never heard of again. Lockwood went down to San Marcial and there opened a saloon which later burned down. Then he went to Corsicana, Texas, and opened a hotel. He never returned to New Mexico after his departure.

The old *la fonda* or hotel in Las Vegas was called the Exchange Hotel. It was a famous hostelry and had been managed since about 1866 by the Kitchen brothers, Charlie and Dick. It was a popular meeting place for all the cattle barons from southern Colorado and northern New Mexico, and all such occasions were signalized by a big poker game, under the auspices of Charlie Kitchen, the ceiling alone being the limit. These games usually lasted for at least two days and nights, meals and drinks being brought to the table so that there would be no break in the playing. Sometimes they lasted for more than two days and became an endurance test. Generally two days was about all that the nerves of even those inveterate and reckless fellows could stand. Among those who sat in at these games were such men as Wilson Waddingham, George W. Thompson, Marcus Brunswick, Henry L. Waldo, Thomas B. Catron, Abraham

Staab, Mariano S. Otero, Jesus M. Perea, Mariano Perea, Lucien B. Maxwell, Jesus M. Luna, William T. Thornton, Tranquilino Luna, Eugene A. Fiske, Charles H. Gildersleeve, John Chisum and many other lesser lights.

I recall an amusing incident in one of these games. The cards had been stacked against Wilson Waddingham by George W. Thompson, who knew Waddingham had just arrived in town from New York and would soon be looking for a game. As it so happened, Marcus Brunswick, who was Waddingham's warm friend, insisted upon sitting in at the game. Inasmuch as the entrance of Brunswick would render useless the stacked pack of cards which was arranged for only a certain number of players, they tried in every way to keep Brunswick from sticking to his purpose. But Waddingham finally said, "If there is no room at the table for my friend Brunswick to play, then count me out, for we came in here together and I refuse to sit in the game without him." This made the situation more complicated, since in order to carry out their plot and get Waddingham into the game, they must make a place for his friend.

But the brain of the arch conspirator and master strategist of the group, George W. Thompson, stimulated by the big haul of several thousand dollars he anticipated making, concocted a plan to save the day, which at the same time would not arouse any suspicion that might break up the game. He managed to seat Brunswick next to him on his left. Then Thompson himself, without a word of warning, fell back in his seat, calling loudly, "I'm sick, mighty sick. Send for the doctor! My God, I'm sick! Send for the doctor!" At the same time he acted out the part. He was hurriedly carried to a near-by sofa and placed on his back, while he continued to groan and call for a doctor.

But in a moment or so his groans died down, and the game began. After several deals, the deck of cards with which they had been playing was exchanged for the one that had been stacked. On the first deal with the new pack, Waddingham and Brunswick both thought they held wonderful hands, and the betting became brisk and earnest, as both Waddingham and Brunswick were so placed at the table that they had to call or raise a bet. When all the money on the table was up, including the amounts which had been declared before the start of the game, a show-down was called for, with the result that Waddingham and Brunswick lost over $30,000.00 on the hand.

As soon as full settlement had been made, George W. Thompson suddenly recovered, and after a good drink of brandy dropped into his old seat, cursing loudly because he had not been in on the "big pot." Undismayed by their loss, Waddingham and Brunswick continued to play and succeeded in adding to their losses. Some years afterwards the secret history of this game leaked out, but neither Waddingham or Brunswick ever raised a voice in protest. In fact, I have often heard Brunswick tell the story, and at the same time mimic George Thompson when he cried so dolorously, "I'm sick. Send for the doctor!" The old-timers were not only good losers, but they knew how to enjoy a joke, even at their own expense.

About this time the Territorial Legislature passed a bill prohibiting gambling and making it punishable by a fine of $50.00 and costs. At that time, such a bill was very unpopular and received no support in its enforcement from many of the people. The story in connection with the origin of this bill was that it had been introduced with the expectation that the gambling fraternity would contribute a reasonable sum of money to have the bill defeated, but for some cause this expectation was not realized and the bill became a law of the Territory.

Soon after the passage of the law, Judge Benedict was holding court at Las Vegas in the old Exchange Hotel. It was a matter of common knowledge that Charlie Kitchen and his brother were conducting in the hotel the best arranged and most complete gambling rooms in northern New Mexico. Speculation was rife as to what would be the outcome of this conjunction of law and lawlessness in the Exchange Hotel.

The law made it the duty of Judge Benedict to charge the Grand Jury particularly on this matter of gambling, and Judge Benedict carried out the full requirements of the law in this respect, giving a most definite and specific charge and insisting positively that they investigate fully all cases of gambling brought to their attention. The Grand Jury began its work and had been in session for a few days, when it became generally known that every lawyer in attendance on that term of court was to be indicted for gambling, even to the Hon. Thomas B. Catron.

When the latter heard of this, he became very warm under the collar and fussed and fumed like a caged hyena. Indict him? ... Why it was not for a moment to be thought of. ... To fine him $50.00? ... Why, that would be adding an injury to an insult. ... Although Tom Catron was a liberal man with his money, he could not stomach the thought of being made to give up any of his coin in that manner. So he definitely declared his intention of fighting the payment of any fine, even though it was the paltry sum of one dollar.

Rumor or gossip played into his hand. Hearing that Judge Benedict (who, after all, was human enough, despite his seat upon the dais of justice, to enjoy a good drink of liquor or a quiet game of poker) had taken a hand in a "little private game" in a certain room of the hotel. Catron made an informal investigation to see if the fact was as reported. On finding that such was the case, he engineered an indictment against Kirby Benedict for gambling.

The next day the Grand Jury presented a large number of true bills, most of them being for gambling. The Judge, after looking through them, handed the whole batch to the Clerk. He then dismissed the Grand Jury, and requested the sheriff to call all the defendants named in these indictments and to have them enter their pleas. All the members of the bar against whom the Grand Jury had found indictments were easily and quickly brought to court. One by one they entered pleas of guilty as the easiest way out, and were assessed in each instance the $50.00 fine and costs.

The Clerk in the mean time was giving various other names to the sheriff, who was bringing them into court as promptly as possible. Finally the sheriff called, "Kirby Benedict, for gambling." Thereupon the Judge stood up, and after listening to the indictment, said in a loud voice, "Kirby Benedict enters a plea of guilty, and the court assesses his fine at $50.00 and cost; and, what is more, Kirby Benedict will pay it." That last assertion was a knock-out blow for the others; it left them, even the Hon. Thomas B. Catron, no loophole of escape from paying the fine.

Many very interesting stories have been related regarding the judiciary in the early days of New Mexico, and Chief Justice Kirby Benedict seems to come in for many. He was without doubt one of the most learned judges that ever occupied a seat on the New Mexico Supreme Court; a man of great ability and unswerving integrity.

Probably the best anecdote about Judge Kirby Benedict is that told relative to his sentence of death pronounced upon one José Maria Martin, who was convicted of murder in the District Court of Taos County, New Mexico, under a statement of facts showing the greatest brutality, with absolutely no mitigating circumstances.

The Judge said:

"José Maria Martin stand up. José Maria Martin you have been indicted, tried and convicted by a jury of your countrymen of the crime of murder, and the court is now about to pass upon you the dread sentence of the law. As a usual thing, José Maria Martin, it is a painful duty for a judge of a court of justice to pronounce upon a human being the sentence of death. There is something horrible about it and the mind of the court naturally revolts from the performance of such a duty. Happily, however, your case is relieved of all such unpleasant features and the court takes positive delight in sentencing you to death.

"You are a young man, José Maria Martin; apparently of good physical constitution and robust health. Ordinarily you might have looked forward to many years of life and the court has no doubt you have, and have expected, to die at a green old age; but you are about to be cut off in consequence of your own act. José Maria Martin, it is now the spring time; in a little while the grass will be springing up green in these beautiful valleys and on these broad mesas and mountain sides, flowers will be blooming, birds will be singing their sweet carols, and nature will be putting on her most gorgeous and her most attractive robes, and life will be pleasant and men will want to stay; but none of this for you, José Maria Martin. The birds will not carol for you, José Maria Martin; when these things come to gladden the senses of men, you will be occupying a space about six by two beneath the sod, and the green grass and those beautiful flowers will be growing above your lowly head.

"The sentence of the court is that you be taken from this place to the county jail; that you be there kept safely and securely confined, in the custody of the sheriff, until the day appointed for your execution.

"Be very careful, Mr. Sheriff, that he have no opportunity to escape and that you have him at the appointed place at the appointed time.

"That you be kept so, José Maria Martin, until — Mr. Clerk, on what day of the month does Friday about two weeks from this come?"

"March 22nd, Your Honor."

"Very well, until Friday the 22nd day of March, when you will be taken by the sheriff from your place of confinement, to some safe and convenient spot within the county. That is at your discretion, Mr. Sheriff — you are only confined to the limits of the county.

"And that you be there hanged by the neck until you are dead and — the Court was about to add, José Maria Martin, 'May God have mercy upon your soul,' but the Court will not assume the responsibility of asking an All Wise Providence to do that which a jury of your peers has refused to do.

"The Lord couldn't have mercy upon your soul. However, if you affect any religious belief, or are connected with any religious organization, it might be well enough for you to send for your priest or your minister and get from him — well, such consolation as you can, but the Court advises you to place no reliance upon anything of that kind.

"Mr. Sheriff, remove the prisoner."

Note: José Maria Martin was never hanged; he made his escape from jail, and never was heard of again.

Money was plentiful in Las Vegas. In addition to what would have been the ordinary business development of the town, the railroad was building south, and the Las Vegas commission houses got the bulk of the outfitting for the different outfits. All the contractors, from Raton tunnel to Lamy, did their business in Las Vegas with either Otero, Sellar & Co., or Browne & Manzanares, and all their pay checks were handled by one or the other of those firms. So there was a considerable amount of money in very free circulation. No sooner did the employees receive their wages than it began to flow at once from their pocketbooks into the dance hall, gambling joints, saloons and restaurants.

In the new town of East Las Vegas it was a problem to secure living quarters. While my father's new residence was being built my mother and sister went back to Denver and did not return to Las Vegas until the house was completed. In my own case, I joined forces with Jacob Gross and Thomas H. Parker in building a small residence on the lots we had bought adjoining the four lots my father was building on. Many a good time did we have in our bachelor quarters when the house was finished, but in a comparatively short time I found myself the only one of the trio left. Jacob Gross got married and was willing to sell his interest to Parker and me; then poor Tommy Parker died of smallpox and I paid his mother in England the value of his share. That left me the lord of the manor.

Chapter XV

SOON after the resignation of Mr. Gross and his departure for St. Louis I found myself for a time entirely in charge of the firm of Otero, Sellar & Co. Mr. Sellar and his family were in Philadelphia for a visit and my father had gone south on railroad business. I remember that in one instance I showed business judgment which turned out well for the firm. The Government contracts in those times were the great business plums, and often two or three firms would join forces in securing one of them. In this instance Otero, Sellar & Co. were joint partners in a contract with Browne & Manzanares and with Colonel Marcus Brunswick of Las Vegas.

For some reason it was necessary to make a large advance in cash in connection with this contract, and Colonel Brunswick called upon me for the part of the advance that Otero, Sellar & Co. were to pay. The amount seemed to me entirely out of proportion to our firm's interest in the contract, and I declined to pay it until I had first obtained authority from either my father or Mr. Sellar. I promised to telegraph at once, but my attitude greatly displeased Colonel Brunswick, who took it to mean that I questioned his authority. "I will give you twenty-five hundred dollars cash right this minute for the interest of your firm in this contract," he shouted angrily, "provided you accept the offer right now, and then I will make the necessary advance myself."

Some sort of hunch told me to accept his offer even though I had to act in the matter on my own responsibility, and I let him write out a check for $2,500, in return for which I signed a temporary assignment, which was later followed by a formal assignment duly executed.

Shortly after the transfer had been made Mr. Sellar re-

"The Court takes positive delight in sentencing you to death."

turned from the East, and, learning of my action, began his old fault-finding treatment of me, which I could never endure with equanimity. So for the second time I resigned abruptly from my position with the firm, and with my brother Page struck out for St. Louis. When my father returned to Las Vegas he telegraphed for us to come back, and we did so, I again falling heir to my former position of manager and cashier.

My course in selling the firm's interest in that contract was finally vindicated. Browne & Manzanares and Colonel Marcus Brunswick lost about $25,000 on the contract. So instead of having to bear their share of the loss, possibly about $8,000, Otero, Sellar & Co. stood $2,500 to the good, all on account of my transaction with Colonel Brunswick. Even the stern Mr. Sellar was willing to give me credit for the outcome, and expressed regret for the way he had talked to me about it when he first learned what I had done. As for my father, well, he praised me for my prompt action in assuming responsibility in words which I like to recall even at this late date.

As heretofore related, the Las Vegas *Daily Optic* was ready for business in August, 1879. The paper was well edited and it had the habit of calling a spade a spade. Quite recently in looking through two badly damaged volumes, which were saved from the fire, one in 1879 and the other in 1880, I ran across a great many very interesting items. Some of them I copy, merely to show the manner of make-up of a daily paper on the frontier.

The *Daily Optic* of November 12, 1879, copied this bit of information from the *Trinidad News*, edited by Henry Sturgis, another of the early editors:

KISTLER'S KALAMITY

"Recent arrivals from Las Vegas are full of big conversation bearing on the pusilanimous conduct of one of the young ladies of that jumping-off place.

"Monday afternoon this interesting individual was passing along the street in front of Kistler's office, just as that worthy was reading his last proof for the evening issue, when she blew her nose. Kistler heard a great concussion and everything in the room grew dark to him, bringing a suggestion of a Rocky Mountain Cloud-bust. The fear-stricken young man rushed to the street, and there learned that his window was all plastered over with mucus (sic). His first impulse was to say something not contained in the Great Book, but a glance up the street showed that his neighbors, for three squares, had met a like fate. All he could do then, was to crawl back to his sanctum and laugh so convulsively, as to make the printers think he was dying in a *caniption fit!—Trinidad News*."

The above is true, every word of it. Now, why didn't your informants state whose proboscis it was that went off half-cocked? "Dolly Varden" and "Steamboat" both deny it. It must have been a Trinidad Demi-monde. We still live.

Under the same date appears a letter from Otero, N. Mex., addressed to the *Optic*, as follows:

Otero, N. Mex., Nov. 11, 1879.

Editor *Optic:*

In the *Daily Optic* of Nov. 7th, you state, that the town of Otero is fast sinking into peaceful obscurity — cause, saloons all gone.

Now, we still have six places selling liquors, enough for the health and morals of a much larger place than this.

Miss Darling opened school yesterday with twenty-two scholars. How is that for a school? Can you beat it, according to population?
Yours truly, M.

The stage coach from Silver City to Mesilla yesterday, Nov. 11, 1879, is said to have encountered Indians in the Magdalena Canon, and turned back. We give the report, just as we go to press.

Considering the very high prices of today, I cannot refrain from copying the following paid advertisement taken from the columns of the *Daily Optic* of December 4th, 1879:

Loftus, the butcher, will deliver choice cuts of beef and mutton, to any part of the new town, at four and a half (4½) cents per pound. Choicest meat in the market, or no sale.

One of the principal factors in making the *Daily Optic* an

interesting paper to the community was Lute Wilcox, the local editor. During the last half of the 70's Lute Wilcox had been a local editor on the *Trinidad News*, and when I lived in that vicinity I had come to know him well. I was glad to have a renewal of that acquaintance when he came down to Las Vegas, and he and I became the best of friends, and have remained so to this day. Finally Lute went to Denver and became editor of *Field and Farm*. But blindness developed and he had to give up newspaper work. Before becoming totally blind he published a series of frontier sketches which were very interesting and lifelike. One of these, telling of a Christmas Day celebration in Las Vegas many years before the railroad reached the state, is so characteristic of the care-free spirit of the place that I reproduce it with the author's permission. I knew practically every person mentioned in the story, and give it just as I have often heard it from Colonel Marcus Brunswick and as it appeared in print:

The enterprising proportion of the happy-go-lucky population of Las Vegas decided that it would be un-Christianlike to allow Christmas Day to slide by without some kind of appropriate celebration. The merchants around the plaza, headed by George Houck and Newton Irvin of the firm of Irvin & Jackman, went out among the boys and got up a joint donation to make the day's occasion worth while. Charlie Kitchen of the *fonda* was made treasurer of the joy pool and everybody chipped to the degree that their financial circumstances permitted. The question of funds in those days was the small end of the proposition and the Kitchen treasury soon had several thousand dollars in the pot.

George Houck was made the commissariat-general and supplied enough provender, wet and dry, to feed the Dutch army in Poland. The day dawned bright and fair, as Pepys said in his diary, and the genial warmth made everybody feel like so many kittens in a catnip garden. While the turkeys were roasting in the drum, the town merchants suddenly developed the Christmas spirit and threw great bolts of calico, ribbons, and other dry goods into the open plaza, where the poor people and beggars grabbed the precious fineries like hungry coyotes falling upon a sick calf.

At dinnertime Marcus Brunswick beat the big gong at the Exchange Hotel and the men folks went in for the feed of their lives. The champagne cases were spread around so thickly on the floor that there was not room to navigate. After the banquet was over, the "Jack of Clubs" lead out a buckskin pony and placed it on a pool table, which Sam Kaiser, Bill Shoup, Dr. Knauer, Frank O. Kihlberg, Henry V. Harris, and a lot of other fellows had packed out into the square. The noble Pegasus was given a bucketful of champagne as a starter, and was coaxed to mount the table. George Howe, "with his three-cornered hat, his breeches, and all that" was then placed on the horse's back. The men picked up the loaded table, rested it on their shoulders, and the queer procession marched around the plaza, and there George Howe, under the big chapeau and wearing a military cloak, made a great living tableau representing George Washington reviewing the northern army under the elm tree at Cambridge.

Along about four o'clock in the afternoon, John Dold decided that the pace was a little too speedy for an old duck with wobbly legs and asked to be escorted home. Charlie Cruson got a wheelbarrow and took it up in front of the hotel like a carriage in waiting. Frank Chapman and some of the other Indians packed Dold out, and laid him tenderly across the wheelbarrow, and with wreaths of mistletoe and kinnikinick to mark the spot where he was laid to rest, the band started off down the plaza playing the Rogue's March. Cruson trundled along with his load and just as the procession reached the *acequia madre*, poor old Don Juan Dold was dumped into the raging canal. If the folks had not fished him out he would have drowned, for he was too heavy to float and too tanked up to swim. They finally got the old boy home and stored away for the night.

In the evening a grand supper was given at the restaurant and bakery of John Pendaries, just to show they were all able to sit up and take nourishment, but it was a hard day and a strenuous night at that. The pleasant George W. Thompson operated a monte layout in a little room at the rear of the Exchange Hotel, and during Christmas Day Sam Kaiser and Charlie Kitchen broke the bank and laid Uncle George on the shelf for the time being. He caught his second wind the next day, however; borrowed a bank roll from somebody, reopened business at the old stand and before the midnight bells sounded at Father Pinal's cathedral up the street, George Thompson had not only got all his money back, but had made a profit of $22,000 on the play of the day. It was like picking up shining nuggets on the golden streets, and Thompson was wise enough to know when to quit, for the next morning Jim Olney hauled him out on the Barlow & Sanderson Stage Coach for Trinidad. There he married the widow of Colonel George Bent, got a start in the cattle business, reared a family and became rich — all because he knew when to quit and what to do at the right time.

Charlie Kitchen was a sport of the old school and was never so cheerful as when mixed up in a horse race. The common multiple worked so rapidly in his business that he made a hatful of money every day, but he soon fell into the evil ways of men of that class. He took up with "French Louise," the niece of Father Pinal, and was frequently at her house, half a block up the street. Martha, his wife, soon tumbled to the business and for twelve years an estrangement between them existed. They never spoke as they passed by, nor even stopped to bat an eye. They communicated only through their little daughter Annie, and finally, after long years of unhappy existence, Mrs. Kitchen quit her husband, who paid her the nice sum of $25,000 as voluntary alimony. She returned to the States with her daughter and neither was ever heard of again.

Just as Leadville was breaking out in 1878, Charlie Kitchen went to the great carbonate camp in Lake County and established the Hotel Kitchen, where he soon made another barrelful of money. The old man died a few years ago at Omaha, and this part of the story is told merely to show that some good folks at least did not get along any better at that time than they do now, for human nature is pretty much the same the world over, and in all kinds of weather.

I have already given indications that the commission-house boys were a lively, fun-loving set of young men. Many of them were from places back East, and they had come West because of the greater business opportunities or because of their liking for the freer life of the West. They were not scapegraces sent away from their homes as a good riddance. Far from that, in fact, for in order to qualify for the positions they held they had to show stability of character. At the same time, they had not sworn to eschew the cakes and ale of life. The fact that they were a jolly, gregarious lot led to the formation of clubs of various types.

The first social club we organized in Las Vegas was called "The Firing Out Club." The object of it was to "fire out" from the ranks of bachelors into those of the benedicts any young man who announced his intention of getting married. As soon as the wedding was officially announced, either by wedding cards or in some other way, the club put on foot plans for the firing-out ceremony. An evening was designated for a dinner in honor of the prospective bridegroom, at which all the members of the club, including the married ones, assembled. It was a fixed requirement that every member of the club was to drink alone with the bridegroom-to-be; the result was that by the time this part of the ritual had been completed the prospective bridegroom was very unsteady on his pins. While in this condition, he was securely bound with a rope and tossed in a blanket, an experience that added to his befuddled condition.

Then the married men gathered themselves in an adjoining room and sang home-made verses from "The Poor Old Sailor," finally ending with a sort of marriage march. Then the lights in this room were turned down until almost the only light in the room came through the transom of the door connecting to the one where were the married men still singing loudly. In the darkness the unmarried men marched in a circle around the prospective bridegroom, who was all the

My Life on the Frontier

while lying on the floor, tied with the rope. Suddenly, he was picked up by six or eight, and, with the aid of two stepladders, he was lifted up until he was on a level with the open transom. Finally, at a given signal, he was tossed headforemost through the transom, to be caught on the other side by the married men in a blanket, and so most heartily welcomed among the benedicts. After the firing-out ceremony the young men would for a time have no further use for the "renegade," as they dubbed him.

The days at Las Vegas fifty-five years ago were almost always bright and fair. The consumptives at the Plaza Hotel had nothing else to do in whiling away the idle hours than to sit on the long bench at the south front of the house and bask in the genial warmth of the golden sunshine. At times there were twenty or thirty of those unfortunate scions of the white plague in this collection. Most of them were fairly well-to-do young fellows with no other fault than that they were desperately ill from the dread malady. Yet they were remarkably cheerful through the somber hours of their impending fate and never murmured or complained. One day while indulging in their usual pastime and wondering each within himself as to which one would be the next to go, Fred Conde, a rich and handsome young bachelor from Rochester, N. Y., proposed that they should form some kind of an organization for their mutual benefit. The idea materialized in the "Lunger's Club," as they called it. It was the custom of this ill-starred order to line up on the long mourner's bench whenever the bus returned from the railway station with its usual load of passengers whom the coon porter, Shakespeare, had caught in his drag-net. Finally some poor consumptive would be helped tenderly down and carefully escorted in to the desk, where Harry Simpson registered him and then stored him away.

Every time one of these new-comers showed up the scamps on the long bench looked dubiously at one another with a knowing glance that spoke volumes. Somebody would invariably remark deprecatingly in a sepulchral voice that seemed to harken from the tomb: "I wonder what that fellow came out for? He will not live until morning," and only too often it did look that way to them. Then Ed Kirkpatrick or some other substantial member would suggest between a gasp and a sigh that it was about the third drink time, whereupon the whole miserable bunch arose wearily and toiled painfully, in Indian file, up the iron steps that led into the barroom. There they all sidled up to the rail, some of them hanging on for dear life, but all of them chaffing and joking while Tom Harper got busy compounding the various stimulants each was to receive.

It required the skilled training of a registered apothecary to get the tansy dose individually correct. Jack had to have cod liver oil from his special bottle. Edward took the acid phosphate, while Fred's portion was cinchona bitters. The next man needed the bromide of potassium as his dash on the side. It was anything from rock and rye to a shot in the arm, and everything from rum and gum to the milk of the wild cow. There were interlocking jolts of Gordon gin, Burton Dognose, fernet, brancha, Hungarian blackberry cordial, Maginnis' stout, Three-star Hennessey, rainbow cocktails, gin rickey or a Red Raven split for the weak constitutions of the "Lunger's Club" contingency. Then they lock-stepped back to the long bench in the glorious sunshine that destroyed the microbes and increased the appetite for more life-giving hootch in the dark bottle.

There was surely no use of repining, for tomorrow the sun was pretty sure to be shining. A day or two after the arrival of the stranger guest there was a new candidate to belong to the "Lunger's Club."

But what became of them finally? Well, under their diabolical manner of existence, by eating little and guzzling much McBrayer and all other kinds of liquor, most of them recovered and forgot that they had ever loitered so close to the valley in the shadow of death, there on the threshold of plumb despair, when everybody thought the undertaker would get the best of them before the rise of another welcoming sunup over the old "nine-mile-hill." One or two preferred the exciting life and became sheep herders. Herbert was carried in on a cot; he is now living in great ease and comfort in his elegant home in Brooklyn, N. Y. Fred Conde is still manufacturing woolen underwear at his large mills at Rochester, and I enjoy meeting him whenever I get to New York. He is now in the best of health and looks as though he were good for forty more years. He is always anxious to meet any of his old friends and talk over the days gone by. The last of the pulmonary Mohicans was Jack Crawford, who died only a few years ago, while serving in the judicial capacity of city magistrate at Albuquerque.

In the spring of 1880 those of us who liked hunting organized the Las Vegas Gun and Rod Club. Kroenig's Lakes, twelve miles north of Las Vegas, were always well-filled in season with large flocks of duck, geese, brant, large white pelicans, ibis, curley, jack-snipe, plover and many other kinds of water fowl. When we wanted to hunt, we usually drove out to the lakes on a Saturday afternoon so as to enjoy the early-evening shooting. Then we would camp for the night at our clubhouse, and early the next morning, before daylight, would be at it again and would continue hunting throughout Sunday. When we returned to Las Vegas Sunday night we would have hundreds of ducks, with a fair sprinkling of the other kinds of water fowl.

One thing that contributed to our bagging such a quantity of duck was our familiarity with the routes taken by the birds when flying from one lake to another. We would build our blinds on the ridges between the lakes, and when we were on a hunt we would divide ourselves sufficiently to have some at each blind. Then when we were all in our positions we would send one of the crowd on horseback to the upper end of the lake and have him fire off a few shots from his pistol. The noise of this shooting would send the ducks and other birds from the water in a perfect cloud, and as in their flight to another lake they passed over our blinds we would stand up and fire, dropping them by the dozens.

Just such a hunt as I have described above took place on Saturday afternoon, March 6th, 1880.

During the duck season we would arrange a hunting party for every Saturday afternoon to go out to Kroenig's Lakes, and on this particular occasion the party consisted of the following named members of our club: Jacob Gross, Page B. Otero, William Hazen, Frank A. Blake, Harry W. Kelly, Thomas H. Parker, David C. Winters, Godfrey F. Radcliffe, James L. Leavitt, Charlie T. Humes and myself. We had a large two-horse wagon which carried all our bedding, provisions, horse feed, ammunition and other necessary articles for the trip. This wagon started for the lakes several hours in advance of the hunters. The driver also took charge of all the horses in the party. The helper, or camp-man, went with the wagon, so as to have everything arranged and in proper order for our arrival late in the afternoon. This helper also did the cooking, for our time was devoted entirely to hunting. Permit me to add that before starting on our hunts we were always particular to have our office work finished and we would usually get on our way about three o'clock in the afternoon, in time to reach the lakes for the evening shooting.

On our arrival we found the lakes alive with all kinds of water fowl, such as geese, brant, ducks, snipe and ibis. There were thousands upon thousands of them in each of the five lakes. We lost no time in getting into the blinds and continued shooting until it became too dark to distinguish the flying birds. We all started back to the clubhouse, each carrying as many birds as he could handle. We arrived at about 9 o'clock at night, and after eating supper all hands rolled in for some much-needed sleep. We were all up and dressed at 4:00 A.M. and after a light breakfast started again for the lakes. We had fine shooting for five hours and then returned for a good meal and a few hours' sleep. Most of us went back to the lakes for a couple of hours' hunting, and at five o'clock we started for home with a bag of four hundred and sixty-one ducks, eight geese and a large quantity of snipe, ibis and curlews. This was not an unusually large number of birds, considering the size of the party. On reaching Las Vegas, we drove around the town delivering game to all our friends, but reserving enough for a big game dinner at Watson's Restaurant.

Chapter XVI

DURING 1879 and 1880, Las Vegas was the headquarters for all kinds of criminals from every known locality in the United States and Mexico. It was even, for a time at least, a place of harborage for Jesse James. In the *Daily Optic* of December 8th, 1879, appeared a disclosure of this fact, in the following words: "Jesse James of Missouri was a guest at the Las Vegas Hot Springs from July 26 to July 29, 1879. Of course it was not generally known." This statement is true, for I met Jesse James during his three days' stay at the Hot Springs. This is how it came about:

The hotel at the Hot Springs, known then as "The Old Adobe Hotel," was being excellently run by Mr. W. Scott Moore and his wife Minnie. They made it a pleasant place for a few days' stay, and I had formed the habit of going there on Saturday afternoon, remaining until Monday morning, and participating in the meantime in one of Mrs. Moore's Sunday dinners, which were feasts indeed. Everything served was of the best. It was on one of these visits that I happened to meet Jesse James. At the hotel was an acquaintance of mine from Missouri, and it chanced that he was the selfsame person whom Jesse James was visiting. So the meeting came about very naturally, but with the proviso that I would keep mum about it. I kept the secret until it became public property through the item in the *Daily Optic* that I have quoted.

The friend through whose good offices I was brought into contact with Jesse James was Scott Moore, whom I had known for many years, our friendship going back to the early seventies, when he was a freight conductor in Kansas. He and the James brothers, Frank and Jesse, had been boyhood friends in Missouri, where they had grown into manhood together. This friendship had begun before the James boys and their kinsmen, the Younger brothers, through the cruel and inhuman treatment their families had received under the infamous "General Order No. 11," had been forced into guerrilla fighting against the Federal Army located at that time in western Missouri and eastern Kansas. This friendship had persisted when, with the termination of the war, the James and Younger groups had become the outstanding figures among the post-bellum outlawry west of the Mississippi.

In the late seventies their names were in everyone's mouth and I, like all the rest, had been thrilled by what I had heard about them.

In appearance and dress the man I saw was far from suggesting a noted desperado. He was of medium height — about five feet seven or eight — not heavy but compactly built; his eyes were blue and rather severe, what might be termed piercing; his hair was dark brown and he had a full beard, not long, possibly an inch and a half or two inches below the chin. He was attired in the usual style of the period. His suit was brown with a coat on the order of a short Prince Albert. His hat was a soft black felt with a moderately wide brim and a rather low crown. The face was an interesting one to study; his blue eyes seemed to give tone to the whole visage.

His manner was pleasant, though noticeably quiet and reserved. He listened attentively to every word that Scott Moore or I uttered but he himself said little. Occasionally he would ask some question about the country and the opportunities for stock-raising. But all the time I was conscious that he was alertly aware of everything that was said and done in the room. He never made the slightest reference to himself, nor did he show the least trace of self-importance or braggadocio. Had I not known who he was I should have taken him for an ordinary business man receiving a social visit from two of his friends. But his demeanor was so pleasant and gentlemanly withal that I found myself on the whole liking him immensely.

I never knew just why Jesse James happened to come out to Las Vegas Hot Springs. Nothing was said in our conversation about the subject, and when in later years I tried to draw out from Scott Moore the true reason, all that Moore would vouchsafe was: "Jesse just came out for a visit and to get a little rest with some of his trusted friends. There was in his mind some notion that he might locate under an assumed name in New Mexico, Arizona or somewhere in the Republic of Mexico, for the sole purpose of trying to live a peaceful and quiet life with his family."

This explanation seemed plausible enough. All the time I was talking with him he seemed to be doing considerable thinking about something very near to him, and perhaps the subject on his mind was this plan to try to find a place where he might "go straight" for the rest of his life unbeset by consequences from out of his past. Scott Moore also told me that Jesse James came directly from Kansas City to Las Vegas, and that he returned directly to Kansas City after his short stay. While I cannot say definitely, I believe this was his first and only trip to New Mexico. From his remarks and questions, I gathered that he had never been in the Territory previously, and I feel sure that he never returned. He left Las Vegas as quietly as he came, accompanied by a close friend, who was a conductor on the Santa Fé Railroad. I doubt very much if at the time anyone outside the inner circle of three, this conductor friend, Scott Moore and myself, knew that the quiet and unobtrusive visitor at the Hot Springs was the notorious Jesse James.

Of course after my meeting with him, I followed more eagerly than ever the subsequent developments in his career, which closed three years later, when he was killed by Charlie Ford, assisted by his brother, Bob Ford, at his "unknown" home in St. Joseph, Mo. Both of the Fords were members of the "James Boys" band, and they murdered their leader in a most cowardly and cold-blooded manner just to get the reward that Governor Crittenden of Missouri had offered for his capture. Not suspecting any treachery from members of his band, Jesse James was hanging a picture in one of the rooms of his house while the Ford boys ostensibly rendered assistance. While Jesse James was standing with his face toward the wall, Charlie Ford shot him through the back of the head and he fell to the floor dead.

The dastardly way in which Jesse James was killed created a great deal of sympathy for him the country over, and a corresponding bitterness toward the Ford brothers. The latter had expected to pose as heroes in the eyes of the world, but instead they found themselves in jail on charges of first-degree murder. They were subsequently tried, convicted, and sentenced to be hanged, but two hours after the court had pronounced sentence, Governor Crittenden issued pardons to both of them.

Charlie Ford became severely stricken by remorse for what he had done, and about four years afterward committed suicide by shooting himself. Bob Ford lived on for about ten years after the killing of Jesse James. He drifted west, and again Las Vegas became identified with the "James Boys" band of outlaws. For a time Bob Ford, in association with Dick Liddel, a notorious member of the band who had turned state's evidence and had been pardoned by the governor, conducted a saloon in Las Vegas. Bob Ford never made any headway in the community, and he soon sold out his interest in the saloon venture, and went to Creede, Colo. There he was eventually shot and killed in a dance hall by Ed Kelly over Ford's mistress, Nellie Watterson, who passed as his wife. Dick Liddel stayed on, but eventually he too sold out his interests in Las Vegas and went East with a string of race horses belonging to J. W. Lynch of Las Vegas. During the time that Bob Ford and Dick Liddel were in Las Vegas, I knew them both quite well. So it might be of interest for me to add my impression of these two men, as they appeared to me at that time.

Bob Ford was a good-looking young man, not tall, but slightly above the average in height and solidly built. His hair was dark brown and inclined to be wavy; his eyes were gray, and he was clean-shaven and neat in dress. He was neither quarrelsome nor morose; on the contrary, he was pleasant to meet, rather boyish and good-natured and always endeavored to make friends. In appearance he would remind one of Jack Dempsey as he looked in his younger days.

Ford seemed to realize that he was in bad with the community for people shunned him as they might a mad dog. The saloon was advantageously located on Bridge Street in the Old Town, about the center of the block between the river and the plaza, on the north side of the street, and it was first class in every respect. But do what they might, the proprietors failed to get the business. The saloon was losing money so rapidly that Ford became despondent over the outlook, sold his interest and left for Creede.

His partner, Dick Liddel, was a rather small man, very slight in build, with dark, straight hair, and a small brown mustache. He was a natural horseman and took more interest in Mendenhall, Hunter & Co.'s livery stable next door than in the liquor business. Dick Liddel was far from being a bartender, neither did he understand the saloon business. He was rough in his dress and general appearance, and much better suited to stable work and attending to horses. So he finally arranged with J. W. Lynch of Las Vegas, who had quite a string of fine running horses, among them a noted racer named St. John, to take them all back East and enter them in the eastern and southern circuits. He immediately sold out his interest in the saloon and soon left Las Vegas with the horses. The horses made good under the manage-

George Howe as General Washington — a Christmas prank at Las Vegas, New Mexico, in the early days.

ment of Dick Liddel, and he soon paid Lynch his price and became sole owner of the entire string.

Though Jesse James did not stay long enough to become an integral part of the crime history of Las Vegas, there were a number of others who were able to give the place an unenviable reputation. In the remainder of this chapter I shall try to present a picture of this side of the life of Las Vegas and to give some idea of the efforts of the more law-abiding element to clean up the forces of lawlessness.

The coming of the railroad was accompanied in Las Vegas, as in almost all of the terminal towns that marked, for the time being, the progress of the transcontinental lines, by an influx of bad men of all sorts, especially gamblers and killers. New Mexico was located so as to receive the backwash from two streams. From one side Texas, Kansas, Colorado and the Indian Territory deposited their flotsam and jetsam of humanity, while from the other side Utah, Arizona and California spewed their human refuse. New Mexico became a sort of catch-basin for this type, and Las Vegas in particular the rendezvous for them.

For more than a year after the entry of the railroad, it can be stated without fear of contradiction that Las Vegas was the "hottest" town in the country. Such a statement would be substantiated by the record, for one month, which the old files of the *Daily Optic* establish. They show that twenty-nine men were killed in and around Las Vegas, either murdered outright or shot in self-defense or hung by the well-regulated Vigilance Committee. Such a record, I am certain, would be hard to parallel in the history of any of the wild towns of the West. It will be of interest to study some of the special conditions that gave support to so much criminality and to follow some of the more striking cases.

For the general impression among underworld characters everywhere that Las Vegas was a promising field, there was a very excellent basis. That section of the town known as East

Las Vegas, or New Town, owing to its having developed with the coming of the railroad, fell under the control of as vicious and corrupt a set of scoundrels as could be found anywhere in the West.

When the New Town section of Las Vegas organized as Precinct No. 29, and held an election of officers, the justice of the peace chosen was a "mystery man" named H. G. Neill, who afterward became known more generally as "Hoodoo Brown." This very appropriate nickname was given him by one of the dance-hall girls in Close & Patterson's, in commemoration of one of her old lovers, the word "Hoodoo" meaning one who brings bad luck to anyone having anything to do with him. Neill seems to have appeared first on the western scene at Trinidad; then he migrated successively to Otero, and eventually to East Las Vegas. It was understood that he came from a good family in St. Louis, but if so, he certainly left all his goodness with the family, for during his stay in East Las Vegas he showed nothing approximating decency or honesty.

Associated with Hoodoo Brown as constable was a criminal who went simply by the name of Dutchy. These two succeeded in assembling in East Las Vegas a group of notorious confidence men, gamblers and killers, who went locally by the designation of the "Dodge City Gang." Joe Carson was appointed city marshal, ably assisted by David Mathers, better known as "Mysterious Dave." Bill Goodlet, a former sheriff and peace officer of Colfax County, New Mexico, was hand in glove with this bunch. The result was that collectively they were able to handle East Las Vegas as they liked, which of course was always to their personal interest.

Conditions went rapidly from bad to worse. Killings took place with such regularity that the first question a man asked on reaching his place of business in the morning was, "Well, who did they have for breakfast this morning?" In the case of these killings, it was usually a question as to which was the more undesirable member of the community, the man killed or the killer. But there was always one satisfaction for the peaceable and law-abiding: the community had one less objectionable character to contend with. Frequently, however, within twenty-four hours would come the arrival of someone to step into the gap in the community who might be ten times as dangerous.

My introduction to the killings of Las Vegas came very soon after my arrival in the town. At first Jacob Gross and I rented a room in the second story of the Davis building that stands just across the street from the Old Exchange Hotel. In fact, Charles Emil Wesche, the proprietor of the Exchange Hotel at that time, used the second floor of this building as an annex to the hotel. In the room just across the hall from ours were two splendid men, good friends of ours, and likewise associated with the firm of Otero, Sellar & Co. They were Henry V. Harris and William L. Hazen.

One evening we were all together in the room belonging to Harris and Hazen, having a quiet game of poker, when our attention was attracted to some loud talking across the street in the direction of the barroom of the Exchange Hotel. Next we heard a pistol shot, followed a minute later by the tread of many feet, seemingly coming up the steps leading to our rooms. We went out in the hall to see what was happening and ran into a number of men, carrying the limp form of a man, who had registered that afternoon at the hotel.

The wounded man was carried into one of the vacant rooms and laid on a bed. Some of those who brought him up the stairs attempted to undress him and make him more comfortable in bed, while others scurried around in search of a doctor. Just as the doctor arrived on the scene, the man died, without having uttered a word.

As well as could be ascertained, the circumstances were as follows: Just before going to supper, the stranger dropped into the hotel barroom for a drink. Someone in the bar objected to his drinking alone, and insisted that he invite all those standing before the bar to drink with him. The stranger paid no attention to this demand, and when he had had his own drink, turned to leave. The man who had demanded drinks for the crowd, blocked the stranger's progress toward the door. The latter again pushed him aside and continued in the direction of the door. Thereupon the drunken rowdy pulled his pistol and fired. The man who did the killing was also a stranger in the town, and he promptly disappeared from sight. It was such things as this that started the Vigilantes to work, for the peace officers of the town were not interested in the enforcement of law and order.

While the grading of the railroad bed was continuing south of Las Vegas, many camps were established along the route especially through the Glorietta Pass, and practically every camp had its saloon and gambling tent. Sometimes these necessary adjuncts belonged to the contractors, but where such was not the case the owners paid a handsome price for the privilege of having the exclusive right to conduct their business over the mileage under the control of certain contractors. Frequently, three or four soiled "doves," or camp followers, would have a tent or two at the rear of the saloon and assist the bartender in entertaining the patrons all during the night. Of course bad men and confidence men followed these camps and many an innocent wandering boy was relieved of all his belongings by running against them. Frequently, during these hold-ups the victim would become despondent over his losses, and either a killing or a suicide would ensue. In the case of killings, usually the right man got killed, and when that happened, rejoicing took the place of grief and the drinks were freely ordered.

One of the largest grading outfits between Las Vegas and Santa Fé was located at Cañoncito, N. Mex. The commission houses were in close contact with all these camps and had men visiting them daily for orders. On December 4th, Rattlesnake Bill, a notorious desperado, for whose body, dead or alive, large rewards had been offered, was killed at Cañoncito by one Frank Page, a late arrival from the States. Page was tending bar in the saloon of Rhodes & Hogan. Rattlesnake Bill came in and demanded a drink in an insulting manner and then refused to pay for the same. Words ensued and threats were made by Bill. Page secured a pistol and, without a word of warning, fired. The ball passed directly through Rattlesnake Bill's heart. Page surrendered to the officers of Santa Fé County and was placed in the county jail at Santa Fé. At the trial he was acquitted of murder and turned loose. New Mexico was rid of another bold, bad man. On the same day, December 4th, 1879, at Glorietta, N. Mex., only a few miles east of Cañoncito, the sheriff of Santa Fé County entered the saloon and restaurant of the Pearson brothers, not unknown in Las Vegas, for the purpose of arresting them. They immediately set upon him, beating him unmercifully over the head and body, and breaking his arm in the mix-up. The sheriff was kept a prisoner in the saloon overnight. The Pearson brothers escaped and were never arrested.

One of the most celebrated characters living in the Old Town of Las Vegas was Chata Baca, who ran a dance hall in Precinct No. 5. Chata was a large woman. She had a sister named Maria who was about the same size, and the two kept Chata's dance hall in orderly condition. Chata catered more to the newcomers. Her girls were selected for beauty and neatness and it was generally known that all these girls danced well, dressed well, never were quarrelsome, and seldom indulged in liquor, save an occasional drink of light wine. Chata watched her girls like a good mother and never permitted them to use bad language or to become boisterous or too familiar with anyone during the dances. They were scrupulously clean and quite decent. So Chata had no trouble in securing the patronage of both the commission-house boys and the railroad-office boys.

The best regulated family is sometimes very apt to "slip

a cog" when least expected, and thus it happened one bright night when Harry Kelly and myself were over at Chata's dance hall. On this occasion some of the native boys became involved in a little dispute among themselves over a partner for the following dance, two of them claiming the same girl, a beautiful young woman named Donaciana Trujillo. Words were quickly followed by blows; then one of the boys pulled out a very small pistol and fired, striking his opponent about one inch to the left of the navel. The wounded man, Santiago Angel, fell to the floor groaning as though in great pain. Doctor William R. Tipton was sent for. He quickly examined the young man's wound while Harry Kelly and I assisted. Angel never recovered from the shock and died before the doctor could get him to the operating table at his office.

Chata herself, as well as her sister Maria, were out of the dance hall when the quarrel occurred; had either of them been there it would never have happened. Chata deeply regretted the incident and did all she could to show on which side her feelings were. She closed her dance hall for several days, and even made a liberal contribution to the mother of the dead boy. The murderer, through the good offices of his friends, secured a fast horse and immediately departed for parts unknown. He was never arrested or brought to trial.

Again, during the latter part of January, 1880, a freighter named Theodore Caston left Las Vegas for Santa Fé with a load of merchandise and other goods. It was rumored he had $1,500 in cash on him. While he was sleeping near his wagon the following night, he was brutally murdered. His head was chopped open by an axe in the hands of some unknown person. No arrest was ever made of the murderer.

Chapter XVII

THURSDAY night, January 22, 1880, was a night long remembered in Las Vegas for the excitement it offered. For several days four horse thieves had been walking around the town visiting the different saloons and drinking considerable quantities of red liquor. They had left their Winchesters, as well as their horses, at the livery stable of Llewellyn & Olds, but each carried two pistols in his belt, despite the fact that Joe Carson, the city marshal, had told them it was against the town ordinance. To his more positive demand that they remove them, they paid no attention. So these four — Tom Henry, John Dorsey, William Randall and James West — continued to drink and talk loudly in the saloons, and ultimately entered the dance hall belonging to Close & Patterson, with pistols displayed openly in their belts.

Marshal Joe Carson accosted them and again requested them to lay down their guns. All four were drunk and not only laughed at Carson's demand, but made their refusal in rough and offensive language. Thereupon, Joe Carson asserted his authority, and a brisk gun-fight began. At least forty shots were fired, and when it ended, the casualties were: Joe Carson, prostrate on the floor with nine bullet wounds in his body; William Randall, mortally wounded; James West, too badly wounded to make his escape; Tom Henry and John Dorsey, wounded but able to escape from the dance hall.

The two last-named desperadoes made their way to the livery stable, to get their horses and their Winchester rifles, so as to make a quick get-away. Tom Henry, with rifle in hand, stood guard at the gate of the stable yard, while John Dorsey saddled the horses. This done, they mounted and made a run from the stable, going north in a direction that soon brought them to the Mora Wagon Road. They dashed up this road until they were a little beyond the town of Mora, where they stopped at a friend's ranch, dressed their wounds and had something to eat.

In the meantime, what were the other survivors of the shooting doing? James West, though badly wounded in the side, was taken to the county jail in the Old Town. William Randall died a few minutes after the fight. His body was placed in a cheap coffin and buried in the pauper's lot without any ceremony. The sheriff, Joe Carson, with nine bullet-holes through him, crawled from the dance hall on his hands and knees in a pathetic endeavor to reach his home and see his wife once again before he died, but just as he met her at the door he fell forward on his face — dead.

Excitement over this affair was at fever heat for a week or more, but no definite clues as to the whereabouts of Henry and Dorsey were forthcoming. Finally, it leaked out where they were hiding and a posse consisting of J. J. Webb, William L. Goodlet, Bill Combs, Dave Rudabaugh, Lee Smith and a man known as Muldoon, all heavily armed, left Las Vegas on February 5th to get Henry and Dorsey, dead or alive.

They surrounded the house where the two were staying and Dorsey and Henry were convinced it was best to surrender but, before doing so, they insisted on a promise of protection from mob violence and a fair trial. The posse started back to Las Vegas at once, but the prisoners seemed dissatisfied and brought the matter to the fore again. Tom Henry went so far as to say:

"I very much doubt if we will be given any show. Now, here's what I propose: If you boys will give me my horse which you are trailing behind the wagon, and allow me a start of a hundred yards, you may shoot at me with all your rifles, and I'll take a chance of getting away." The deputies declared they could not do that, but renewed the promise of protection.

When they reached Las Vegas, the two prisoners were placed in the county jail. The next morning they were interviewed by reporters from the local papers and the writer was present when the following information was drawn from them: They claimed that the purpose of their presence in Las Vegas was primarily to have a good time, though they admitted that they intended to steal as many valuable horses as they could safely get away with. They declared that they had no intention of killing anybody and attributed the whole "bad mix-up," as they expressed it, to drinking too much whiskey. Tom Henry admitted that his real name was Thomas Jefferson House, and that he had lived with his aged father and mother in Pueblo, Colo.

He gave his age as twenty-one, but young as he was, it was evident that he was the leader of the gang. John Dorsey, who said that he was thirty-three and had come from Texas, would give out nothing further about himself. James West admitted that his real name was James Lowe and that he, like the others, was from Texas. He said he was twenty-two. He was most profane, and expressed the opinion that Tom Henry and John Dorsey were "God damn' fools to be taken alive." From these three it was learned that the dead member of the crowd, William Randall, had lived in Texas and was thirty-six. Beyond these facts they seemed to know little about him.

But the citizens of Las Vegas were not inclined in this affair to wait the slow operation of the judicial machinery. At midnight on Saturday, February 7th, a large but orderly gathering collected at one of the vacant store buildings on Railroad Avenue. Thence it marched, two abreast, toward the county jail. As it proceeded, recruits were added, so that the line was finally about half a mile long. When it reached the jail, it met with no resistance. The jailor promptly handed over the keys, and it was an easy matter to take Tom Henry, John Dorsey and James West out and march them to the old wind-mill in the center of the plaza.

They were mounted on the platform and ropes placed

about their necks. The first one to receive attention was James West. For some reason his hands had not been tied and this permitted him to grab the rope as he was being pulled up, to prevent its breaking his neck. At the same time, he called loudly for his mother. He did not have on his belt, and as he was being pulled up, his trousers began slipping down to his feet but were held up somewhat by his shackles. Tom Henry, the young leader of the crowd, looked at him for a moment, and then said, "Can't you see they intend to kill you? So stop your crying and die like a man." These words brought Lowe, alias West, back to himself, and with the exercise of will-power he removed his hands from the rope above his head, and drew them down sharply and forcibly against his sides. At the same time, there was an involuntary kicking of his legs, which caused his trousers to drop still farther down.

Just at this moment a shot was fired by one of the leaders, whom many have believed was the widow of Joe Carson in male attire. Tom Henry immediately dropped to the platform and rolled over, saying, "Boys, give me another in the head." These were his last words, for about a hundred shots followed. At the end of the fusillade Tom Henry and John Dorsey were lying dead on the platform, and James West was hanging at the end of the rope, stone dead — his body also riddled with bullets.

Without doubt these fellows received their just dues at the hands of the mob, but one regrettable feature in the affair was that the members of the posse that captured two of this gang and who had made them such strong promises of protection, were among the leaders of the crowd that perpetrated the hanging and shooting.

While Las Vegas was still in ferment over the killing of Joe Carson, another lurid incident occurred. On January 26th, some railroad workers in charge of Joe Castillo got drunk and raised a disturbance in front of the dance hall of Close & Patterson. One of the proprietors hunted up Joe

Castillo, who had retired for the night, and asked him to come over to the dance hall and quiet his men. Castillo was about to do so when the new peace officer, Dave Mathers (better known as "Mysterious Dave") appeared on the scene and started making arrests.

Not knowing that Mathers was an officer, Castillo resented what he took to be arbitrary interference. Hot words were bandied between the two men for a few minutes; then Castillo pulled out a small pocket pistol of only .22 calibers, thinking that it might serve to intimidate Mathers. But Castillo reckoned without his host, for Mathers pulled his gun and fired, killing young Castillo instantly. The outcome was wholly without warrant. Young Castillo had not intended to shoot anyone, but under the code of the time the display of even so harmless a weapon as a .22-caliber gun was enough to warrant the other man's firing. This left no other course open to the jury that sat on the case when it came to trial, than to render the verdict that it was homicide in self-defense.

Las Vegas had by no means a monopoly of killings, justifiable and unjustifiable. The next one occurred at Santa Fé. I chanced to be over there on February 10th on some business for Otero, Sellar & Co., and found considerable excitement over a shooting scrape that had taken place that day. A man named Jack Armstrong, accompanied by a friend, entered the saloon kept by Noah Dunn directly opposite the jail on Water Street, and after taking two drinks handed Dunn a five-dollar bill. Dunn returned Armstrong four dollars and seventy-five cents, the correct change. But Armstrong demanded five cents more, perhaps under the impression that the drinks were ten cents each. Dunn refused, at the same time explaining that in his place drinks were fifteen cents or two for a quarter. This angered Armstrong, who drew his pistol, remarking: "I'll have my change, you son of a bitch," and fired, killing Dunn instantly. Armstrong managed to escape and was never captured.

But to come back to the killings in Las Vegas: About this

time occurred the execution of Manuel Barela at the hands of the Vigilantes. Manuel Barela was a brother of Don Mariano Barela of Las Cruces, one of the most prominent members of the community. He had come up to Las Vegas in charge of a large mule train belonging to his brother, Don Mariano. Being an inveterate gambler, Manuel, on reaching Las Vegas, had at once sought out in a *tendijon* a suitable monte game. His gambling was of course accompanied by heavy drinking, whether he was winning or losing, and with this excessive drinking went a tendency to become quarrelsome. And in the bargain Manuel always carried a gun on his person.

After playing at monte for several hours, and losing about one hundred dollars, he walked out of the building and proceeded in the direction of the plaza. When he reached the corner, he thought of his pistol, and perhaps with a desire to lift his spirits a little he pulled it out of its concealed holster and fired one shot into the air. Then catching sight of an inoffensive old man crossing the street in his direction, Manuel remarked to a bystander, "I'll bet fifty dollars I can shoot the third button off that man's vest." Taking deliberate aim he fired, the bullet striking the old man near the heart and killing him instantly. Manuel was promptly overpowered by the officers of the law and placed in jail to sober up and repent at his leisure, as well as to await trial.

The members of the rich and influential family to which Manuel belonged came to his support and secured for him the very best lawyers in the Territory. These attorneys used every device to save their client, and it looked as though the case would be hard-fought and long drawn out, with the wealth and prominence of Manuel's family finally turning the scales of justice in his favor. But it so happened that a few weeks later a man named Beckworth got into trouble by handling his pistol in much the same braggadocio manner, and that entirely altered the situation.

Beckworth's pistol went off while he was merely twirling it in his fingers, and killed a man who was standing just behind him. He claimed it was an accident, but the one accident did not seem to satisfy his ambition to show himself an expert in handling a gun, for he kept on twirling his pistol. Again it went off, this time killing a woman who happened to be standing in the doorway of her house. Two accidents of the same kind proved too much for the community, and Beckworth was arrested and placed in jail. That same night the Vigilantes paid their respects to him and strung him up on the old wind-mill in the center of the plaza, pinning on his breast a placard inscribed, "This is *no* accident."

As the Vigilantes were about to disband and return to their homes, someone among them suggested that they go back to the jail and get the other murderer, Manuel Barela, adding as argument that his case had been pending too long already. The proposal met with unanimous favor. The crowd marched back to the jail and securing Manuel Barela, took him to the wind-mill and hung him alongside of Beckworth. This was one of the rare cases where the Vigilantes acted entirely on impulse.

In the furore created by Beckworth's rash deeds, the Vigilantes possibly were overzealous in creating an impression that they meant business. As a matter of fact, most people believed that Barela would have been acquitted at the next term of court, and as this would have been due to the influence of his family connections or to the connivance of his lawyers, there were many in the community who viewed the action of the Vigilantes as meet and proper.

The next killing I have to record came more closely home to me than the others I have been recounting. On Thursday night, March 2nd, 1880, a group of the commission-house boys had gathered in the office of Otero, Sellar & Co., and spent the evening until after midnight in talking over old times. The occasion was a visit from our old friend and associate, Jimmy Morehead, who had been connected with the firm of C. R. Morehead & Co., of Leavenworth, Kans., at the same time as my father and Mr. Sellar. The St. Louis house finally went out of business, and Mr. Morehead travelled west in the interest of several large wholesale houses. Of course he always secured large orders from the commission houses, and his visits were invariably enjoyed by his numerous friends. When the group broke up, James Morehead, Jacob Gross, Thomas H. Parker and I started for our homes. Morehead was living at the St. Nicholas Hotel, while the other three of us lived in our bachelor quarters two blocks farther on.

As we walked along Morehead told us of the impudence of a waiter at the hotel who had that morning refused to bring him eggs because he was a few minutes late, and as we approached the hotel, he closed the story of this affair with the remark, "The same thing is liable to happen in the morning, for I am getting to bed late tonight and I don't intend to regulate my hours of sleep and my habits to suit the waiters of a hotel where I am paying a good price for the poor service I am getting." We then parted from him at the front door of the hotel and went on to our place.

The next morning about 9:30 a boy came running into the office of Otero, Sellar & Co., with the startling announcement that Morehead had just been shot by Jim Allen, a waiter in the hotel. The boy added that Morehead wanted my father to come at once to see him. My father happened to be in the Old Town and could not get away. So I felt that I should act in his stead and, dropping my pen, I ran as fast as I could to the St. Nicholas Hotel, closely followed by Charles O. Cole, the receiving and forwarding clerk.

We both reached the hotel at about the same time and found Morehead sitting in a chair in the main office, evidently in great pain as the result of his wound. I asked if a doctor had been called and the clerk replied "No." So, thinking that it was high time that one was summoned, I ran out of the front door, and seeing Doctor M. M. Milligan on the other side of the street in the act of getting into his buggy, called to him to come over quickly, which he did.

We then managed to get Morehead upstairs to his room and into his bed. Taking off his coat and vest, we discovered where the bullet had entered his stomach, just over the lower vest pocket on the left side, but we could not discover where it had come out. We went on undressing him and next removed his trousers. Then the doctor, in order to make a closer examination of the wound in Morehead's left side, lifted up his shirt and noticed on the right side a small blue spot on the skin. Guessing what was underneath, the doctor made an incision with a small lance, and then pressed on both sides of the blue spot with his thumb and forefinger, the bullet popping out on the bed.

We finished undressing Morehead and made him as comfortable as we could. He was suffering a great deal and the doctor told him to be as quiet as possible, and especially not to talk much. Then calling Cole and myself aside, he told us that it was only a question of a few hours, as Morehead could not possibly get well. In a short time others heard of what had happened and a number of people called to see how the wounded man was getting on, among them my father, Mr. Gross, Mr. Mennet, and virtually all the commission-house crowd, for Jimmy Morehead was one of the most popular salesmen on the road.

About ten o'clock that night, Morehead began to suffer greatly. Cole and I were alone with him at the time; in fact, we had not left him for a moment since we arrived in the morning. One of us asked him whether he wanted a drink of water, but he was only able to shake his head to indicate no, and just at that moment a gurgling noise began in his throat, which seemed to presage the end. An instant later he drew a deep breath and all was over.

Jim Allen, the waiter who had committed the crime, had been arrested and placed in jail shortly after the shooting. The town was in a state of excitement all day long over the affair, and groups of men could be found on every corner discussing what should be done. By early evening public opinion had decided upon a meeting at 11 o'clock in a vacant building on Railroad Avenue and the sequel was rather clearly forecast. But when the news of Morehead's death at about 10:30 was spread abroad, the excitement was intensified to such a pitch that the people were ready to take Allen without more ado and hang him on the old wind-mill in the plaza.

No doubt this would have occurred had not J. J. Webb and "Mysterious Dave" Mathers come up to the room where Morehead had just died and, beckoning me out into the hall, requested that I go to the lot where the mob was gathering and tell them not to go towards the jail, for it was guarded by a dozen picked shooters, who would shoot to kill should there be any attempt to attack. I felt that they were telling the truth, and I was entirely willing to do what might save a great deal of bloodshed. So I hurried over to the place where the mob was assembling and told the fifty or more gathered there exactly what Webb and Mathers had said. They readily saw the lack of foresight of proceeding with a lynching in the face of such odds, and with the general understanding that the matter would be dropped for the time being but would come up at another time when circumstances were more favorable, the meeting was adjourned.

At this point I must go back a little in the sequence of events. In view of the serious nature of Morehead's wound, I had sent over to Old Town for a justice of the peace to come to the hotel and take his dying deposition. I did not want to have "Hoodoo" Brown in this capacity, for I had surmised from the beginning that all the officers of the town were in sympathy with the gang of thugs and murderers, of which Jim Allen was a full-fledged member.

Jimmy Morehead shot by a waiter — for ordering eggs.

As soon as a justice of the peace arrived, I told Jimmy Morehead that the court wanted him to make a sworn statement of everything connected with the shooting, and I suggested that he take plenty of time in doing so. He was perfectly willing to give his account, and after he had been duly sworn and informed by the justice of the peace that he was making his dying declaration, he proceeded to give his version of the incident:

"Yesterday morning this waiter, James Allen, refused to bring me eggs for my breakfast after I had ordered them and he became very impudent towards me, a guest in the hotel and paying for all the service coming to me as a transient boarder. It is true that on that morning I was about five minutes late in entering the dining-room, but surely that was not sufficient cause to have a waiter abuse or insult a guest of the house. I drank my coffee and ate what was given me and left the room.

"This morning I entered the dining-room exactly at 9 o'clock and took my seat at the table, just as they were about to close the door. Allen, the waiter, came up to me showing that he was quite plainly out of temper. I gave him my order, including some poached eggs on toast. He said, 'You are too late to get eggs; you will have to take what you can get.' I did not like the manner in which he addressed me, and replied, 'Look here, young man, I want no more of your impudence and abuse. I am a guest in this hotel, paying for what I get, and as such must insist on courteous treatment.'

"Allen then came up close to where I was sitting and said, 'To hell with your courteous treatment. I'm just as good as you are in any way you want to take it.' I got up from the table very mad, saying, 'You damn' scrub, I want no more of your impudence.' He then advanced towards me, saying, 'You are a damn' sight more of a scrub than I am.' I picked up a chair, intending to strike him, saying, 'You damn' son of a bitch, don't you open your mouth to me again.'

"He then started towards the kitchen, and I walked out

of the dining-room, intending to settle my bill and leave the hotel. On entering the office, I stopped in front of the water cooler at the end of the counter to take a drink, and as I was lifting the glass to my mouth, Allen came rushing into the office, from the same door I had just closed on leaving the dining-room. He had a cocked pistol in his hand and said, 'You infernal son of a bitch, get down on your knees and beg my pardon, or I'll kill you.'

"I made a jump for him and he fired. After shooting me, he turned and went back into the dining-room and closed the door. Only one shot was fired. I was suffering great pain and sat down in the chair, where my friends found me."

The day after the shooting Allen had a preliminary hearing before the District Court, which was in session, and a change of venue was granted to Santa Fé County. But before the trial took place, Allen and three other prisoners made their escape from jail. They were closely followed by a posse, which located them sitting around a campfire eating supper near Aguilar Hill, close to the town of Chaperito in San Miguel County. The posse fired upon them without warning, and they were all killed instantly.

The bodies of all four were stacked up in a farm wagon with no more regard than if they had been sheep carcasses, and brought back to Las Vegas. There they were all laid in a row on the same platform of the old wind-mill where but a few weeks previously Tom Henry, John Dorsey and James West had been hanged and shot by the Vigilantes. All day hundreds of citizens visited the old wind-mill to see the bodies of those who had played their last card. Late in the afternoon they were taken to the paupers' lot and buried in one grave.

The true facts regarding the escape of Allen and the other three men were never given out at the time for many reasons, but after the lapse of fifty odd years, they may be disclosed. The Vigilantes were thoroughly aware of the deplorable situation in the government of the town. They knew that no worse a crowd of murderers than Dutchy, "Mysterious Dave" Mathers, J. J. Webb, Billie Wilson, "Sport" Boyle, had ever gained control of a town. They realized that it was only a question of time until this mob, with the backing of "Hoodoo" Brown, the justice of the peace, would effect the release of Allen and the others.

So the Vigilantes sought to checkmate this procedure by actually bringing about the escape of the four men. They bribed one of the jailers to go to the four prisoners and offer to help them escape provided they would pay him a certain amount of money, which they were to secure from their friends and confederates in East Las Vegas. This they were able to do, and thus their escape was brought about. But the Vigilantes had no intention of permitting them to escape in reality. They had a posse ready to follow them, with the result already noted.

This explains why the posse when it surrounded the four fugitives sitting about their campfire did not go through the usual formality of demanding their surrender. The posse was instructed fully as to its part in the grim business of acting as the understudy for the Vigilantes, and they proceeded accordingly.

Chapter XVIII

ALL during the spring of 1880 killings continued to be the order of the day. About this time a prosperous livestock man, Michael Kelliher, arrived in Las Vegas from the north, well supplied with cash for the purchase of cattle for his range in Wyoming. He frequented the many saloons then in Las Vegas, and took an occasional drink, usually with stockmen with whom he had become acquainted. He made no effort to conceal the fact that he had a large sum of cash on him, and the news soon reached Hoodoo Brown through his faithful ally, Dutchy.

The information was detailed, even to the fact that the money was carried in a large black leather pocketbook kept in Kelliher's inside coat pocket. A scheme was at once formulated in the brain of the genial Hoodoo Brown, and there can be no doubt that he engineered and put through every detail of the plan that led to the killing of Kelliher in the saloon of Locke & Brooks on Central Avenue, where the American Railway Express Company's building now stands. Sport Boyle, a brakeman on the Atchison, Topeka & Santa Fé Railroad, was the confederate selected to take Kelliher into the saloon for a drink. Boyle's instructions were to start something after he and Kelliher had had a drink but the exact details were left to his mother-wit. What he actually did was to order the drinks himself and then refuse to pay for them, saying that Kelliher had ordered them, averring further that he came as the latter's guest. Kelliher was perfectly willing to pay, but naturally resented some of the uncalled-for remarks with which Boyle had accompanied his refusal.

The two men began to quarrel in loud voices, and this brought to the scene two other confederates, Dutchy and Webb, who had been posted outside the saloon. They ran toward the bar at which Kelliher and Boyle were standing, still quarreling, and without a word of warning, shot Kelliher through the back of his head. He fell to the floor dead, just in front of the bar.

A farther step in the plan that was carried out was the immediate locking of the front door of the saloon while Sport Boyle went for the justice of the peace, Hoodoo Brown, who promptly repaired to the saloon and took charge of the body of the murdered man. The first thing Brown did was to remove the leather pocketbook with the cash, together with the watch and other jewelry, including two beautiful diamond studs, each of about two and a half carats.

Then a hand-picked coroner's jury was summoned, consisting chiefly of his henchmen and office bums, which promptly exonerated Dutchy, Webb and Boyle, declaring that the killing was justifiable in the discharge of their duty as peace officers. In truth, no more deliberate or premeditated murder was ever committed anywhere.

That same night, Hoodoo Brown and Dutchy disappeared from the town, taking with them all the belongings of the murdered Kelliher. They also took along with them the widow of Joe Carson, mentioned in another chapter as the woman who fired the first shot the night of the lynching of Henry, Dorsey and West to avenge the killing of her husband.

The District Court was in session at the time, and indictments were promptly brought against Hoodoo Brown, Dutchy, Boyle and Webb. Boyle made a successful getaway with the bunch, and Webb was the only one that was arrested. He was placed in the county jail on March 5th, 1880. Michael Kelliher's brother came to Las Vegas from his home in Wyoming and offered a large reward for the capture of Hoodoo Brown and Dutchy, but neither of them were ever found. The general opinion was that Dutchy was the one who fired the shot that killed Kelliher, and for that reason he was especially wanted.

The search for the two was engaging the attention of the town when April 1st came around, and Russ Kistler, editor of the *Daily Optic*, could not resist the opportunity to play an April fool on the community. So on April 1st, the *Daily Optic* carried a lengthy account, under large headlines, of the capture of Hoodoo Brown and his companion, Dutchy, accompanied by the information that they were to arrive in custody on the evening train.

The town fell for the hoax completely, even the Vigilantes being at the station in full strength to meet the train. When they discovered that they had been tricked, some became much incensed at the editor, but finally all reached the point where they thought it a good joke.

Webb's trial was conducted on March 10th, 1880, and the same day the jury brought in a verdict of "Guilty of murder in the first degree." Three days later Webb was sentenced to be hanged, the date being fixed for Friday, April 9th. Those who knew the situation freely forecast that Webb would not be hanged. It was naturally supposed that his friends in the Hoodoo Brown crowd would in some manner attempt to secure his release. This turned out to be the case. I, curiously enough, witnessed the early stages of the attempt, although at the time I was not aware of the significance of what I beheld.

In those days a line of hacks ran between the towns of Las Vegas and East Las Vegas, at a charge of twenty-five cents a passenger. On the second of April, I had to go over to Old Town on a matter of business and availed myself of the hack line. Mrs. Adolph Mennet was going over also, and we started from New Town together. Before we had gone very far, two other passengers hailed the hack and got in. These were Dave Rudabaugh, a notorious "bad man," who was handy with a gun, and Johnny Allen, house painter and well-known associate of Hoodoo Brown. I knew both Rudabaugh and Allen quite well, and, of course, spoke to them when they got into the hack, which was a three-seated open affair. They occupied the center seat, while Mrs. Mennet and I sat on the rear seat.

When the hack reached the plaza in the Old Town, Mrs. Mennet and I got out at the First National Bank corner, and the hack-driver proceeded with the other two passengers, evidently taking them to their destination. As I found out afterward, they had the hack-driver take them to the county-jail entrance, where they got out, ordering the driver to wait for them.

Both Allen and Rudabaugh entered the jail, and encountered the jailor, Antonio Lino, a quiet man, who asked them what they wanted. Rudabaugh drew his pistol, and pointing it at Lino, demanded the jail keys. Instead of complying with the order, Lino attempted to jump back into the yard, perhaps with the idea of gaining time to defend himself. Rudabaugh, however, fired — killing the jailor instantly. Then he and Allen secured the keys from the dead jailor's pocket, and tossed them to Webb, the prisoner they sought to help. But he for some reason made no effort to get away and instead went to the assistance of the jailor, who he found was dead.

Whatever Rudabaugh and Allen may have thought of Webb's refusal to leave the jail with them, they did not deem it expedient to linger and debate the question. So they hurried out to the hack which was waiting on the outside of the jail, but on this trip they considered it necessary to assume complete control of the vehicle. So they pointed a pistol at the head of the driver and ordered him to get out. Then Allen took the reins, while Rudabaugh sat beside him with a pistol in his hand. They drove down the side street and entered the plaza. Then they drove down Bridge Street at break-neck speed and over to New Town, where they stopped at the hardware store of O. L. Houghton and procured rifles and ammunition, being in too much of a hurry to pay for them.

Then they drove the horses on a dead run across the railroad track and out on the road leading east toward Olguin Hill. It must be remembered that in those days there were no telephones, so it was possible for Rudabaugh and Allen to drive over to New Town and provide themselves with guns and ammunition and be well on their way toward escape before the news of the killing reached New Town.

A large posse was quickly formed and followed the desperadoes for many miles. Indeed, more than a hundred men, well-mounted and armed with rifles and pistols, joined in the chase. Whenever their pursuers got within shooting distance, the two men in the hack would stop, and, getting out of the vehicle, would shoot at the posse with their long-range guns. The posse, knowing the desperate character of the two men it was pursuing, was not inclined to follow or be foolhardy about taking chances with them. So the posse never overtook Rudabaugh and Allen.

At the foot of Olguin Hill, the two desperadoes traded their tired team for a fresh one, and continued on to a ranch, where they exchanged their entire outfit for two good saddle horses, fully equipped. Here they also refreshed themselves with plenty to eat and drink, besides filling their saddle bags with provisions. Then they departed in the direction of Fort Sumner, which at that time was the headquarters for Billy the Kid and his gang. When they reached Fort Sumner, Rudabaugh threw in with Billy the Kid and during the next few months was an active member of his gang. Johnny Allen continued on to Texas and was never heard of again.

Webb, as it will be remembered, had refused to escape from the jail when the opportunity was offered by Rudabaugh and Allen, although he was under sentence of death. This act on his part counted much in his favor in the eyes of the community, and his friends made use of it in an effort to persuade the Governor of the Territory to extend clemency. They also showed that the evidence seemed to indicate that Dutchy had done the actual killing and that Webb had been somewhat unwittingly the tool of Hoodoo Brown. After going into the case thoroughly, the Governor commuted Webb's sentence to a short term in the penitentiary. But his friends continued active in Webb's behalf, and their efforts, supplemented by those of that able attorney, Judge Sydney M. Barnes, finally secured his pardon. He left almost at once for his old home in Indiana and was never heard of again around Las Vegas.

On April 8th, 1880, another horrible murder was added to the catalog of violent deaths in Las Vegas. Nelson W. Starbird, one of the best-known hack drivers plying between the Old and the New Towns, was assassinated in cold blood by someone who fired into the hack from ambush. It was generally thought that the intended victim was George Poindexter, who was being driven home to his residence in the Old Town shortly after midnight by Starbird. The murderer's bullet lodged in Starbird's back. Poindexter drove the hack to Starbird's home, but the former died before the doctor could get to him.

This killing was so appalling that the Vigilantes began to bestir themselves. On the night of the 8th of April a mass meeting of the law-abiding citizens of the town was held, with an attendance of virtually one hundred per cent. Speeches were made by such men as my father, James A. Lockhart, Jacob Gross, Robert K. L. N. Cullen and Rush J. Holmes. It was decided to give a warning to the lawless element. Hand bills were printed in large type, scattered over town and posted on the walls of every building.

Here is how the warning read:

Las Vegas, N. Mex., April 8th, 1880.

A TIMELY WARNING

To Murderers, Confidence Men, Thieves:

The Citizens of Las Vegas have tired of robbery, murder, and other crimes that have made this town a byword in every civilized community.

They have resolved to put a stop to crime even if in attaining that end they have to forget the law, and resort to a speedier justice than it will afford. All such characters are, therefore, notified that they must either leave this town or conform themselves to the requirement of law, or they will be summarily dealt with. The flow of blood MUST and SHALL be stopped in this community, and the good citizens of both the old and new towns have determined to stop it, if they have to HANG by the strong arm of FORCE every violater of the law in this country.

VIGILANTES.

This notice had the desired effect. Large numbers of the undesirable element left town within twenty-four hours after the placards appeared. It was well for them that they did, because the Vigilantes in their renewed zeal had gone so far as to appoint a rifle squad, who were charged to shoot on sight from concealed places any of those well-known thugs and desperate characters who might be found lingering in the town beyond the twenty-four-hour limit. The better element had taken control of the situation. The peace officers had become negligible quantities in the effort to make the community law-abiding, and the only course open was to let the better element take the reins into their own hands and handle the situation in a drastic way.

The efforts of the Vigilantes did not result in the complete elimination of killings. On May 27th, 1880, another cold-blooded murder occurred in the saloon of Locke & Lockwood. J. M. Russell, a fireman on the Atchison, Topeka & Santa Fé Railroad, had taken a drink and was standing at the bar talking to a girl who had come into the saloon through a rear door. He was about to leave, when J. J. Tuttle, a brakeman on the same railroad, entered, and seeing Russell talking to the girl, walked up and without a word, pulled a pistol and shot Russell dead on the spot. Tuttle then ran from the saloon and made his escape. The next day the Vigilantes met and passed the following resolution:

We are in favor of hiring forty policemen for East Las Vegas, if that force can do away with the nuisance of pistol-firing night and day.

My Life on the Frontier 207

While this internal lawlessness was going on in Las Vegas, the town was under the shadow of that external lawlessness — the Indians and their forays — which infected the West so long, and which lingered longer in New Mexico than any other part of the land. The Government was wrestling with the problem, but was accomplishing little. The detachments of soldiers scattered throughout the state at a dozen forts and posts were under the command of General Edward Hatch, whose headquarters were in Santa Fé. But for some reason his policy was ineffective in stopping plundering and murdering by the Indians.

My father, thoroughly cognizant of the situation, lost patience with General Hatch, and I find the *Daily Optic* of April 21st, 1880, stating his position in the following item:

> In an interview with Hon. Miguel A. Otero, ex-delegate to Congress, reported in the *Optic*, that gentleman says: "Hatch mismanages everything. If I could be Governor of New Mexico for twenty-four hours, the Indians would have to go. I would call out the militia and volunteer troops, and we would soon wipe out the murderous vagrants. Hatch does not report the many murders committed by the Indians; and the high officials at Washington are ignorant of the real state of affairs."

During May of the year 1880, the Indians were reported to have killed many settlers, burning their homes and driving off much stock. This led many of the larger towns in the Territory to organize military companies. On May 24th, 1880, the young men of Las Vegas held a meeting in the dining-room of the St. Nicholas Hotel and organized the San Miguel Rifles. I was the chairman of the meeting and M. W. Browne, the secretary. So enthusiastic was the spirit of the meeting that sixty signatures to the muster-roll were secured. Jack C. Churchill was unanimously elected captain, and ways and means of getting needed equipment and securing facilities for drilling were discussed. It was understood that each member of the company would pay for his own uniform, rifle and other personal equipment. A committee was appointed to solicit subscriptions to a fund with which to rent a hall to be used as an armory.

The company throve, fired with the ambition to be regarded as the best-drilled company in the Territory. While Churchill was with it, he directed the drilling and kept up the interest. But when his removal to Washington, D. C., forced him to resign the captaincy, we decided to secure the services of the best drill-master in the United States, if he could be had. At that time the Terre Haute Rifles of Terre Haute, Ind., were attracting attention as the best-drilled military company in the country, and so we aimed at none other than its captain, Edward Friend. After some correspondence, he finally accepted our offer of $250 a month in addition to a position as city editor on the *Daily Optic*, which carried additional salary with it.

Captain Friend proved to be a fine fellow and was very popular with everyone who knew him. He was efficient as drill-master and it was not long before he had the champion military company in New Mexico. In the course of time the Indian troubles quieted down. Celebrations were held throughout New Mexico over the joyful news that Chief Victorio of the Southern Apaches, together with his band, had engaged in battle the Mexican troops at Los Castillos, in the State of Chihuahua, and that seventy-five warriors, including Chief Victorio, had been killed on the battlefield. Sixty-eight women and children were reported taken as prisoners of war. From the report received it was evident that every warrior was killed, thus wiping out one of the worst marauding bands the West has ever had to deal with. This was the best possible news New Mexico could have received, as the killing of Victorio's band put an end to massacres of unprotected settlers in the remote sections of the Territory. It also had the effect of our losing interest and enthusiasm in military affairs. The members of the San Miguel Rifles became indifferent about drilling, and dilatory in paying the monthly assessments. So the company expired.

Former President Grant, Mrs. Grant and Mrs. Fred Grant visited New Mexico for the week of July 7th to 15th, 1880. They were publicly received at both Santa Fé and Las Vegas. While in Las Vegas the San Miguel Rifles acted as an escort. The General walked down the line shaking hands with every member of the company. In the evening a grand ball was given in honor of the visitors at the Hot Springs Hotel, and everyone present enjoyed the evening. At midnight a banquet was served and champagne flowed like water. The General in a few well-chosen words thanked the people, and congratulated the "trail-blazers," saying: "I have never been given a better time nor have I enjoyed myself any more at any place on my trip around the world, than I have right here in Las Vegas."

Three months afterward, on October 28th, 1880, Rutherford B. Hayes, President of the United States, Mrs. Hayes, Secretary of War Ramsey, General William T. Sherman and many other members of the presidential party, returning overland from the Pacific Coast through the Territory of New Mexico, visited Santa Fé and were received with a great public demonstration, William G. Ritch, Secretary of New Mexico, delivering the address of welcome. The party took a special train out of Santa Fé for the East, making a brief stop at Las Vegas. There the San Miguel Rifles were lined up on the railroad platform and President Hayes, Secretary Ramsey and General Sherman passed down the line shaking hands with each member of the company.

Chapter XIX

I SHALL close this recital of the turbulent year 1880 with an incident near its end that caused Las Vegas to feel that it was a participant in the lawlessness then rampant in the southern part of the Territory and that brought back to its notice Dave Rudabaugh.

Early on the morning of December 23, 1880, at the little rock house built many years before by Alejandro Perea, near Stinking Springs, N. Mex., Pat F. Garrett, Frank Stewart, Lon Chambers, Lee Hall, Louis Bozeman (alias "The Animal"), James H. East, Barney Mason, Tom Emory (known as "Poker Tom"), and Bob Williams (alias "Tenderfoot Bob") killed Charlie Bowdre and captured Billy the Kid, Dave Rudabaugh, Billy Wilson and Tom Pickett.

The Kid and his companions had taken refuge in the rock house when they felt closing around them the toils of Pat Garrett's determined effort to capture the party. Garrett's posse had besieged the rock house all during the night, and when Charlie Bowdre appeared at the door early the next morning, Garrett had given unmistakable indication of the temper of the quest, by shooting Bowdre, who died in a few minutes. So the Kid and the remaining three of his company decided to propose terms of surrender, which Garrett agreed upon, promising them protection until they could be tried.

In seeking a jail strong enough to hold the quartet, Garrett naturally turned toward Santa Fé, and as the nearest railroad station was East Las Vegas, he carried his prisoners there. The news that these noted desperadoes were coming through Las Vegas, and perhaps would be kept overnight in the Las Vegas jail, brought large numbers of curious people to the plaza.

Albert E. Hyde, who was in Las Vegas at the time, wrote

a magazine article some years ago, giving a graphic eyewitness account of the entry of Garrett's party. As this tallies with what I remember, I shall reproduce it:

> It was a beautiful afternoon, and the elevation of the Grand View Hotel afforded a wide range of vision across the plains, stretching to the blue line of distant hills.
>
> As the hours passed, the crowds began to grow more impatient and distrustful. All had become skeptical, when from our point of vantage we discerned a cloud of dust in the southwest. When the cause of it advanced close enough for the people to descry a wagon outfit accompanied by mounted men, a mighty shout went up. The good news was indeed true. Billy the Kid was a prisoner and Pat Garrett was a hero.
>
> As the wagon, pulled by four mules, approached, we saw four men sitting in the bed, two on a side, facing each other. The Kid, whom Dr. Sutfin had known in his cowboy days and instantly recognized, was on the hotel side of the wagon, chained to a fierce-looking, dark-bearded man who kept his slouch hat pulled well down over his eyes, and looked neither to the right nor to the left. This man was the daring and dangerous Dave Rudabaugh, who, among many other crimes, had killed the Mexican jailor at Las Vegas a short time before. He feared recognition, as well he might, for the Mexican population thirsted for his blood. The other two prisoners were Pickett and Wilson, prominent members of the Kid's gang.
>
> Billy the Kid was in a joyous mood. He was a short, slender, beardless young man. The marked peculiarity of his face was a pointed chin and a short upper lip which exposed the large front teeth and gave a chronic grin to his expression. He wore his hat pushed far back, and jocularly greeted the crowd. Recognizing Dr. Sutfin he called: "Hello, Doc! Thought I'd jes' drop in an' see how you fellers in Vegas air behavin' yerselves."
>
> Heavily armed deputies rode on each side of the wagon, with two bringing up the rear. Garrett rode in front. The large crowd evidently surprised and annoyed him. Fearing for the safety of Rudabaugh, he turned and gave a low order to the mule-driver, who instantly whipped up his team, and a run was made across the plaza to the jail.

Garrett heard enough during the next few hours to convince him that an attempt would be made to lynch Rudabaugh. He promptly increased his force to thirty men, who guarded the jail that night. In the meantime he planned to take the prisoners next day to Santa Fé for safe-keeping. Not a suspicion of this move was allowed to get out.

Garrett placed his prisoners in the jail for the night. The next morning he began preparations to move them to Santa Fé by the railroad. But he experienced considerable trouble in getting the San Miguel officials to allow him to take Rudabaugh along, for local sentiment was strong for keeping the latter in Las Vegas now that he was back on the scene of his crime. Garrett protested that he held his prisoners under a United States warrant and that this fact gave him a precedence over the local officials. But the Las Vegas officers were not inclined to yield.

Finally, despite the mutterings of the Las Vegas people, Garrett placed the four prisoners in a closed carriage and hurried them to the railroad depot in the New Town, where he found a mob assembled, the majority of whom were armed with rifles and pistols. Sympathetic with the mob were the sheriff, Desiderio Romero, and his deputies, headed by his brother, Pablo Romero, generally called "Colorow" on account of his red hair and heavy, bushy, red mustache and chin whiskers. The demand that Dave Rudabaugh be turned over to the Las Vegas officers was renewed, and again Garrett refused.

He had managed by this time to get his prisoners aboard the train and had them in one car under a heavy guard consisting of Cosgrove, Stewart and Mason. The mob surrounded the depot and train, and showed signs of forcing its way into the car where the prisoners were held. But Garrett stood on the platform, calmly, and said: "I promised these men I would deliver them to the sheriff of Santa Fé County or to the United States officer at Santa Fé, and I intend to

Doc Holliday shoots it out with Charlie White in Las Vegas, New Mexico.

do exactly as I promised. Now, if you people insist on trying to take them away from me, I can see only one thing for me to do and that is to arm every one of them and turn them loose to defend themselves as best they may. And what is more, all my officers and myself will assist in protecting them."

As Garrett finished talking, my father got up on the car-platform and stood beside him. He first shook Garrett's hand, and then turning to the sheriff and his deputies, as well as to the mob, said: "Gentlemen, these prisoners are in the custody of Mr. Garrett, and he has given his word that he will turn them over to the proper authorities at Santa Fé. This I know he will do. Now, it is a very serious thing for you men to hold up the United States mail as you are doing, and as the train is ready to start, I appeal to you, as your friend, to retire at once; otherwise the consequences may be very severe. I will give you my personal guaranty that Mr. Garrett will do exactly as he has said. The judge of this judicial district resides in Santa Fé, and on their arrival there, he will immediately take full charge."

This speech had the desired effect. The officers and the mob withdrew, and the train, which had been held up for about an hour, pulled out on its way to Santa Fé. While the mob was holding the train and seemed determined to take Rudabaugh away from the officers, Pat Garrett stepped back into the car. To the prisoners Garrett said: "Do not be uneasy. We are going to fight if they try to enter this car, and if the fight comes off I will arm you and allow you to take a hand." Rudabaugh was excited and considerably worried, but not so Billy the Kid. At Garrett's promise, the Kid's face beamed and his eyes fairly glistened, and he replied: "All right, Pat; all I want is a six-shooter. There is no danger though; those fellows won't fight."

I really believe, however, that the Kid was disappointed that the mob did not attack the car, for it would have unquestionably resulted in an opportunity for him to escape. Undoubtedly he had many friends among the crowd, for it was well known that he was on good terms with the native element of the country and had protected and helped them in every possible way. In return the native citizens were ready to do all in their power to assist him. If there had been an attack, the chances are that Garrett and his companions would have been killed in their effort to keep their prisoners. Rudabaugh would have fallen into the hands of the mob, and possibly lynching would have followed. But the quick and elusive Kid would probably have lost himself in the crowd and disappeared from the scene. My brother and I were so much interested in the whole thing that we secured permission from my father to go along on the train to Santa Fé, and we enjoyed ourselves immensely in the company of Garrett and his guards and their prisoners. On the way over, we talked much with Billy the Kid and Rudabaugh. The latter we knew quite well, as he had been on the police force in East Las Vegas for a time together with Mysterious Dave Mathers. The Kid we had never seen before, though we were of course familiar with his part in the Lincoln County War and in the reign of terror he had afterward created.

During our stay in Santa Fé, we were allowed to visit the Kid many times at the jail, taking him cigarette papers and tobacco, as well as chewing gum, candy, pies and nuts, for he was very fond of sweets and asked us to bring him such things. My impression of the Kid was that he was just about the same, so far as general appearance went, as most boys of his age. Sitting very close to him in the railroad coach, I observed quite plainly his apparent interest in everything taking place inside and outside of the car in which we were riding. He seemed to be intent on some weighty matter involving himself, and possibly was at the time evolving plans as to what to do in the event of an attack by the mob.

To be frank, I found myself liking the Kid, and long

before we had reached Santa Fé, nothing would have pleased me better than to have witnessed his escape. He had his share of good qualities: he was pleasant to meet; he had the reputation of always being kind and considerate to the old, the young, and the poor; he was loyal to his friends and, above all, loved his mother devotedly. He was simply unfortunate in starting life, and became the victim of circumstances. I had been told that Billy had an ungovernable temper; if so, I never saw it in evidence, for he was always in a pleasant humor when I happened to meet him. Mrs. Jaramillo at Fort Sumner said of him: "Billy was a good boy, but he was hounded by bad men who wanted to kill him, because they feared him, and of course he had to defend himself." Don Martin Chaves of Santa Fé said: "Billy was a man with a noble heart, and a perfect gentleman. He never killed a native citizen of New Mexico in all his career, and the men he killed, he simply had to in defense of his own life. He never had to borrow courage from any man as he had plenty of it himself. He was a brave man and did not know what fear meant. They had to sneak up on him at dead of night and then murder him."

Mrs. Jaramillo I have known for many years. She is a lovely woman, kind and gentle. Don Martin Chaves is a quiet, unassuming and kindly gentleman. He is well up in the seventies and is in perfectly good health today. Most of the older citizens of Santa Fé are well acquainted with him, and he holds the respect and esteem of everyone knowing him in his community. So the testimony of these two regarding the real character of the Kid carries considerable weight. My own personal impression corroborates that of these other persons. In looking back to my first meeting with Billy the Kid, I have no hesitancy in saying my impressions of him were most favorable ones, and I believe I can honestly say he was "a man more sinned against than sinning."

Dave Rudabaugh remained in jail at Santa Fé for a time

and was then taken back to Las Vegas and tried for the killing of Antonio Lino, the jailor. The outcome was conviction and a sentence to be hung, but Rudabaugh escaped from jail and went to Old Mexico, where he got into serious difficulty by killing a Mexican officer. The man whom he killed was very popular, and his friends went after Rudabaugh in great numbers and with more success than did the friends of Lino. They finally surrounded him, and in the fight that ensued, Rudabaugh was killed. His head was cut off and carried on a long pole around the Mexican plaza where Rudabaugh's victim had lived. After this display, the head and the body were given to the vultures to devour, and the well-picked bones left to bleach on the hillside. Grim as was this ending, I am inclined to think it was deserved, for Rudabaugh was one of the most desperate men of those wild days.

Of this same period, another episode occurs to me, which I believe will be of interest. During the early days following the entrance of the railroad, there was a saloon located on the southeast corner of the plaza just where the old First National Bank building now stands in the Old Town of Las Vegas. The bartender in this saloon was a man named Charlie White, thought to have been a member of the gang hailing from Dodge City. Several rooms in the rear of the saloon were used for different kinds of gambling, and were run by a tough lot of confidence-men and crooks. The barroom itself was usually crowded with bums and cappers working in the interest of the gamblers.

During the year 1880, Doc Holliday arrived in Las Vegas from Dodge City. He was quite a noted character in those days. He had been a dentist in some small farming town in central Illinois, and had become involved in a love affair which terminated by his being jilted by the young lady for another gay Lothario, who had been introduced to the family by Doc himself. This became the turning point in his life, and he decided to "Go West" and take his chances with killers and bad men. To fulfill such an ambition, he wisely selected Dodge City as the best locality to acquire a thorough education in the manly art of self-defense. After he had made what he thought was a sufficient advancement to enable him to rate himself as expert on the draw, quick on the trigger, a perfect marksman with a gun or pistol, as well as an experienced horseman, he qualified at once for an appointment under the celebrated Earp Brothers, who had undertaken the job and did finally succeed in "cleaning up" the town of Tombstone, Ariz.

Holliday had had some serious difficulty with Charlie White back in Dodge City, which was the immediate cause of White's departure from that place, but Doc had traced him to Las Vegas and had promised himself that if he ever passed through that town while White was there, he would certainly pay him a visit. Being a man of his word he stopped off in Las Vegas while en route to Tombstone to join the Earp Brothers, simply to square matters with his enemy. Holliday had no sooner gotten off the train than he started out to discover White's whereabouts. After locating him, he went back to the New Town for his supper. This done, he took the shortest trail for the saloon on the plaza. Doc entered the saloon with a cocked revolver in his hand and began hostilities at once, without previously making his presence known. White was in the act of serving some thirsty customers, but recognizing his old enemy from Dodge City, he ducked behind the bar just in time, while the customers ducked to the floor. White quickly emerged with a six-shooter, and the duel began in dead earnest, many shots being exchanged at short distance without effect.

The meeting was so sudden that both participants were evidently somewhat off their accustomed good marksmanship, but finally White dropped to the floor. At first it was thought that the shot had killed him, and Holliday feeling that he had fulfilled his mission to Las Vegas, departed for the New Town, to mingle with his old friends of Dodge City. A doctor was called at once for White, and it was found that while the bullet had only grazed the skin, it had been so near the spine as to stun him temporarily. He was up and around in a couple of hours as good as ever.

Doc Holliday remained a few days in Las Vegas before taking his departure for Arizona, and I met him quite frequently and found him to be a very likable fellow. After leaving Arizona he went to Colorado, where he died a natural death. White had evidently tired of frontier life for he left for his home in Boston on the very first train going East. No arrests were made. It was simply allowed to pass, as no one was interested in either Holliday or White, and the peace officers in Las Vegas were much too busy looking after their own games.

Chapter XX

AT the close of the Civil War my father, who was then residing in Leavenworth, Kans., became by accident a pioneer in the mining development in New Mexico. He happened to be interested just then in a large Government contract to deliver freight to some of the outlying military posts in the Southwest. As the contract was a time contract he went himself with the large outfit to prevent unnecessary delay en route. But when they reached the Jicarilla Mountains they found the roads impassable, owing to an unprecedented snowfall. The snow became so deep that it was impossible to move the outfit, so they went into camp and made preparation for a lengthy stay. My father, knowing of the reputed richness of the placers, decided to employ his men in washing dirt for gold in the many gulches. He built many earthen tanks and melted the snow by building fires and heating large boulders and rolling them into the tanks filled with snow, and in this crude manner he secured sufficient water to wash the dirt. They were unable to move the outfit for nearly three months, and during that time my father took out $16,000 in gold dust.

Some years prior, Don Bonifacio Chaves, my cousin, who had a store in the Jicarilla Mountains, was surprised by a band of Indians making a raid on the small settlement close to his store. He escaped on horseback, taking with him two large jars filled with gold dust. As the weight was too heavy for him to carry, he buried the treasure, intending to return later when the Indians had been chased back to their reservation. When he returned he was unable to locate the spot where the jars were buried.

This mining experience of my father, as mentioned above, was but a "flash in the pan." The great interest came later.

About the time I went to live at Las Vegas, the Territory of New Mexico began to pass through the period of mining excitement.

Among the clerks in the employ of Otero, Sellar & Co., was Professor Charles Longuemare, a jaunty little Frenchman who hailed from a celebrated school of mines located near Paris, France. The professor was an authority on mining; at least, we all believed him to be. He was a very small man, not much over five feet in height, and weighing about one hundred pounds. He had a very high forehead with a scanty growth of hair, and wore a Van Dyke beard.

It was the professor's intense enthusiasm, his absolute confidence in his ability to find gold, that made us all sure of acquiring great wealth. No sooner had we crossed the Raton Mountains and settled at the town of Otero, than he began to take trips into the foothills west of the town. When he returned he usually had his pockets bulging with rocks of all kinds, which he would take out one at a time, telling us in the scientific language just what each specimen contained. We all marvelled at his wonderful knowledge of minerals, and were prepared to believe all he told us, for this was our first lesson in mining.

The professor erected a small shack at a safe distance from the warehouse and established a laboratory, equipped with a furnace, mortars and pestles of all kinds and sizes, as well as crucibles, acids and blowpipes. He explained to us that we were in a mining region of unpredictable wealth, and his small grey eyes would sparkle as he told us of the fortunes in store for each of us.

Frequently a few of us would accompany him on his prospecting trips. In fact, practically the whole clerical force in both commission houses at Otero, went out with him on Sundays and holidays, and at the professor's suggestion we located many mines in the foothills, which, as he stated, "had great promise of eventually becoming large producers."

One thing I shall always remember with much pleasure; the professor started me on the road to make untold fortunes in mining, and, in a way, I have ever since been following his early instructions. It is a fascinating sport, and we were all very happy in our anticipation of what the next few feet might bring forth. Not one of our group ever struck "pay-dirt," not even the little professor, who later toyed with us at Las Vegas and then Socorro, where he finally settled. But the mines near Otero proved worthless and soon fizzled out. However, we were perfectly well satisfied with the explanations made by the professor, who proved to all of us beyond any question of doubt that the tertiary formations surrounding our claims were entirely at FAULT, and that the MICACEOUS conditions of the ore bodies prevented values from predominating; as quite naturally AZURITE when fused with FELDSPATH would, to be sure, LIQUIFY by heat in a CRYSTALLINE formation which frequently produces SILICATES of ALUMINA with a VITREOUS luster resembling MALACHITE, and thus proving DIFFUSIBILITY by TRANSMISSION through POROUS SUBSTANCES and therefore eliminating the possibility of MINERALS in place.

We agreed with him thoroughly, answering, "Quite so." His explanation seemed so very honest, we found ourselves expressing sorrow because we had not spent more money in proving all his points, but he promised us that when we reached Las Vegas he would make geological investigations in the foothills, and when completed in all details, would certainly make millionaires of all of us. We all carried a pocket dictionary to learn the meaning of some of his scientific terms, and in time fondly imagined that we were profound mineralogists. We could hardly wait until we reached Las Vegas, as we felt that the professor was our one hope of wealth. We were indeed happy in his company and followed him like a pack of hounds.

One day early in January, 1880, real excitement broke out in Las Vegas. Nels Newell, an employee of Otero, Sellar & Co., and Professor Longuemare, the recognized geologist of the firm, came into town from a prospecting expedition with some pretty good-looking ore samples, which they said had been found in the San Carlos District, not more than ten miles from Las Vegas. No sooner did that news get abroad than the whole town became convinced that a new Leadville would spring immediately into being.

A number of overeager souls, among whom were several commission-house boys, were for striking out that very afternoon for the new gold field and locating claims, but it was finally agreed that everyone would be a good sport and not start until the next morning. We all felt that this would give time for us to get in on the ground floor before the outsiders began to come.

There was, however, one group among the citizens of Las Vegas, which took the view that they had no part in this gentleman's agreement, and they cleverly stole a march on the rest of us. Very quietly they went to Don Oakley's livery stable and hired a six-seated rig in which they made their get-away from town. To clinch the secrecy of their move, they took strips of burlap and wrapped the tires of the wheels, thus eliminating noise as well as forestalling any trail to be followed over the short grass of the mesa.

It was after midnight when the rest of us learned of their departure. At three o'clock in the morning we had decided on a course of action. We started in the wake of the pirates, the trail leading around through Kearny's Gap and out onto the open and pathless mesa through piñons and cedars. This caused considerable additional loss of time, so that when we reached what we thought was the San Carlos District, all the land had been staked out by the other crowd. Doctor Severson, Doctor Milligan and Doctor Bailey nearly laughed their heads off when we pulled up, while Ike Hilty and Frank

Whitelaw, admitting that it was a dirty Irish trick on their part, sarcastically remarked that we ought to have been a little quicker on the trigger in such a spry country. They added consolingly that if we wanted the really choice claims on the mother lode, they would sell us an interest in the one lying farthest out.

We swallowed our chagrin and struck off to look at the proffered location. It did not look good to any of our party, so we followed the phantom of hope farther. On and on we went out through the Tecolote and up to San Geronimo, and by the time we reached that place we were hot and as starved as March wolves on a hunger strike. Soon it was our fortune to reach the home of Juan José Herrera, a good friend, who took us in and not only quieted our hunger with chili con carne and tortillas, but built up our battered hopes by telling us that the San Carlos District was "no good nohow" and promising to show us where to find "the real stuff" up in the Mineral Hill District, a few miles farther on.

Being now in much better spirits, we gladly followed our friend on his old white horse as he led the way toward the main range on the west. By ten o'clock we had come to a lovely little cove in the hills and, staking out our horses, we set out up the gulch. In half an hour we had uncovered a vein of porphyry carrying free gold, and we set up stakes for two claims apiece. Then we hurried back to town, made our filings, and sprang the mining sensation of the season by disclosing in the evening paper the news of the great find. To prove our story, we had Uncle John Robertson's assay certificates, and that night we and some of our friends met at the fire station and organized the Mineral Hill Mining District. It is perhaps unnecessary to state that none of the San Carlos crowd were admitted to the inner circle.

The stampede that followed was one of the epochal events in the mining history of New Mexico. The camp at the Mineral Hill District grew like a June mushroom in the night. But like many another mining location, its duration was a short one. Two or three of us were lucky to sell out in time to save something, but as it was, we could out-brag the San Carlos pirates, for their venture proved the truth of Herrera's contemptuous opinion and piddled out completely after the pirates had spent two years and a lot of money trying to develop it. When they became convinced of the uselessness of further endeavor, it was too late for them to sell out.

But there is another chapter in this rivalry with the San Carlos crowd. When my companions and I returned from the Mineral Hill District and it became known how the other group had tricked us in the San Carlos District, the original discoverers, Nels Newell and Professor Longuemare, joined forces with us and volunteered to take us to the exact spot where they had procured the fine ore specimens which started the boom.

Wariness and stealth were of course essential in our movements, because everyone was suspicious of even his brother and anxious to overreach him, too, if possible. So the six of us who were in the party agreed to start at the same hour, about daylight, but to take different routes, until we reached an agreed-upon meeting place about one mile below Romeroville. Of course all this concealment only added spice to the whole affair, and we enjoyed relating, when we had all come together, how we had given everyone the slip.

When Nels Newell and Professor Longuemare had conducted us to the spot of their remarkable find, we were overcome with joy to discover that it was several miles south of the area where our rivals had located their claims. We proceeded to stake claims by the dozens, naming them after every girl we knew. After we had located everything in sight and for miles around as well, we returned to Las Vegas, feeling that we had again scored on the pirate group.

The next day we went back accompanied by laborers,

whom we put to work building four log cabins suitable for the various activities that were soon to come into full blast. One was to be a storehouse for keeping of supplies, including blasting powder, fuses and caps. Another was to be a mess-room and kitchen for the miners. The other two were to be used as bunk-houses. A few days later Tom Parker and I bought four medium-sized mules, complete sets of harness, and a three-inch Schuttler wagon with spring seats.

All during the month of January, 1880, the mining excitement took precedence over everything else, and legitimate business in Las Vegas was relegated to second place in the universal desire to get rich quick. Meetings were being held every morning, noon and night, and new companies were being organized every day. Sometimes the capital stock of these ran into the millions, there being no "blue sky" laws in those times. But I would give it as my opinion that there was more real development and far less swindling under the conditions then prevailing than we have today in spite of our laws. Perhaps the secret of the popularity of "blue sky" laws is that they provide more offices for the politicians and more fees for the attorneys who seek a loophole for their clients, while the meek and greatly burdened taxpayer, as usual, pays the bills.

One of the important companies organized during the excitement was the Las Vegas Consolidated Mining & Milling Company, with a capital stock of $25,000,000. It was altogether a closed corporation; the membership was limited to twenty-five and not a share of the stock could be placed on the market, as it was entirely too valuable to dispose of to the public. Each member thought himself a millionaire from the very start, and regarded his stock as being worth its par value from the day it was issued.

The millionaire-to-be members of the company were the following:

Hon. Miguel A. Otero (I)..................President
Hon. Henry L. Waldo...............First Vice-President
Hon. Caldwell Yeaman...........Second Vice-President
Mr. Jacob Gross ....Treasurer
Mr. Frank A. Blake ....Secretary
Mr. Louis Sulzbacher......................Counsel
Mr. Page B. Otero.................General Manager

Mr. Oliver L. Houghton	Mr. John Perry Sellar
Mr. Adolph Mennet	Mr. Charles Longuemare
Mr. M. A. Otero, Jr.	Mr. HarryW. Kelly
Mr. G. F. Radcliffe	Mr. Thomas H. Parker
Mr. Thomas D. Bell	Mr. Herbert C. Blythe
Mr. Cliff W. Able	Mr. Millard W. Browne
Mr. Alfred Rossier	Mr. J. C. Churchill
Mr. Lee Chick	Mr. A. M. Blackwell
Mr. Frank B. Nichols	Mr. Charles O. Cole

Those who became infected with the mining fever had one common characteristic. Every spare bit of energy was thrown into the many valuable mining claims, and there was always a kind of ticklish feeling creeping up and down our spines for fear we might have allowed some hidden treasure to escape our vigilant and wary explorations. So more claims were constantly being located, some lapping over other claims to prevent the possibility of even a fraction of the ground being lost to our company.

The great San Carlos Mining District now presented a most active and prosperous appearance, and visions of a large mining camp similar to Leadville, Creede or Victor, Colo., made us feel sorry for all those who failed to get in on the ground floor. However, later events proved that they were the lucky ones, and that we were the ones needing sympathy. The real "fly in the ointment" was that Charles Longuemare, professor of geology and mineralogy, had us all going south.

Page B. Otero and Cliff W. Able had been duly elected general manager and superintendent, respectively, with unlimited powers for spending not only the money in the treasury, but more if needed.

These two young executives signalized their assuming the responsibilities of office by a great display of engineering ability. They effected a consolidation of the four log cabins erected on our mining properties into quarters for the general manager and the superintendent, and then proceeded to give a generous welcome to anyone who cared to visit the camp.

The very few real laborers were forced to herd together in one small wall tent, where they conducted their own frugal mess. One of the cabins that was built originally as a bunkhouse was elaborately fitted out as a club-room: a large refrigerator was installed and abundantly supplied with ice, not only for the purpose of preserving the butter, eggs, vegetables, fruits, salad oils, sauces and raw oysters (in season), but also to keep at a cool and palatable temperature the large supply of bottled beer, light wines, champagne, Hennessey brandy, whiskies and gin. Like all mining camps, the management kept a log, but in this instance the log was not for recording the different strata in the San Carlos District, but rather to show that no man or woman ever left the camp hungry or thirsty.

Every Sunday or holiday large parties visited the camp, where roast turkey, roast pig, roast beef, spiced ham and many other dishes were served. Both Page and Cliff prided themselves more on their cuisine than on auditing their accounts, the latter performance being undignified and intolerable when they were authorized to expend company money at their own sweet will. To tell the plain and unvarnished truth, the principal shafts sunk by these officers were into the pockets of those liberal contributors who were willing to hold the stock of the company and pay regular assessments.

This, however, was but one mining company among many. Mining was all the rage and new companies were organized in all directions from Las Vegas. The commision-house boys were involved or inveigled into nearly all of them, inasmuch as, in the eyes of the community, they were regarded as "good spenders" and "easy marks." Here are the names of a few of these companies:

Coyote Mining & Milling Co., of Mora County
Guadalupita Mining & Milling Co., of Mora County
Elizabethtown Gold Mining Co., of Colfax County
Moreno Valley Mining Co., of Colfax County
Red River Placer Mining Co., of Taos County
St. Louis & Las Vegas M. & S. Co., of Socorro County
White Oaks Consolidated Gold Mining Co., of Lincoln County
Jicarilla Placer Mining Co., of Lincoln County
Tres Hermanos Mining Co., of Santa Fé County
Las Animas Gold Mining Co., of Sierra County
The Buckeye Mining Co., of Socorro County
The Water Cañon Mining Co., of Socorro County
The Stone Wall Mining Co., of Socorro County
The Deep Down Mining Co., of Grant County
The B. O. B. Mining & Milling Co., of Grant County
The Mammoth Consolidated M. & M. Co., of Santa Fé County
The Carbonate Hill Consolidated M. & M. Co., of Leadville, Colo.
The Corona Queen Mining & Milling Co., of Lincoln County

The writer was to some extent in all of these different mining companies, and still possesses enough handsomely lithographed stock certificates to paper the walls of a good-sized room. Nevertheless, he prizes them highly, for though they are intrinsically of no value, they are priceless because of the memories and associations that cluster around them.

Though these mining ventures proved virtually a total loss, none of us regarded ourselves as stung. We felt that we had made our contribution to the development of our section of the country and argued with ourselves that if we had not invested this money in mining we would have speculated in something else. The spirit of "take a chance" was strong in the land, and along with it went the belief that he was a poor sport, indeed, who would cry over spilled milk.

After a few years of disappointment we traced back over the numerous claims located by our "Little Professor," the talented geologist and mineralogist from France, and were happy in the final summing up that it was no worse. During these years we met another professor, but this one hailed from the British Isles. He was Professor John Robertson, F.R.A., a scientific scholar from England. He opened the only assay office in Las Vegas, and fairly coined money. He was busy all day and most of the night, as we miners were extremely anxious to know results. Suspicion hovered around the assay office of the professor, and one day, to test his ability and knowledge of minerals and at the same time to satisfy ourselves, we pounded up an old jug handle and gave it to him to assay for gold, silver, copper and lead. The returns were marvelous and showed that the jug handle contained all the different minerals in paying quantities, but predominated largely in gold. From that day on the professor's business began to lag, and our confidence in the integrity of this scientific foreigner began to lessen. The next day we mailed him a dried herring, and merely asked: "Would you designate the sample herein as being a true fish-er vein, and, if not, then why?" On still another occasion we sent him a ball of horse manure and asked: "Is this sample an indication of horse carbonates in place, and will it pay to work?" The professor soon lost his reputation as an assayer and departed for another mining district farther south.

After discarding the two professors, we sent to Colorado

for an experienced prospector, and on his arrival gave him a complete outfit, with three good pack mules and a man to look after the camp and do the cooking. About that time one Cruz Naranja, from Coyote, N. Mex., arrived in town with a sack of fine copper ore, and at once brought it to the office of Otero, Sellar & Co. The new prospector thought well of the ore, so we promptly headed him for Coyote, in Mora County. Two days afterward James Leavitt, Tom Parker and I hired a good team and accompanied Naranja to his home.

Our prospector had arrived at Coyote the day before and had established his camp close to the discovery holes made by Naranja. Our first work was to locate claims before making our discoveries known, so we started at once and did not stop until we had located fifteen claims. One of us drove over to Mora the next day to have the notices recorded. Naranja was appointed superintendent and instructed to hire laborers and start work at once. On our return to Las Vegas a new company was organized, and each member was assessed $250 to commence operations. Of course, inasmuch as Naranja had brought the matter to our attention, we gave him an equal interest. He was not required to pay any assessment, besides receiving a salary and his board as superintendent.

We worked these prospects for several months, sinking one shaft down to the 110-foot level, and the deeper we went the less ore we found. The very best ore we ever recovered from those fifteen claims was what Naranja brought in on his first trip, and we later decided among ourselves that he must have gotten all there was in the district at that time. The name "Cruz Naranja" translated into English means: Cruz — a Cross or Crucifixion, and Naranja — Orange. After many months of labor and expense we became convinced, beyond a shadow of doubt, that Mr. Orange had passed us a lemon.

While we were still spending money at Coyote, our prospector returned to Las Vegas from Guadalupita, where he had been prospecting for several months, bringing with him a sack of very rich copper ore, together with the startling report that he had at last located the mother lode or vein. His story impressed us all so strongly that another company was formed at once, carrying with it the usual assessment. We kept the information entirely within our little group, and the next morning Tom Parker and I left for Guadalupita in company with the prospector, and, on our arrival, proceeded to locate claims enough to cover all the ground selected by our man. As soon as this was done, we left for Mora to have the location notices recorded and then continued on to Las Vegas and spread the news. By this time Tom Parker and myself began to figure that the opportunity was ripe for us to "play safe," so we sold one half of our interest for more than we had paid out in all our previous mining investments. This was done entirely upon the report made by the prospector and the sack of specimens he brought in, and the man who bought our shares thought at the time that we were doing him a favor by selling. The mines turned out the same as the Coyote mines, and both companies ceased business. Parker and myself had the laugh on the other boys, for it was now too late to unload any of their stock certificates.

About this same time, the spring of 1880, White Oaks, in Lincoln County, was enjoying a good-sized mining boom, and to all appearances it looked as though it might even rival some of the large camps in Colorado. A party of gentlemen hailing from Denver, headed by Colonel George W. Prichard, then a resident of Denver, arrived in Las Vegas en route to White Oaks. They had with them some of the richest gold specimens I had ever seen up to that time; some pieces were as large as a man's hand and almost solid gold. All of these specimens came from White Oaks and had been secured by Colonel Prichard on a former trip.

The North and South Homestake mines were producing much of the rich gold ore, and old J. E. Wilson, the discoverer, gave away enough of those rich specimens to have made any man comfortable for the balance of his natural life. Besides the two Homestake mines, there were: the Little Mack, Old Abe, Confidence, Comstock, Rip Van Winkle, Miguel A. Otero and several others, all big producers of gold.

White Oaks was growing rapidly and soon had a population of two thousand people. Main Street reminded one of the old frontier days with dance halls, saloons, gambling dens, restaurants and houses of prostitution. At night everything was wide open. The usual bad men were in evidence, and much shooting was the order of the day and night. In the prosperous days many large brick buildings went up, occupied by business firms carrying large stocks of merchandise, dry goods, hardware and furniture. Several beautiful brick residences were built by the wealthy miners and it looked as though the little mining camp might soon be a full-fledged city. But the rich gold ore and the many rich veins disappeared, and today White Oaks looks like a deserted village. All those fine buildings are empty and the grass is again growing in the middle of the streets.

During the boom days I joined a party of friends on a trip to White Oaks, in the interest of business and pleasure. We had a nice outfit, consisting of one four-horse spring wagon, which carried our provisions and bedding, and one two-horse spring wagon in which we rode. On our arrival we pitched our camp a short distance from the town.

We soon found that every foot of country had been located, but that many interests were for sale. We were offered many good locations at a price, the promoter said, which was like giving it away. However, we did not bite; and after our three days' visit we returned, stopping for a couple of days in the Jicarilla Mountains. We were all more impressed with the Jicarilla placers than anything we had seen at White

Oaks, and after our short visit we started back for Las Vegas. We heard several rumors about Indians, but never ran across any. The hunting was good, and we succeeded in killing many quail and one large black-tail deer, so we were well supplied with fresh meat. While in White Oaks I visited the merchants and sold quite a number of large orders of merchandise for Otero, Sellar & Co. By this time we were all beginning to be a little more cautious about our mining investments, although we all wanted to get rich quick and were always ready to take a chance.

My brother Page beside being a recognized miner and a successful hunter and fisherman, was also a champion billiard player, and had won many fine ivory-finished billiard cues during championship games in Colorado, Utah, Arizona, southern California and Texas. The *Daily Optic* of March 13th, 1880, has this to say:

A large crowd, in other words a curious crowd, gathered at the Monarch Hall last night, to "pipe off" a billiard match between William H. Hays, the great Texas champion and our Page B. Otero.

Page was not in trim, having been roughing it in the mines for the past few months, but Karl thought he could play well enough to tackle the great "I Am." So Page shouldered a cue and boldly waded in, coming out on top in every contest. The first was a three-ball game for 68 points, Otero leaving his opponent 25 points in the rear. Hays scored the best single run 16. The second game was a four-ball game 500 points, Page winning by 150 points. In this interesting match the best run was credited to Otero, which was 80 points. Page nursed the ivories in a masterly manner to do this. The Texas champion found more than his match in Otero. Although making no pretentions, Page is the undisputed champion of the Great Southwest, Texas included. Good for you, Old Rusty. I'll bet fifty cents on you, although I don't know the game. Hays is a very good fancy-shot man, but when it comes down to hard-pan billiard-playing, Page B. Otero can discount him out of sight, and walk away with him as a cat would with a mouse.

Chapter XXI

THE year 1881 was an eventful one in many ways. It was not by any means as wide-open and filled with deeds of violence as were the preceding two years, but it brought substantial business developments in which my father and I were involved.

Soon after the election in November, 1880, my father and his partner, John Perry Sellar, became estranged in both their business and social relations. In truth, trouble began to brew some years back, as early as 1873, to be exact, when my father became active in railroad matters; and this ill feeling continued between them for some years, finally culminating near the close of 1880. Early in 1881, matters had become so unpleasant that it was decided that they had better wind up the business of Otero, Sellar & Co. and go into voluntary liquidation. Almost immediately a new firm sprang into existence, organized by Jacob Gross, Arthur M. Blackwell, Alexander Stockton and Harry W. Kelly, all of Las Vegas and former employees of either Otero, Sellar & Co. or Browne & Manzanares. They organized under the firm name of Gross, Blackwell & Co. and at once took over the business of the old firm, assuming the task of winding up the affairs of Otero, Sellar & Co.

In January, 1881, I was elected cashier of the San Miguel National Bank, again succeeding my old friend Jacob Gross, who resigned after the merger, while my father continued as president of the bank. The San Miguel National Bank was still doing business on the southeast corner of the plaza in the Old Town of Las Vegas, in a building owned by J. Rosenwald & Brother. This location was not what might be considered a desirable one, either from a business standpoint or for the convenience of the customers, so the board of directors decided at a meeting early in the year to move over to East Las Vegas as soon as the Union Block was completed and ready for occupancy. The bank had already anticipated the move to the New Town and had secured a lease on the lower south half of the building. The room was equipped with new counters, partitions and railings, and on Saturday afternoon, immediately after banking hours, the safes, books, stationery and furniture were moved over to the new quarters. Sunday was devoted to getting everything in readiness; on Monday morning we were settled and doing business as though nothing had happened.

Banking was a very prosperous business at that time. The prevailing rate of interest paid by borrowers was eighteen per cent, and there was an additional charge of ten per cent commission whenever it became necessary to re-discount our paper in New York. Usury laws had not been enacted in the Territory, and money was worth as much as you could get for it.

The banking establishments in the West had little to worry about during those early days, for money was plentiful and there never was such a thing as a bank failure. The profits in buying and selling cattle, sheep and horses were enormous, so those who engaged in that line of business were quite willing to allow the banks to take a good share of their profits. Frequently, a customer would see an opportunity to buy a bunch of cattle at a low price and then hold them for several months. On such occasions he would go to the bank and borrow $10,000 for six months, paying eighteen per cent interest, the note reading "from maturity," so the interest, amounting to $900, was deducted and an additional ten per cent commission was charged; for the banks would stress the fact that they were short of money and would have to re-discount the note in the East. So the borrower would get $8,100 cash for his $10,000 note. The note was re-discounted in New York at four per cent interest. Banks readily earned from twenty per cent to fifty per cent on their capital stock each year. Losses were few and far between. Dividends were usually twelve per cent and the remainder of profits was passed to the surplus account, which gradually increased the value of the stock to many times its par value.

While banking in general was most successful, I recall an occasion when the San Miguel National Bank came within an ace of being held up by a gang of robbers. The leader was a man named Tom Jones. His lieutenants were Tom Brinkley, one of the old Stockton gang, and David Kelly, one of the notorious Sam Bass gang; the fourth was a young man named Crommitt. It appeared that Crommitt did not go into the plot with his eyes open and after fully realizing the enormity of the crime and the dangers of the undertaking, he weakened and resolved secretly to give the whole thing away and get the protection of the citizens. He accordingly posted Jacob Gross, giving him all the plans of the robbers: the day and the hour when the attack was to made, and the manner of the escape by horseback. Gross related the full story to Harry Franklin, the city marshal, who at once called in Arthur Jilson. Together they arranged to kill or capture the entire party.

For some reason the robbers decided to postpone the date a few days, and in the mean time Franklin determined to arrest them, one at a time, holding them separate and apart. In this way he secured a full confession from Tom Jones which tallied exactly with the original confession made by Crommitt to Jacob Gross.

The Vigilance Committee met in the A. C. Schmidt Hall with ropes, but finally, after several hours of deliberation, agreed to send the trio to the county jail to await the sitting of the next grand jury.

It was the general belief that had Tom Brinkley been the leader instead of Tom Jones, who was somewhat of a coward, the bank would have been robbed and many of us working in the bank would have been killed. Had the leaders of the Vigilance Committee left it to a vote of those present, the telegraph poles on Grand Avenue would have borne fruit the next morning.

Although my father was the president of the bank, he was now devoting practically all his time to the building of a branch railroad to the Jemez Hot Springs, starting from the town of Bernalillo, at present the county seat of Sandoval County. Surveys had been made and grading had begun and finished for a distance of one mile out of town. William B. Strong, president of the Atchison, Topeka & Santa Fé Railroad, George Hazelton of Boston, and several other Santa Fé railroad directors and officials became interested in a new company, the object of which was to take over not only the Jemez Hot Springs but also the Sulphurs and Baca Location No. 1. Mariano S. Otero, my father's nephew, owned the Sulphurs and Baca Location No. 1, the latter a land grant containing 100,000 acres and no less than 750,000,000 feet of saw timber, besides an abundance of running water, beautiful farming land and fine grazing land for cattle or sheep. The Jemez Hot Springs were owned equally by my father and his nephew. My father had been elected president of the new company, and he and his nephew were both named as directors.

New bath houses were to be constructed at once as well as a good-sized stone hotel adjoining the bath houses. Everything connected with the enterprise had the endorsement of eastern capitalists and it had every appearance of becoming a great success, as it surely would have been had my father lived. The Jemez Hot Springs are without a shadow of doubt the greatest medicinal mineral hot springs in America. With railroad facilities and good hotel accommodations these springs will advertise themselves, and eventually become the most celebrated curative mineral waters in the world. What was known as the "Otero Original Spring" has a temperature of 178° and throws out a volume of water several feet high when confined to a pipe. Adjoining the hot springs are cold springs of soda and iron delightful to drink. For humanity's sake, these springs should be purchased from the present owners by the Government, together with the Sulphur Springs and the Baca Location No. 1, and made into one of the greatest health resorts in the world.

Much notice was being taken about this time of the Star Route Swindles in New Mexico. Fortunes were being made by men who started with absolutely nothing except the backing of men in Washington who had influence. The Whiskey Ring had no sooner died out than the Star Route Mail Contracts sprang into prominence through the manipulations of such men as Stephen W. Dorsey, Richard C. Kerens, Stephen B. Elkins, Thomas B. Catron, Numa Reymond, John H. Riley, Michael Cosgrove and numerous lesser lights, as well as others in Washington higher up and behind the scenes. The idea was gigantic. Imaginary mail routes were being laid out, postoffices established, postmasters named, and the Government swindled out of millions of dollars. While it was quite true that the pioneers had a devil of a time to get their mail in out-of-the-way places, their wants were never really considered by this group.

One of these numerous routes was, perhaps, the longest mail route in the world, and was successfully handled by one buckboard, operating between Vinita, Indian Territory, and Las Vegas, a distance of six hundred miles, as the crow flies. From the horrors that haunted the weary trail with its meanderings in and out, one could mentally calculate the distance at a good thousand miles. To many a poor driver, it was more than this, for it meant the final end of his mortal relay. Many an unfortunate chap never reached the end of his route. The line followed closely the thirty-sixth parallel, encountered no towns and was in no sense a necessity, but was simply worked politically, as a private graft, by plunder-

My Life on the Frontier 239

ers and their knights-of-the-inner-circle at Washington. Thus the Vinita mail service, starting nowhere and ending nowhere, was registered as making tri-weekly trips across the Panhandle through buffalo country inhabited almost entirely by savages, outlaws and desperadoes; in reality it made about one trip every three weeks.

About the only persons who could possibly be served en route, were a few isolated ranchmen or cattle men, nearly all of whom were itinerants — here today and there tomorrow like a vagrant wind. The route passed through the entire length of the neutral strip or No Man's Land, as it was commonly called, the garish abode of cutthroats, wherein a decent man's life was not worth more than fifteen cents for more than fifteen minutes at a stretch — and he was a lucky dog not to have his neck stretched, at that. It was as somber and gloomy as were the secrets of Enoch, and the tragedies of that gruesome trail will never be written for the reason that the most of them never came to light. Every day or so there was a stick up when a driver or a passenger was ambushed and killed between the relay stations on the lonesome prairie and no record was ever kept of the incident. Dead men tell no tales and the unknown missing have no friends to notify or damages to pay.

At Las Vegas I often saw the buckboard arrive from its ten-day trip from Vinita, and it was frequently pretty well bespattered with the dried blood of some poor devil who had been shot en route, but nobody knew the first thing about it, for it did not always pay in those powder-stained days to know too much. E. W. Parker, the sub-contractor, was a good man who used to grieve sincerely over the murders that occurred so frequently, but he was powerless to stop the crimes or cut down the death rate; besides he had a right smart run of troubles of his own. The last driver on the out trip was Johnny McNulty. We often commiserated with him over the dangers of his job, but he only laughed with his graveyard grin and remarked that they would never get him, as everybody knew he was not worth getting. This bluff on himself, however, did not come out very gayly, for one evening in the midsummer of 1881, the Vinita buckboard pulled in with a new face on the seat and the through pouch missing. Johnny had been killed back on the Concha by Tom Pickett, one of Billy the Kid's band, whom Pat F. Garrett branded as the most cowardly brute he ever met.

The affairs of the Vinita mail route, like all of the other Star Route frauds, finally resulted in a great national scandal and the house of cards builded on the sands of No Man's Land took a great fall. Senator Dorsey was selected as "the goat," indicted in the federal courts and defended by Robert G. Ingersoll in one of the most celebrated legal battles ever tried before the Washington courts. Bob took a big slice of the Senator's Palo Blanco ranch at Chico Springs in Colfax County, N. Mex., as a part of his fee. Colonel Ingersoll was afterward a frequent visitor to Las Vegas and the writer has often enjoyed meeting him. Senator Dorsey was put out of politics. He was no worse than many of the others, but he was caught with the goods. I knew Senator Dorsey quite well and rather liked him. He was a jovial fellow — kind, congenial and full of fun. Mrs. Dorsey was very beautiful, besides being a charming woman of great ability. Her latter life was clouded with sorrow and grief and it was really pitiful to see her a short time before her death.

All this time we were extending our telephone lines in Las Vegas and getting many new subscribers. The county commissioners of San Miguel County evidently did not believe in the necessity of encouraging new inventions, for they declined to allow the different county officials to put in a telephone, saying it was merely a toy, and besides it could not speak Spanish and the expense was too much. We did our best to convince them that the telephone was here to stay, and that it could speak Spanish fluently, when the proper man was at the transmitter. Finally we had to give it up as a bad job, for nothing we could say would convince them that the telephone would ever become a necessity. We had just extended our line to Las Alamos, a distance of twelve miles north, and the exchange was located in the store of Andres Sena at that point. Mr. Sena reported that all his numerous friends in Las Vegas were calling him up, wanting to talk to him over the new line, and he was so busy talking to them that he could not find time to go home for lunch.

The very next day, April 13th, 1882, after completing the line to Las Alamos, we had a heavy snow storm, the snow falling in Las Vegas to a depth of several inches. Nevertheless, on April 14th, 1882, Mrs. A. G. Hood gave a very interesting telephone concert at her residence. The music was furnished by a piano and a connection of telephone wires conveyed the lady's playing simultaneously to Las Alamos, the *Optic* office and the Hot Springs Hotel. Mr. Hood was director of the wire musicale and initiated the hearers into new telephone marvels.

The success of our local telephone ventures caused my father to aspire to larger successes. Late in the fall he went to Denver to meet General Marshall regarding the organization of a telephone company to acquire the rights of the Bell Telephone Company in the Republic of Mexico. After the meeting both General Marshall and my father went to Boston and succeeded in their efforts, the Mexico Telephone Company being incorporated with my father as president and General Marshall as secretary and treasurer. On their return from Boston they proceeded to the City of Mexico, where they made satisfactory arrangements with the Government of Mexico, and immediately returned to Las Vegas. General Marshall remained as a guest at my father's home for a couple of days and then proceeded to Denver, my father returning to the Jemez Hot Springs to note progress in the buildings under erection.

My Life on the Frontier

In January, 1882, my father was reëlected president and I cashier of the San Miguel National Bank. The banking business continued good, and conditions at the Jemez Hot Springs looked most encouraging.

The Atchison, Topeka & Santa Fé Railroad reached Deming, N. Mex., on March 10th, 1881, and made connection with the Southern Pacific Railroad, thus making an all-rail route across the continent by way of New Mexico, and Arizona. In July, 1881, the Atlantic & Pacific Railroad, building west from Albuquerque, reached the Arizona line en route to California.

The Las Vegas Fair Association and Racing Park was organized during the summer of 1881 and I was elected president with Felix Martinez as secretary and treasurer. At the opening of the fair grounds we had several good running races, during one of which a horse ridden by Harry Blake, son of Frank A. Blake, flew the track and struck a young boy on the head, killing him instantly. About the same time the Las Vegas Fair Association started, a similar association was organized in Albuquerque, and a driving and race track circuit established in New Mexico. The first fair was held at Albuquerque on October 3-8, 1881, and as president of the Las Vegas Fair Association, I was honored by being named one of the judges for all horse races during the meeting.

Chapter XXII

EARLY in 1881 the Knights of Pythias entered New Mexico with Hon. George W. Prichard as Supreme Chancellor and Representative for New Mexico, and El Dorado Lodge No. 1 was instituted at East Las Vegas. All the young men connected with the commission houses, banks, railroad offices and social clubs joined the order, and soon El Dorado Lodge No. 1 was one of the largest and most prosperous lodges in New Mexico. We organized a Uniformed Division and on parades the black frock coats with red bandoleers, red belts and swords with silver trimmings and helmets with red and blue plumes were much in evidence. I was one of the early members, joining in 1881, and have kept in good standing ever since. In connection with the Knights of Pythias I recall an amusing incident which deserves relating.

The Frederick Ward Theatrical Company happened to be playing in Las Vegas for a week's engagement at the Rosenthal Theater on Railroad Avenue. The repertoire, as I remember, was made up entirely of Shakespearian tragedies — *Hamlet, King Lear, Macbeth, Julius Cæsar* and *Romeo and Juliet*. The theater was crowded every night, and in addition we had a great time entertaining the troupe, driving them out to the Hot Springs to enjoy some of Scott Moore's elegant meals and arranging house parties, for they were pleasant to meet and thoroughly nice people. In the middle of the week something happened in the community which called for a general turn-out of all citizens, orders, societies, clubs and military organizations. Of course, the new uniforms of the Knights of Pythias had to be in the parade, and not a member was missing. Colonel Prichard in command wore a helmet with a beautiful yellow plume, while the others wore the red and blue plumes. Frederick Ward, noticing the great amount of interest taken in the Knights of Pythias, offered to have his troup produce *Damon and Pythias* for the following Saturday-night performance. In making the announcement he asked the members of the order to attend in uniform. The front rows of seats were reserved for the Knights and their ladies, and the theater was sold out completely even to the standing room.

It being Saturday night and the last performance, many of the actors had been busy saying good-bye, and by the time they were to go on the stage they were feeling their oats to such an extent that most of them had forgotten their lines. The two leading men who took the parts of Damon and Pythias were considerably under the weather, and during the scene where Pythias was appealing to the tyrant Dionysius to let Damon go to his wife and child, he completely forgot his lines and stepped back into one of the wings; Damon, who was standing there, tried to coach him — this developed a dispute. Damon felled Pythias and they had a real fight, which of course brought down the house.

As soon as order was restored Pythias again appeared on the stage with blood flowing down his cheek, caused by one of Damon's blows. Shortly after Damon had parted with his wife and daughter, he called loudly for his horse, and his slave appeared quite noticeably under the influence of liquor. He had completely forgotten his part, and wore a pair of spectacles and carried a small book, from which he read with difficulty: "My lord, to save your life I slew your steed." This was more than the audience could stand, and they fairly yelled with laughter. The slave stood in the center of the stage, and finally throwing down his book, he faced the audience and said: "Well, what is eating you? If you can get up here and play this part any better than I can, just come up." Everyone in the house was pleased, for it was well worth the price of admission, and we remained to the last, the Knights of Pythias with their ladies escorting the troupe to the hotel.

where we ordered plenty to eat and drink, then cleared the dining-room, sent for music and danced until Sunday morning.

Las Vegas Hose Company No. 1 was organized by the young men of the town and was entirely composed of volunteer firemen. A subscription list was passed around and the citizens were so liberal in their donations that in a few days we had raised sufficient money to pay for the hose cart, the hose, nozzles, and all the necessary equipment, as well as the rent for a small building, along the side of which we erected a derrick and added a fire-alarm bell. I was treasurer of the organization and also ran with the cart. We all got plenty of exercise and some amusement, for we had a fine running team and won many races. The organization of our fire company was timely, for the big fire, which threatened to destroy the entire town of East Las Vegas, occurred in the fall of 1881. The fire started in a restaurant just across Railroad Avenue from the Casteneda Hotel and soon the dance hall of Close & Patterson was in flames, as well as all the other buildings in the block.

A dance was in progress on Zion Hill, the abode of the aristocracy of East Las Vegas, who were commonly called the "silk stocking brigade." Most of the young men of the town were there with their best girls, all in full dress with silk socks and dancing pumps of patent leather. When the bell sounded the alarm, we were in the midst of a waltz. We all made a wild rush from the dance, leaving our partners standing in the center of the room. We reached the hose house in a bunch, and in a moment were running for the scene of the fire. Before many people even knew of the fire, we had made connections with hydrants and were playing several streams on the burning buildings. The restaurant was one mass of flames and the fire was just reaching the dance hall when we arrived. Many of the girls had retired to their rooms in the rear of the hall, and we created quite a commotion when we ran down the hall pounding on each door and yelling, "Fire! Fire!" Many escaped in nightgowns, carrying their clothing in their arms. A number of heroic acts were performed by the volunteer firemen. It was strange to see them in full dress fighting a big fire, and they stayed with it until noon the next day, tired, muddy and wet to the skin. A paid fire department could not have rendered more faithful service than did those boys. All the frame buildings in the block were in ashes, but we saved the adobe and brick buildings and prevented the fire from spreading to the next block.

The fire, however, brought about one loss which I greatly deplored. The *Daily Optic*, with all its valuable files, was almost a total loss. Editor Kistler did manage to save enough type, together with what he could borrow, to get out an edition of his paper the following afternoon, but the files were burned. My good friend Lute Wilcox was still connected with the *Daily Optic*, and just before the fire he had written an article on "The Oldest Human Habitation in America," referring to the Old House at Santa Fé, which I think well worth repeating:

THE OLDEST HUMAN HABITATION IN AMERICA

Santa Fé, New Mexico, boasts of having the oldest residence in America and that antique piece of bric-a-brac is in a way one of the most interesting curios of the ancient city. It is adjacent to the Old Church. This structure of mud is the last remains of the ancient Tegua Pueblo of Analco. Until recent years it was entered through a scuttle in the roof as are all Pueblo houses. The sides were afterwards pierced with doors and windows and the occupants came and went like their neighbors. The house at present contains but two rooms which are not larger than ten by twelve feet each. The bare floor is almost devoid of furniture but the faded walls are plentifully adorned with pictures. The evidences of age confront one at every turn and the traveler who sets out to explore the nooks and corners of the quaint old town will find himself submerged in a sea of historical data and speculation concerning the strange people that lived in caves before American history began. In the central part of the city extending the entire length of the north side of the plaza square and covering several acres of ground is the Old Royal Palace whose one-story adobe walls are five feet thick. It is the oldest building used for government purposes on the continent, its age being over 300 years. Though now mainly used for purposes of modern commerce its venerable walls are covered with the dust of historic lore.

Here the courtly grandees of Spain held the reigns of sovereignty, issuing royal edicts and with a flourish of the pen sending prisoners to the tender mercies of the Inquisition. The palace has been a prison house for the innocent as well as the guilty. This old building has served as a fortress for people who fled from the cruel savages; a long line of Governors and Captain-Generals have here made their homes; the royalty of Spain and distinguished visitors in every department of official and civic life at home and abroad have been welcomed as honoured guests; declarations of war have been issued; republican laws promulgated and treaties of peace negotiated in this adobe landmark, but its chiefest interest lies in the fact that on August 22nd, 1846, General Kearny with his boys in blue planted the stars and stripes upon its pancake roof and took possession of the town without a struggle. It stands today in a state of fine preservation.

The above article was written fifty-four years ago, but the Old House and the Palace of the Governors are still in perfect state of preservation, cared for by the Historical Society.

Jacob Gross, Thomas H. Parker and myself were living together in our bachelor quarters on the corner of Seventh and Main Streets (the corner now occupied by the Baptist Church). Jacob Gross, however, was soon to marry Miss Caroline Linton of Saint Louis, leaving Parker and myself alone. I purchased the interest of Gross in the quarters as soon as he returned from his bridal trip. He and Miss Linton were married at St. Louis on January 12th, 1881, and they reached Las Vegas about the middle of February following.

Jacob Gross was about the closest friend I ever had, outside of my own immediate family, and that friendship continued up to the time of his death. He was associated with my father and Mr. Sellar in the house of C. R. Morehead & Co., at Leavenworth, Kans., in 1864, and went with Otero, Sellar & Co., as bookkeeper, in 1867, remaining with the firm until 1880. In 1881 he succeeded the old firm under the name of Gross, Blackwell & Co., at present Gross, Kelly & Co., of Las Vegas. All my knowledge of bookeeping, as an accountant and as cashier was taught me by Jacob Gross. He was most thorough in his business education and had no such thing as a superior in office work.

Mrs. Gross was a refined and most charming woman and, naturally, was a leader among the younger set in East Las Vegas. I was as much at home in the Gross residence as I was in my own or in my father's, and I always called Mrs. Gross "Sister Carrie." She was a talented musician, played the piano and had a pleasing contralto voice. It was not long before we organized an amateur opera company, as Las Vegas had considerable talent in that line. Those taking the principal parts among the ladies were Mrs. Gross, Miss Hattie Knickerbocker, Miss Emily Tetard and Miss May Dunlop, and among the gentlemen were Page B. Otero, Harry J. O'Bryan, Dr. D. H. Rust and Earnest L. Browne. Some of the operas we gave were *The Little Tycoon, Billee Taylor, Pinafore, Mikado, Chilperic* and others. The rehearsals were great fun and always ended with a midnight supper, including plenty to eat and drink.

Our Firing-Out Club had been quite busy with several deserters from our bachelor club; so it was decided to organize another club to be known as the Sitting-Out Club, which might be a counteractive. We all wore a silver badge; on the bar was our name, and from two small chains from each end of the bar was suspended a solid silver triangle with the letters S. O. C. on each point. In the center of the triangle was an eye surrounded with these words: "We never sleep." The sole object of the club was to ascertain when any one of our bachelor friends was paying marked attention to any of the young ladies, and if it looked serious we would meet at a certain room and at intervals of every fifteen minutes one of us would call on the young lady until all had arrived and they would never leave as long as the victim remained. It finally reached my turn, and the young lady, with the approval of her parents, agreed to sit up all night with me, and between two and three in the morning they began to weaken and one by one left. The young lady was Miss Grace Keller, and she afterwards married Valentine Carson.

There were no automobiles in those days, but we all had fine trotting and saddle horses and beautiful turn-outs. I still had my old pony Kiowa, who was now ten years old and just as frisky as ever. I broke him to work in single harness and had no trouble in doing so, for he seemed to know at once what I wanted, but on the road he objected to any fast team passing him, and whenever one tried he would break into a run. Often when he was running like a blue streak and I happened to have one of the girls with me in the little red-wheeled wagon, I would throw the reins out on his back to frighten the girl, but when I spoke to him he would slow down to a trot, or if I told him to stop he would obey so suddenly as to almost jar us out of our seat. I never had to tie him unless I happened to stop in front of a saloon, which frequently occurred in those days. If I failed to tie him, he would wait until I entered the saloon, then he would shake his head and go directly home to his stable and wait there until I returned and took off his harness. At any other place or house or while hunting he would stop for hours and never think of moving until I appeared. He never objected to shooting and would walk between me and the game until I was ready to shoot, when he would stand perfectly still while

I emptied two barrels of my shot-gun from under his neck, over him, under him or across his back. He seemed to understand every word or command given him by me.

Early in the fall of 1881 at Las Vegas, N. Mex., while on a fishing trip up on the Pecos River, I fell in the stream and of course was drenched from head to foot. I was several miles away from camp and when I arrived it was found I had contracted a severe cold, which forced me to return immediately to my home at Las Vegas and go under the care of Doctor C. C. Gordon. The cold soon developed into pneumonia, and after several weeks' hovering between life and death I finally recovered sufficiently to undertake a trip to St. Louis, as my physician thought the change would be beneficial to my weakened condition.

My good friend Jacob Gross had just been called to St. Louis in anticipation of an early arrival in the family.

The fact that Mr. Gross was in St. Louis led my father and mother to decide on my going there, but, unfortunately for me, I left home too soon, and while en route, instead of improving, I took a relapse. I was alone and without a nurse, but a good friend of my father, who had volunteered to see me safely landed in St. Louis, to which place he was going, took charge of me, as we were traveling on the same Pullman sleeper, and on our arrival in St. Louis he took me at once to the Southern Hotel. It was during the celebration of the anniversary of the surrender at Yorktown, the hotel was crowded, and everybody connected with the hotel was too busy to give any attention to a sick man, so I found myself greatly neglected. My room was anything but pleasant, and when I reached it I was entirely too weak to undress. Sometime during the night I left my room for the toilet, and as I was returning I fainted and fell on the floor in the hallway. Just how long I remained in that condition I never knew. A gentleman occupying a room on the same hallway and close to mine discovered me lying in the hallway and quite naturally thought I was intoxicated, but he very soon realized that I was sick, and he carried me to my room. As it happened, he was a member of the Knights of Pythias, and, noticing my badge of the order attached to my watch chain, he immediately got in touch with a Knight of Pythias Lodge and a member called on me at once and soon had Doctor Glasgow, a relative of my mother, call. The doctor got word to my friend Jacob Gross, and he came the next morning with a buggy and horse and drove me out in the country to the home of his cousin, Doctor Sol Steigers, and there I remained, under the watchful care of his two lovely sisters, until the attending physician suggested that I be taken to the Mullanphey Hospital and my parents advised by telegraph of my serious condition. How I lived through all these circumstances is still a mystery. My father chartered a special engine to take him to La Junta to catch the Denver express for Kansas City, as my mother and sister were in Denver at the time and had taken the first train out. My brother Page followed my father on the following day, and on the arrival of the entire family in St. Louis they all secured quarters at the hospital.

A report got into circulation in New Mexico that I had died and my obituary was written by my old chum, Captain Edward Friend, City Editor of the *Optic*, but a quick answer to a telegram prevented it from being printed in the evening paper, and it was afterwards presented to me on my return to Las Vegas some months later. It seemed a miracle that I recovered.

About the middle of December my attending physician advised another trip, so my mother and sister joined me on a trip down the Mississippi River, on the Steamer *John C. Scudder*, to New Orleans, where I remained for several days at the old St. Charles Hotel, managed by Mr. Rivers. I had a letter to him from Mr. Adolphus Busch telling Mr. Rivers to give me anything I wanted and to charge it to him. It was a splendid letter; of course, I did not take advantage of its contents, but I thanked Mr. Busch from the bottom of my heart.

Leaving New Orleans, we all took passage on the *S. S. Hutchinson* of the Morgan Line for Cedar Keys, Fla., and from there we took the train for Jacksonville, Fla., where we remained for a month at the St. James Hotel, taking side trips on the St. John's River to Sanford and Enterprise; to Lake George, then to Palatka and up the Oklawhaha River, which is one of the most beautiful streams I have ever seen. We next went to Key West and from there took a steamer for Havana, where we remained for a couple of weeks. We visited Matanzas and the great caves.

Completing our visit in Cuba, we returned to Jacksonville, Fla., and from there, after a few days' rest, headed for our home at Las Vegas, as my health was greatly improved; in fact, I was feeling as though I had never been sick, and was eating everything in sight and gaining nicely in weight.

We arrived home early in February of 1882. *The Optic*, in mentioning my homecoming, had this to say:

It was agreed upon by a few of the many friends of M. A. Otero, Jr., to extend a serenade to him last evening. Some twenty or more accompanied by Boffa's orchestra, quietly approached the residence at 10:00 o'clock and made their presence known by a sweet refrain, which swelled and floated out upon the frosted air only to be broken in upon by a generous request to "walk in."

Once under the hospitable roof of Don Miguel, the hours sped fleetly by, entwined with vocal and instrumental music, alternately. This greeting to one of Las Vegas' most conspicuous and popular young men, whose life was so recently despaired of in an eastern city, licenses the assertion that it was truly a heartfelt offering.

The recipient of this compliment experienced no greater joy than those who bestowed it. Whether prostrated upon a bed of suffering, or traveling in quest of returning health, his thoughts always wandered back to his home among us. The surging Mississippi, the swelling ocean, tropical Cuba, or the Everglades of Florida, were admired and passed by. He was only to be made truly happy by being once more in his cañon home. The joys of the evening were not alone his, for the whole family shared alike the favors tendered the invalid. Let this greeting to our young friend alienate him from any tempting offers from distance. Rather let it confirm the hope that here, in Las Vegas, must be his home, for we all love him and welcome him "Home Again."

In a very short time I had sufficiently recovered my good health to permit me to go back to my work in the San Miguel National Bank.

Just about this time the entire territory was shocked by an occurrence which happened in the little village of Los Lunas, Valencia County, N. Mex.

It seems that the jail in Los Lunas was somewhat crowded, so a number of citizens residing in the town took it upon themselves to visit the jail, and, as they remarked at the time: "We will clean it up properly." The party was made up of the "leaders in society," and was headed by sons of one of the leading families of Los Lunas who had mustered up their courage by indulging in frequent libations of "Mistela," a most palatable and delicious beverage.

It was on March 7th, 1882. They found the jail contained the following prisoners:

Charles Shelton, charged with murder.

Johnnie Redmond, charged with murder.

Henry French, charged with complicity in a murder case. These three prisoners they took to a well-known tree near Los Lunas and promptly hung all three, until they were dead. When they returned to the jail they found two negroes who had been accused of stealing. These were severely flogged with a "bull-snake" whip and ordered to leave town and never return, under pain of death, and it was stated that they were still running when last seen. Two other Americans who were inmates of the jail were released and set at liberty.

The whole affair was most disgraceful throughout, and the perpetrators of it should have been arrested and adequately punished, even though the leaders were prominent men and of the first families of Los Lunas.

The young men in those early days were constantly playing tricks on one another, and I remember an amusing one which happened at this particular time: One of my very good friends, Price Lane, General Manager of the New Mexico Bell Telephone Company, was the victim of what we all considered a very good joke. Price had been down to Silver City, N. Mex., on some important telephone business which required his personal attention and a stay of a week or ten days. While he was away, his Las Vegas chums, so to speak, "put up a job on him," by agreeing to inform him immediately upon his return to Las Vegas that he was the victim of a scandalous rumor, which the newspapers had gotten hold of and would soon spring on him. The matter was broached in such a delicate and sympathetic way that Price fell into the trap. He rushed right over to *The Optic* office and paid $25.00 for the suppression of the alleged scandal. Of course, it was not published and the money was turned over to Price's friends, who spread a champagne lunch at Lord Locke's saloon, and invited Price to attend. It then flashed upon him that he had been most outrageously "sold," but he seemed perfectly satisfied with the happy outcome of the tragic affair — which to him had looked so dubious that he had lost a night's sleep, made an affidavit for *The Optic*, setting forth, under oath, his innocence in any flagrant scrape, and for fear of utter disgrace had packed his grip and was cogitating on a passage to Chihuahua, Old Mexico. The crack of champagne corks buried the odium of the hoax and Price was the gayest at the spread, which was paid for with his good dollars.

Early in September, 1881, a large gathering of railroad officials were meeting in Denver, Colo., for the purpose of discussing proposed plans for the building of a railroad from Arkansas Pass, Texas, on the Gulf of Mexico, thence northwest to Las Vegas, N. Mex., and on in the same direction through Utah, Oregon, Washington, to Vancouver, B. C., Canada.

The Las Vegas & Gulf Railroad had already been incorporated and everything connected with the building of the said railroad looked most favorable, and there seemed but little doubt in the minds of those interested that the project was going through at once. However, Frank and Charlie Springer and the Maxwell Land Grant Company, in which the Springers were largely interested, were doing all in their power to prevent the building of the proposed railroad from Arkansas Pass, fearing that such a route would open up the coal fields of Utah and possibly destroy the coal mines surrounding Raton, in Colfax County. To be sure, Trinidad and southern Colorado joined with the Springer forces, and, of course, this involved the whole of the State of Colorado.

My father, Miguel A. Otero (I), Oliver L. Houghton of the Las Vegas & Gulf Railroad, Mr. A. G. Hood and Miguel A. Otero, Jr., both interested in the building of the Las Vegas & Gulf Railroad from Arkansas Pass to Vancouver, all left Las Vegas for the meeting in Denver. The following item is taken from a Trinidad *Times* reporter, who is scared a good deal more than hurt, when he speaks, as follows: "Don Miguel A. Otero (I), who passed through here on last Saturday night, was bound for Denver. He is a high official on the N. M. & S. P. R. R., and said important business demanded that he should be in Denver by Sunday night. There has been a gathering of railroad officials in Denver for several days past, and it is generally concluded that startling railroad changes are about to take place, and before long."

On this day the Tabor Grand Opera House of Denver was to be opened, with Miss Emma Abbott as the prima donna. Possibly, the railroad officials had purposely timed their meeting to fit in on this great society event, when Denver, with Tabor's help, was doing the grand, "And the night shall be filled with music, And the cares that infest the day Shall fold their tents like the Arabs, And as silently steal away."

One thing was very much in evidence; the railroad officials very materially helped to crowd the Opera House every night.

Tabor's private box was on the lower right side facing the stage, while the delegation from Las Vegas, N. Mex., had the lower left side, directly opposite to the Tabor box, and on this particular occasion, Tuesday night, September 13th, 1881, Emma Abbott appeared as Marguerite in the opera of *Faust*, and I believe the Las Vegas delegation acquitted itself with great honor and *éclat*.

The Las Vegas *Optic* has this to say:

ABBOTT'S ADMIRERS

Las Vegas people generally conduct themselves nicely at home, but abroad they act admirably. During Emma Abbott's rendition of *Marguerite* in the opera of *Faust*, at the Tabor Grand, in Denver on Tuesday night, a Las Vegas delegation, in one of the magnificent boxes of the theatre, presented the charming little lady with a floral parasol — a tribute of their admiration and a recognition of her talent. The papers of that city are wild over the presentation, which it seems, was conceived by Don Miguel A. Otero (1), Oliver L. Houghton, Mr. A. G. Hood and Miguel A. Otero, Jr., comprising the Las Vegas, New Mexico, delegation, and the *Optic* takes the liberty of producing what they had to say about it. The *Tribune* says editorially:

"Las Vegas distinguished itself last night. Some of her representatives now in Denver gave the thriving New Mexican city a first class advertisement and paid Miss Abbott a very pleasant compliment."

A reporter on the *Republican* made use of the following artistic language:

"A very pleasing feature of last evening was the presentation to Emma Abbott of a silk parasol, covered entirely with choice flowers, really a work of art. It was presented by a deputation from Las Vegas, New Mexico, who had come all this distance to hear the favorite prima donna."

The *News*, generally rather of a stiff-backed conservative order, gushed as follows, in the editorial column:

"A very pleasing affair occurred at the opera last night which was not down on the bills. This was the presentation to Miss Abbott by a delegation from Las Vegas, New Mexico, of a beautiful and unique floral design. It was a parasol, full sized, and composed of the choicest and rarest flowers, inlaid with this inscription: — 'Las Vegas to Abbott.' This well-merited tribute to the sweet songstress was an entirely new and original design. * * * The unique and handsome floral design was the subject of universal commendation."

The following is taken from the *Optic* of September 17th, 1881:

OTERO'S OBJECT

A Scheme to Organize the Denver, Las Vegas and Socorro Railroad.

The *Optic* stated in a previous issue that Don Miguel A. Otero (1) was in Denver on important Railroad business, the nature of which could not be divulged at the time. It now transpires, however, that a long-legged reporter on the Denver *Republican* has had a talk with Don Miguel and the cat has been let out of the pouch.

The *Optic* reporters were fully posted on the scheme before Mr. Otero left Las Vegas, but as the fruit was not ripe for the plucking, the *Optic's* pole was restrained from knocking it off — hence the "scoop" goes to the credit of the Denver paper.

The plan is to organize a local company in Las Vegas and build a road from this city to the Colorado line, where connections will be made with Governor Evans's Denver & New Orleans road, now in course of construction south from Denver. Don Miguel A. Otero (1) has been identified with railroad building in the West for quite a number of years, and no man understands the topography of the country, status of commercial interests, peculiarities, wants and demands of the people better than he. It is an open secret that he has been in correspondence with Governor Evans ever since the *Optic* mentioned the advisability of courting that magnate's favors, and it is further understood that Mr. Otero has been requested by the governor to visit Denver and have a confidential audience with him upon this all-absorbing subject, and it is in compliance with this summons that Don Miguel is now in Denver.

The scheme is to organize the Denver, Las Vegas & Socorro Railroad Company, and as the project has been favorably considered by territorial and eastern capital, there is no reason, with good workers at the helm, why the plan should not be speedily consummated. The organization will be effected in this city next week and an assessment of 10 per cent, of the capital stock will be made, with which to conduct the survey and commence the actual work of construction. The line will be constructed from Las Vegas north, and after an outlet has been effected to the north and communication opened to Denver the road will push south to Socorro, and there connect with Socorro & Pacific, a line that is to reach down into the Black range country and probably onward into Chihuahua. As yet no alliance has been made with the New Orleans faction, but it is intended to use their line as the most advisable outlet to Denver — that city once approached, and Las Vegas is delivered from thralldom.

It begins to look as if our new railroad hopes are to be realized, and we are glad to see that a striving effort has been made to bring the scheme to a focus. Capital and brains will do wonders in bringing out imperative needs and desired effects.

This latter railroad proposition does not in any way interfere with the building of the Las Vegas & Gulf, in fact railroad building is on the move and Las Vegas figures in all directions.

When our delegation returns from Denver, let us get busy and strike while the iron is hot.

About the close of the winter and the beginning of spring in 1882, East Las Vegas, the Old Town, and all of the surrounding country were visited by an epidemic of smallpox.

Many deaths occurred in both towns, in spite of the precautions taken by county and city officials. Doctor E. H. Skipwith was appointed health officer in the Old Town and given extraordinary powers in enforcing the health regulations, and insisting on cleaning and disinfecting all premises within the town limits. Pest-houses were erected outside of the city and town limits. In East Las Vegas, Doctor C. C. Gordon was appointed health officer, and he and Dr. Skipwith were authorized to appoint special physicians, and many immune nurses were provided to help in meeting the situation. The Masonic bodies, the Odd Fellows and the Knights of Pythias joined together and erected a building known as "The United Lodge Hospital." We secured as our head nurse a man named William Cox, who had acted in that capacity before, for he had had smallpox himself and believed himself immune. In the conducting of this hospital I was the executive member for the Knights of Pythias and was kept constantly on the go. One of our brother Knights, named Elkins, who had recently purchased the stock of books and stationery owned by Ticer & Co., on Bridge Street near the Gallinas River, was down with the smallpox, less than a week after he had taken his inventory. He became the first patient to enter the United Lodge Hospital and was given the best of care. Mr. Cox reported each morning that the patient was improving, but in a few days his case developed into a terrible case of black smallpox, from which he died. Mr. Cox, who had been nursing him, contracted the same malady and also died within the week.

Mrs. Elkins, unknown to any of us, had visited her husband at night and talked with him through an open window. She was at the time stopping at the Central Hotel, where the Meadows Hotel now stands in East Las Vegas. A few days later she developed smallpox and everyone at once left the hotel. The proprietors wanted to turn Mrs. Elkins out of the house and put her in a pest-house. The doctor said it would mean certain death if they attempted to move her at that time. The owners of the hotel appealed to the authorities and orders were placed in the hands of the officers to eject her from the building.

The Knights of Pythias called a hurried meeting and decided to put an inch rope around the entire hotel and place an armed guard over the building, permitting no one to enter. Each guard carried a shot-gun. The officers were not anxious to enter the building; so Mrs. Elkins was not disturbed. In a couple of weeks she was well enough to leave the hotel, which immediately underwent a thorough fumigation and cleaning. The Elkins' store was cared for during the time by the Knights of Pythias, and on the recovery of Mrs. Elkins she very quietly sold out everything and departed with the money, without even saying good-bye, and the Knights of Pythias had to settle all her unpaid bills. Such sometimes is the return made to the liberality of benevolent organizations.

Our bachelor quarters were even invaded, and my roommate Thomas H. Parker was stricken with the dread malady and died. I was now the sole member left. I bought Parker's interest from his mother in England. The *Daily Optic* fought gallantly for Las Vegas and jumped every newspaper in New Mexico that dared to mention smallpox as being in either the New or Old Towns.

On April 1st, 1882, Clark D. Frost, late manager of the Lindell Hotel of St. Louis, left that city with two carloads of men and women, sixty odd in number, who were to take positions in the Montezuma Hotel at the Las Vegas Hot Springs, which was to open and be ready for business on April 17th. Among the party was a well organized band of jubilee singers and minstrel performers, and immediately the young men of Las Vegas were laying plans for serenading parties with good old southern songs.

Charlie Dambmann was one of the many young men who

had migrated from New York, or one of the New England states, to the West. His parents possessed more money than common sense, for they fondly imagined that the West was a good place to start reformations after their offspring had already been spoiled by overindulgence in the free use of money in that wonderful city of New York, where it only took ready cash to provide and supply any venturesome youth with all the enjoyment found in wine, women and cards.

In broadcasting his crop of wild oats, Charlie Dambmann, the scion of a noble tribe, had considerable to do with the world, the flesh and the devil in New York. His good Dutch father came to the conclusion soon that the proper place for such a heathen would be on a ranch out West. Charlie was just thirty-five, and squandering wealth was his peculiar art. The old man calculated that all these things should not deter Ma from giving her consent to the transition of the rich silk importer's lad who never before had been so far away from the scent of salt water. With Fred Althof sent along as manager of the sub-treasury and guardian to see that the 250-pound youth might not go astray or pick up any bad change in the wicked West, and with "Teddy" Hart as valet and lady-in-waiting, the spendthrift from Gotham arrived at Las Vegas in the boom days of 1881. Some kind Samaritan lost no time in selling him Fred Hooper's Box Ranch at Red River Springs.

Young Dambmann brought a lot of fool notions with him. It was all right enough to entertain aristocratic ideas so long as they did not conflict with the customs of the country, but in this particular the young man fell down in at least one instance. He had not been down on the cattle ranch very long before he came up to Las Vegas for a lot of ranch supplies. Among the accoutrements most desired of all was a pagoda for the back yard. As he wanted something unusually fancy regardless of cost, he was taken to F. L. Baker's carpenter shop, where he bargained to have one made for $250.

Then he went over to Paul Marcellino's music store and bought a Chickering grand piano for $1,500, after which he returned to his Box Ranch. When his order had been completed and was ready for shipment, nothing quite so gay in the way of a commode had ever been seen in the whole cattle kingdom, and, like the pimple on Katasha's shoulder, people came for miles to see it.

One morning a letter was received in Las Vegas from Fred Althof, manager of the Dambmann Cattle Company, to hurry up and send out the contraption and piano. A four-horse outfit was secured from Captain Hutton and both were loaded and securely tied on the big flat dray. For fear something might happen to the precious load in going the 120 miles, four of us young bucks got out our saddle horses to form a sort of escort.

A house-warming was given that night at the Box Ranch after we had set up the pagoda on its roost a hundred steps back from the ranch house. The cowboys eyed the improvement contemptuously and said: "Nobody needed all that style out there on the lonely prairie." After remaining there a couple of days to rest ourselves and the stock, we pulled out for home.

It seems that the cowboys took such a dislike to Dambmann's *retirada*, looming up there like a lighthouse in a mist, that it created a vendetta which resulted in disaster to the peace and dignity of the isolated neighborhood. They did not relish the slips of tissue paper they mistook for cigarette papers flying recklessly here and there over the range; so one dark night they got even with the nuisance by hitching their combined lariats onto the pesky thing and dragging it far out on the prairie. Then they set fire to it, and this was the last of such fancy privadas in that locality.

Dambmann was a pleasant fellow to meet, jovial, liberal and withal considerable of a sport, and nothing suited him so well as a game of poker. A few of us in Las Vegas, including myself, were always ready to accommodate him whenever he came to town. He was always accompanied by his valet, "Teddy" Hart, who, of course, rode about ten feet in the rear. I happened to be one of a party going to the Las Vegas Hot Springs on horseback, in which were also Althof, Dambmann, Blake, Dold, Nichols and Houghton. Just behind Dambmann at the regulation distance rode the faithful valet. As we entered the plaza in the Old Town, the horse Dambmann was riding took fright and bolted. We could easily see that Dambmann had completely lost control of his horse and was powerless, having dropped the reins and was now holding on to the pommel of the saddle for dear life.

Just as he reached the southwest corner of the plaza, a man ran out in front of the horse, in an attempt to stop him. This act caused the frightened animal to stop suddenly, and the big boy went over his head, fortunately escaping the stone curbing. The jolt of 250 pounds was terrific, and he was badly bruised, several of his front teeth being knocked out. "Teddy," who was following his master closely, was on the spot about as soon as Dambmann, and, jumping from his mount, assisted the injured man to his feet. Of course we all followed and were there about as quickly as "Teddy." As soon as Dambmann recovered from the shock he began spitting out teeth and blood, and then discovering poor "Teddy" he yelled out: "Say! Teddy, why in hell didn't you stop the damn' beast?" "Teddy" was standing at attention and quickly answered: "Hi did my best, Sir, but my 'orse 'e could not hovertake you, Sir." Dambmann brought "Teddy" from dear Old London, and as he was a regular cockney-English, he dropped his H's at the right time and picked them up again, as they all do. We all laughed except Dambmann and "Teddy." Another horse was brought from the stables of Mendenhall, Hunter & Co., and we continued our ride to the Hot Springs. Many a night have I seen Dambmann in a poker game while "Teddy" was outside holding the horses until daylight, never daring to leave his post.

The Dambmann Cattle Company purchased a good-sized herd of longhorns which was added to the Hooper stock, and they were soon in the cattle business good and plenty. Things seemed to be going on nicely at the Box Ranch and everyone connected with the outfit appeared happy and contented. At an unguarded moment Dambmann gave Althof the slip and took the train for New York, leaving word that he had gone on to visit his father and mother, although neither had expressed any desire for such a visit so soon after his reformation in the West.

The young man happened to strike Broadway just as Maurice Grau returned from Europe with the greatest grand opera company ever seen in this country. The leading lady in the opera company was the Russian diva, Madame Nixau, and she not only captivated all of New York, but also the partially reformed young man from the Box ranch, Red River Springs, N. Mex. After finishing a brilliant week in New York City, the opera company moved to Philadelphia, and the New Mexico cattleman went along as part of the leading lady's wardrobe.

She was to sing *Carmen* that night, and every seat in the house had been sold. The Quaker aristocracy were seated, but the curtain did not go up for a long time. Then it was whispered around that the prima donna had not only jumped her contract under a $50,000 forfeiture, but had taken the westbound train for New Mexico in company with Charles Dambmann, Jr. Grau, forced to put on an understudy, got through the season with a tremendous loss financially and suffered as well a great jolt to his professional reputation, from which he never recovered.

The Eastern papers were full of the scandal, and the next day when the news reached Las Vegas that the loving couple were coming in a private car all of his friends began to get busy. A meeting was called to ascertain what was the best thing to do, as it was a splendid chance to get a lot of free advertising for Las Vegas, and, besides, it would please our money-spending cattleman, who was, after all, quite an asset in our town. Well, the vote was unanimous in favor of a big reception, with a brass band and a banquet fitting the occasion. It was a great success and the talk of the town for years, for it was pulled off entirely by the men, much to the horror of the women who were not in on the festivities.

When the excitement was all over the couple settled down for a long honeymoon in the Montezuma Hotel at the Hot Springs. They took the east bridal suite, which, with extras, cost Mr. Dambmann about one hundred dollars per day, and some kind of entertainment was pulled off every night. The town was well populated with rich young Englishmen who had been caught in the cattle swirl and they were the favored guests at the blue suite. A game of baccarat was set up in true Monte Carlo style, with Madame "Neezo," as she was called, sitting at the head of the table as banker, and every one had a good time and pleasant games. In one night the beautiful and talented prima donna won $21,000 in cold cash.

Such gayety could not last forever, and one evening the couple headed for the East, but not in a private car, nor was Chris Wiegand there with his brass band. Madame Nixau never sang in America again, but returned to Europe with a good-sized fortune. As for the forfeiture, Dambmann compromised the breach of contract with Maurice Grau for $40,000. The Dambmann Cattle Company continued on for a few years and finally went on the rocks, but genial Fred Althof saw that all the debts were paid.

> "Look 'round, the wrecks of play behold,
> Estates dismembered, mortgaged and sold."

Dambmann in after years accepted a position with a life insurance company and went as its representative to Austria, where he remained until his death. Fred Althof I afterwards met in New York, where he was representing a champagne house. "Teddy" Hart remained in New Mexico. He had saved up some money and finally settled in Gallup, N. Mex., where he opened a hardware store and made considerable money, got married and reared a family of two girls, who in time married and settled in the West.

Soon after the Atchison, Topeka & Santa Fé Railroad reached Las Vegas the directors of the railroad authorized the purchase of the Las Vegas Hot Springs and the building of the Montezuma Hotel and a branch railroad running from the main line at Las Vegas to the Hot Springs, a distance of six miles. They at once began a wise system of advertising which brought many people of prominence from all over the world to the Hot Springs as a health resort. The Marquis of Lorne and his pretty little wife, the Princess Louise, daughter of Queen Victoria, were among the many visitors. They remained several days and then departed for California, where they were so well pleased with their reception on the coast that they concluded to linger in those parts much longer than they at first intended.

Both were very popular at the Hot Springs, and all those who had the good fortune of meeting them expressed the wish that the climate of California might be of benefit to the princess, for she was in rather poor health at the time of her visit to the springs. Of one thing I am quite sure: everybody at the Hot Springs was quite in love with the little princess, including myself.

About this same time another family connected with British royalty arrived at the Las Vegas Hot Springs for a visit, Captain Manners and his beautiful and charming wife. They were enjoying a trip through the western part of the United States and wished to live in true western style — camping out in a large wall tent. The Hot Springs Company gladly welcomed them, and their tent was pitched within the grounds adjacent to the Montezuma Hotel, where they dined and roamed about at will with their many congenial friends. They were delightful people to meet, and the captain was a most jovial good fellow and greatly enjoyed an occasional glass of Scotch whiskey with ginger ale or a cool bottle of wine. At this particular time he was a captain in the British army, but some years later succeeded to the title and estate of the Duke of Rutland. They greatly enjoyed their stay of several weeks, and one very important happening, which will always serve to recall the Las Vegas Hot Springs with pleasure, was that during their visit Mrs. Manners gave birth to a daughter, an elder sister of the much admired Lady Diana, who proved such a success in the play, *The Miracle.* An item in the *Optic* under "Spring Sprays" has this to say: "Mrs. Capt. Manners will leave the Hot Springs for London, England, on Saturday. Captain Manners will go on to the ranch of the Dambmann Cattle Company. Springs people will be sorry to see this estimable couple depart, as they have made hosts of friends during their stay here. Their long residence at our favorable resort has made it seem a second home to them, and both the Captain and his wife are loath to leave the place."

Captain Manners, the Duke of Rutland, died some years ago, but his wife and her beautiful daughters are still living in London.

Chapter XXIII

THROUGHOUT these pages dealing with my own experiences on the frontier there has appeared in the background many times my father Don Miguel Antonio Otero (I). I have already given some indication of the long, distinguished service he rendered New Mexico prior to 1862, when he gave up politics in order to devote his whole attention to his business interests. I have also shown how he was called away from these when the Atchison, Topeka & Santa Fé Railroad Company started to build from Topeka, Kans., towards the Territory of New Mexico and desired his services in securing its right-of-way. To accomplish what was necessary, he had to be most of the time at the front, and such items in the *Daily Optic* as the following show his activity.

From the issue of December 11th, 1879:

Hon. Miguel A. Otero joined William B. Strong, General Manager of the A. T. & S. F. R., George O. Manchester, Assistant General Manager, J. F. Goddard, General Freight Agent, George B. Lake, Division Superintendent, A. A. Robinson, Chief Engineer, and many Directors from Boston, on a trip to the end of the track.

Again, from the issue of January 8th, 1880:

Governor Anthony and Hon. Miguel A. Otero came into Las Vegas one day early this week. They were looking after the interest of the N.M. & S.F.R.R., and departed again for the ancient city.

Also, from the issue of January 10th, 1880:

Governor Anthony, Hon. Miguel A. Otero and Judge Henry L. Waldo arrived from Santa Fé on last night's train, and went east to Boston to attend a Directors' meeting of the A.T. & S.F.R.R.

Finally, this from the *Daily Optic* of April 3rd, 1880:

"Hon. Miguel A. Otero, Vice-President of the New Mexico and

Southern Pacific Railroad, the Jay Gould of Montezuma, was met by an *Optic* Inquisitor this morning, and the following confab took place:—

REPORTER: "Back from the south, I see?"

MR. OTERO: "Yes, I have been to Albuquerque and Bernalillo."

REPORTER: "How is Albuquerque panning out?"

MR. OTERO: "The New Town, I suppose you mean. A town company has laid out more than a hundred acres in town lots, which are selling rapidly and many buildings are going up."

REPORTER: "When will the Santa Fé Railroad get there?"

MR. OTERO: "About Tuesday, the 6th instant, possibly a day sooner."

REPORTER: "How about the Atlantic and Pacific Railroad? Will they build out of Albuquerque soon?"

MR. OTERO: "Yes. The money has been secured and there will be little delay," etc., etc.

These several items from the newspaper have been given to show the activity of my father in the construction of the Atchison, Topeka & Santa Fé Railroad through New Mexico. I would not be putting it too strongly if I said that it was entirely through his personal influence that favorable legislation such as was desired by the railroad officials was secured from the Territorial Legislature. It was also largely through his prestige and effort that the right-of-way through the Territory needed by the Santa Fé Route was secured without any compensation being demanded of the railroad, not even by my father himself, who worked untiringly for the railroad from 1873 until his death.

On numerous occasions I acted as my father's secretary, and was present with him at a meeting held in Santa Fé when Governor George T. Anthony, William B. Strong and A. A. Robinson urged my father to submit a bill for his services, saying to him: "Don Miguel, your services would be hard to estimate, for they have been worth to the company many thousands of dollars. We think you ought to put in your bill accordingly, and we will take pleasure in approving it." My father positively declined to do what they suggested, his refusal being put in the short but sincere statement: "I was working for New Mexico, and I am satisfied if my Territory gets the benefit of my labors."

Although my father considered himself definitely out of politics, he was unable to escape one more plunge into the whirlpool, although cesspool might be a better appellation, considering the malodorousness of New Mexican politics even fifty years ago. In the summer of 1880 the politicians of the Territory were busy getting ready for the coming election in the fall. The Democrats in looking around for a suitable nominee for Delegate to Congress felt that my father was the most popular man they could find, and so without his having been at all active in the matter they nominated him by acclamation at the Territorial convention held during that summer at Santa Fé and sent a committee to notify him of this action (he being in Santa Fé at the time) and to invite him to come and address the convention.

When the committee called upon my father, he concluded that the only course open to him was to respond to the wish of his party so strikingly and strongly expressed. So he accompanied the committee back to the hall where the convention was in session and, on his entrance, received an ovation, the delegates standing on their seats and cheering for several minutes. When the demonstration ended, my father was introduced by the chairman of the committee and delivered a rousing speech, which worked the convention up to the highest pitch of enthusiasm, especially when in the peroration he accepted the nomination and promised a vigorous and successful campaign against the nominee of the Republicans, Mr. Tranquilino Luna.

The political pot boiled and seethed all during the summer and early fall, the election taking precedence of everything else in the Territory. Rumors of great frauds planned by the Republicans were rife on the streets of every town in the Territory, and the Democrats made preparations to do what they could to check such tactics. But their efforts were unavailing. When the election came off, the result showed that under any fair and honest count my father would have been declared elected by a handsome majority, but through the basest and most barefaced frauds ever practiced in any country, he was robbed of his victory, and Tranquilino Luna declared elected.

I happened to be sent to Socorro County to watch for evidence of fraudulent practices in the river precincts and to gain all the facts possible as to frauds in Valencia County, where it was said they voted the sheep; and I can speak knowingly of what really took place in that county and which was verified a considerable time after the election. There was a precinct in Valencia County which had been specially created for the sole purpose of stealing the election. The returns from this precinct gave Luna nearly a thousand votes, every one of which was dishonest and fraudulent, while my father secured not a single vote in the precinct. The newly created precinct turned out on investigation to be merely a sheep camp belonging to the Luna family. A few years later Jesus M. Luna, an older brother of Tranquilino, and I were talking over the election in his home at Los Lunas and he admitted to me that my father had been honestly elected, but declared unblushingly that they had to count his brother Tranquilino in by fair means or foul.

I heard Mr. Worth Keene, then a railroad contractor on the line of the Atlantic & Pacific, building west from Albuquerque, tell how he and his camp had contributed to the polling of those thousand votes. In the conversation I was one of the party who heard Mr. Keene telling Solomon Luna, another brother of Tranquilino, how he had carried out the instructions given him by the Republican organization of Valencia County, which were as follows: "You must send from your camp six of your men in a light spring wagon drawn by a good team of mules to the voting place. These men are to vote, and then they will be given a slip of paper from one of the judges of election on which is written six names, which they are to use when they next appear at the voting place. They must then return to the wagon and drive out behind one of the sand-hills in the vicinity of the ranch house being used as a voting place. After each one has selected one of the names on the paper they drive back to the voting place and again vote under the names given them. This same procedure must be kept up all day." "I sent six of my most reliable men and they continued voting from sunrise to sunset, at the end of which time they had cast nearly one thousand votes for Tranquilino Luna. As not a single Democrat ticket was in evidence of course none was voted." All during the story Solomon Luna was noticeably uneasy and worried, no doubt fearing that Worth Keene might tell something they had been holding back from the public. He tried hard to stop him without attracting my attention, but Keene went on with his story, giving full details and seemed apparently proud of the part he had taken in the unlawful act. Finally it reached the point where Solomon's embarrassment became too noticeable, so I said: "Let Worth finish his story, for I heard exactly the same story from your brother Jesus some time ago. Worth has evidently forgotten that it was my father who was running against Tranquilino at the time." There was a death-like silence for several minutes, broken by Solomon inviting us all to take a drink.

What was done in Valencia County was but a sample of what was done by the Republican Party throughout the entire Territory. At the time my father was urged by many of his friends to bring a contest, for the general opinion was that this was one of the most daring and outrageous cases of stealing an election ever perpetrated in New Mexico or elsewhere. But such a contest would have had to be fought out before Congress, and as the House of Representatives was then in the hands of the Republicans, my father thought it useless to go to the trouble and expense of a contest. His feelings were, however, so strong about the matter that I believe had he lived until the next election he would have been willing to enter the fray again and try conclusions with Mr. Tranquilino Luna. It is true that he would in all likelihood have encountered the same chicanery and fraud that again resulted in the defeat of the Democratic candidate, Francisco A. Manzanares, but he might have felt encouraged to make a contest as did Manzanares. The complexion of the House of Representatives had changed by that time and was Democratic, so when the frauds and stealings were shown, Francisco A. Manzanares secured his seat, to the entire satisfaction of the people of New Mexico.

The first telephone company to organize and do business in New Mexico was organized by my father, Page B. Otero, Miguel A. Otero, Jr., A. G. Hood, and Charlie Keimle. The first telephone line built in New Mexico was built by the above-named directors between Las Vegas and the Las Vegas Hot Springs. This was all done in the year 1880. The Las Vegas Telephone Company was organized with Miguel A. Otero as President, and Miguel A. Otero, Jr., Secretary and Treasurer. We put in an exchange under A. G. Hood, General Manager. Miss Nellie Cummings took charge of the switch-board, and I believe was first "Hello Girl" in New Mexico; she held this position for some years, until her marriage with Mr. Otto G. Schaefer on November 5th, 1884, when she was succeeded by Mrs. Anna B. Shout.

Many people were invited throughout the Territory to assist in the ceremonies attending the completion of the first railroad to enter Santa Fé, next to the oldest town in the United States, and I was one of a party to represent Las Vegas during this great event. The Atchison, Topeka &

Santa Fé Railroad reached this city on February 15th, 1880, and the occasion was celebrated by an excursion to the Missouri river in Pullman coaches, given complimentary by the railroad company through the New Mexico representatives, Governor George T. Anthony, Hon. Miguel A. Otero, and Hon. Henry L. Waldo to the 24th Legislative Assembly, then in session, other territorial officials and prominent business men throughout the Territory. The train was in charge of Major Thomas J. Anderson, the General Passenger Agent of the railroad, and visited Topeka, Lawrence, Kansas City, Atchison, and Leavenworth.

In the same year, 1880, on May 14th, the Albuquerque Street Railroad Company was incorporated, and cars were soon running, the first street railroad to be operated in New Mexico. A few months later, on December 20th, the Las Vegas Street Railway Company was incorporated, and cars commenced running shortly thereafter.

In an earlier chapter of this book I mention my uncle, Don Manuel A. Otero, and give a description of his home at La Constancia, Valencia County, and also our family's visit with him during the year 1872. He and my father were the last of the immediate family of my grandparents and were most devoted brothers. We were all greatly shocked at receiving a telegram from my cousin announcing the death of my Uncle Manuel which occurred at his home on Saturday, February 25th, 1882.

The Las Vegas *Daily Optic* of Monday, February 27th, had this mention of his death: "Another link that binds us to the past has been severed by the death at a ripe old age of Don Manuel A. Otero at La Constancia, Valencia County, on Saturday. The disease that carried him off was typhoid pneumonia. Don Manuel was an older brother of Don Miguel A. Otero, and the father of Mrs. Dr. Henriquez of this city. The deceased was surrounded by every comfort that heart could wish; he was an excellent man, kind, considerate, thoughtful, and his life was singularly free from the vices and follies of our common humanity. All respected him for his many virtues. In the several spheres of husband, father, and citizen, he occupied a position worthy of emulation. One by one the old settlers are passing away. They will all soon be gone."

Don Manuel was born on March 20th, 1815, and had not quite reached the age of sixty-seven years.

My father was almost heartbroken over the death of his only brother and never fully recovered from the shock. The family had scarcely become reconciled over this death before another one of the immediate family followed.

Don Ambrosio Armijo died in Albuquerque on Easter Sunday, April 9th, 1882, at the age of 65 years. He was my uncle by marriage, having married Maria Candelaria Otero, my father's youngest sister, who preceded him to the grave. They were the parents of five children, four of whom, Perfecto, Jesus, Mariano, and Mrs. Symington, survive them.

Don Ambrosio Armijo was well and favorably known throughout New Mexico. He was born at Ranchos de Albuquerque in 1817, and was a most useful citizen to the community in which he resided, as well as one of the most prominent men in the Territory. Before the advent of the railroad into New Mexico, Don Ambrosio Armijo owned and operated one of the largest mule trains carrying freight across the plains from the end of the railroad to points in New Mexico. While he never accompanied the outfit himself, it was always in charge of one of his sons. He was a large property owner and besides conducted one of the largest mercantile establishments in Old Albuquerque.

Just at this time great preparations were being made for the opening of the Montezuma Hotel at the Las Vegas Hot Springs by the Atchison, Topeka & Santa Fé Railroad. The day had been set and elaborate invitations were sent out for April 17th, 1882. The directors of the railroad held a meeting in the morning at Santa Fé, and my father was again elected Vice-President of the New Mexico and Southern Pacific Railroad. After the adjournment of the meeting they all came over on a special train to participate in the opening of the hotel. At the banquet and reception Colonel W. G. Dickinson of Topeka, Kans., was the master of ceremonies. Don Miguel A. Otero, my father, was called upon to respond to the toast, *Railroads as a Civilizer*. In being introduced, Don Miguel was mentioned as a man whose name is familiar to everyone who is at all acquainted with the history of New Mexico. After making his salutation, he proceeded in the following classic language:

"I cannot better express my feelings on this auspicious occasion, and in the presence of this brilliant assemblage, than by relating the beautiful and pathetic superstition of the Pecos Indians, whose home, for ages, had been in the valley contiguous to that in which we meet tonight. These brave and simple-minded people implicitly believed that their mighty but ill-fated emperor, the glorious Montezuma, disappeared from view amid the clouds of their native mountains, that he promised to return to his adoring people once more, after ages had passed away. With trusting faith they believed his words; and he promised when the day of his return arrived that he would come in glory from the east — his face bright and fair as the noonday sun, and clad in all the garments of glory. Century after century passed away but still they kept alive their sacred fire, which burned as brightly as their undying faith, but at length the fire in their temple and their faith died out. The last remnant of the faithful old tribe has disappeared from the homes of their fathers and the ancient shrine is in ruins, but we, who fill their places, have lived to see the return of the mighty chieftain. With power and majesty he comes, with the ancient sun-god from the east, and tonight we hail his coming in the new and splendid halls of the Montezuma!

After the banquet the spacious dining hall was cleared of its tables and the floor prepared for the dance. At 9:30 Prof. Helm's famous Fourth Cavalry orchestra sounded the grand

Miguel Antonio Otero (1), the author's father.

march and the ball was inaugurated under most favorable auspices.

There were fourteen dances on the program, which kept the "light fantastic" feet in a bustle till eight in the morning. It was one of the grandest affairs ever given in New Mexico up to that time.

About three weeks after the opening of the Montezuma Hotel, as above related, my father was busily engaged in pushing the work of building the branch railroad from the town of Bernalillo, now the county seat of Sandoval County, to the Jemez Hot Springs, and he was already planning for an excursion, to be made from Las Vegas, Santa Fé and Albuquerque to celebrate the opening of the new hotel at the Springs. At this time the hotel was almost completed and ready for furnishing. About the middle of the month of May my father returned to Las Vegas. While there he met his old friend, J. M. Studebaker, who had just arrived from South Bend, Ind. Stopping at the Hot Springs at this time was another old friend, Michael Spangler, sheriff of Arapahoe County, Colo. They were both anxious for a fishing trip into the mountains, so my father arranged to have me take them out, as he had to return at once to the Jemez Hot Springs. I quickly arranged the details, and the following morning after my father's departure south, we started out with every intention of staying for at least a couple of weeks in the mountains. In our outfit we had two covered wagons and complete camping and fishing equipment and two extra men; one to cook and the other to take care of the camp, look after the horses and attend to all the chores. I rode my saddle pony, Kiowa, while Alex Savajeau took his horse and accompanied me on horseback. In the party were J. M. Studebaker, Michael Spangler, R. J. Holmes, Alex Savajeau, myself and the two men servants.

Late that same afternoon we were camped on a beautiful stream where the speckled beauties were very plentiful, we having caught, in a few minutes, sufficient trout for our supper. We were tired and went to bed soon after eating. The next morning we all started out long before sunrise and returned for breakfast about ten o'clock with our baskets filled with good-sized trout.

Almost immediately after eating my breakfast a queer sensation came over me, something like a premonition which seemed to be calling me home. Finally I could stand it no longer and reluctantly told Mr. Studebaker, and at the same time advised him that my action need not interfere with the party as I would take Kiowa and ride back alone. They, however, would not listen to such a proposition on my part, all of them insisting upon going with me. We reached Las Vegas late that same afternoon and the first man I met was Harry W. Kelly, who asked me if I had been home, saying: "Your father, Don Miguel, is a very sick man; he arrived this morning from the Jemez Hot Springs, on a special train from Bernalillo." I went immediately to our home and found my father very low with an attack of pneumonia. He seemed greatly relieved when he saw me enter the room and said he wanted to have a talk with me, but Doctor Gordon thought I had better wait until the next day. The following morning he complained of feeling cold, and he called to us boys, Page and myself, to go down to Houghton's Hardware Store and bring back a couple of oil burning stoves to put in his room. He got up and walked into my sister's room and got into her bed, saying, "It is too cold in that room." We left him talking to my mother and Judge John F. Bostwick, his attorney, who was joking with him about being sick.

Just as we had selected the stoves and were in the act of leaving Houghton's store with them, Judge Bostwick appeared at the door and said: "Boys, leave the stoves; it is all over with Don Miguel; he died just as you were leaving the house." It happened to be Decoration Day, May 30, 1882.

The news of my father's death spread rapidly over both

the Old and New Towns and people called by the hundreds. The entire Territory was in mourning and telegrams poured in from all over New Mexico and much of the western country.

The first part of the year 1882 in New Mexico had rather a heavy death toll among the prominent old settlers, as Don Manuel A. Otero, Don Ambrosio Armijo and Don Miguel A. Otero all died within ninety days' time.

Our family burial place being in Riverside cemetery, Denver, Colo., where my sister Gertrude is buried, we decided to bury my father there. The Atchison, Topeka & Santa Fé Railroad officials placed a fully equipped train at our disposal for the family and those friends who wished to attend the funeral at Denver, and hundreds went with us from all parts of the Territory.

On June 2nd the Denver *Press* sent out the following telegram to the *Daily Optic:*

THE OTERO OBSEQUIES

THE LAST SAD RITES CONDUCTED WITH GREAT CEREMONY

The funeral services of Don Miguel A. Otero are now begun, with the preparations of the most elaborate order. The Denver lodges of Free Masons have charge of the obsequies and inter the remains with all the beautiful ceremonies of the mystic order. The weather is threatening rain but nevertheless Trinity Memorial Church is well filled with the most prominent people of Colorado, including Governor Pitkin, all the state officials in a body, and a large number of prominent railroad officials.

The floral decorations are very beautiful and appropriate about the altar. The casket is covered with wreaths and festoons, and in the center are the words "Rest" in immortelles. Beneath is the silver plate bearing the simple inscription of the deceased's name, with the date of his birth and death.

The remains are fairly preserved but are not opened to view today.

Rev. Charles H. Marshall preaches the funeral sermon and by the hour *The Optic* goes to press this evening, New Mexico's greatest son will be lying in Riverside, in the vault by the side of his lost daughter Gertie. Miss Mamie, the only surviving daughter, reaches Kansas City this evening, and will arrive in Denver tomorrow night.

THE TRIBUTE OF THE PRESS.

The *Republican* and the *Rocky Mountain News*, of this morning, devote much space editorially to the memory of the late lamented Don Miguel. Other papers yet to issue will contain tributes of respect to the memory of the mighty fallen.

The bereaved Otero family and party of Las Vegas friends return home on Monday.

The *Daily Optic* of June 2nd says editorially:

The well-written obituaries of the late Don Miguel A. Otero, which have appeared, would fill a large sized scrap book, and he deserved every word of eulogy passed upon him. Such men as he do not exist in every community, and such men as he are seldom appreciated until after the dread summons have been served upon them.

I feel that this chapter devoted so largely to the close of my father's long and useful career would not be complete without a biographical sketch which will give in conspectus the outstanding events in his life. While doing this involves some slight repetition of what appears here and there in the book, I believe it gains in weight to be assembled in one place and to be enlarged with some additional material.

Don Miguel Antonio Otero (I), was born at Valencia, County of Valencia, Territory of New Mexico (at that time a province of Old Mexico), on June 21st, 1829, and was the youngest child of Don Vicente Otero and Doña Gertrudes Chaves y Aragon.

He was first sent to a private school at Valencia, conducted by a Catholic priest, where he remained until he was eleven years of age, learning the rudiments of Spanish, arithmetic and religion. In 1841 he went to the St. Louis University at St. Louis, and remained there until the Mexican War broke out in 1846, when he was recalled home by his parents. In the spring of 1847 he was sent of his own choice and at his own request to Pingree's College at Fishkill on the Hudson, New York. His father gave him his own choice of many schools which had been recommended, and he chose a Protestant institution so as to acquaint himself with the difference between the two ruling religions; the Roman Catholic and the Protestant. His mother had destined him for the priesthood, but the two years' attendance at the Pingree College liberalized his views without changing his religion.

At the Pingree College he became a Professor on the Faculty and was made Assistant Professor of Latin and Greek. He was a very studious young man, worked constantly with his books, and soon was made Assistant to the Principal of the College, a great honor for one of his age. This position he held for a term of two years, and to the entire satisfaction of the Principal. His school and college life covered a period of twelve years. Under the advice of the Principal of the Pingree College he took up the study of law. He first began his studies in the office of Hon. James Thayer, a distinguished lawyer of the State of New York, who was at that time living in Fishkill. This was in the year 1849. In the winter of 1849-1850 he went to New York City and entered the law office of General Sanford, remaining there one year, at the end of which time he decided to return to St. Louis, where he at once entered the law office of Hon. Trusten Polk, who was afterwards elected Governor of and still later United States Senator from Missouri. He completed his studies in his office, was admitted to the bar of the State of Missouri early in the spring of 1852, and at once took out his license to practice in that state.

His father having died a year previous, and his mother

being anxious to see him now that his studies had been completed, he decided to return to New Mexico at once and visit at the old home. After a month spent with his mother at Valencia, his brother, Judge Antonio Jose Otero, sent him to California in charge of a large herd of sheep, which he soon disposed of in the mining camps. On his return home he immediately went to Albuquerque and began the practice of his profession in that city, but very soon afterwards he was appointed private secretary to Governor William Carr Lane, the second Civil Governor of the Territory of New Mexico, and he served as such during the entire term of Governor Lane.

In September, 1852, he was almost unanimously elected to the Territorial Legislature as a member of the House of Representatives from Valencia County, and while he was still under the required age of twenty-four years, as provided by the law, the House waived it in his case, as no objections were raised. So he served during the entire Second Legislative Assembly, which convened on the first Monday in December, 1852. In this contest he represented the progressive American element in the Territory. The Otero, Chaves and Armijo families were all for the American Party as against the Mexican Party.

On the acquisition of the Territory of New Mexico, from the Republic of Mexico, in 1846, his oldest brother, Don Antonio Jose Otero, was appointed Associate Justice of the Supreme Court of New Mexico and Judge of the Second Judicial District Court by President James K. Polk. Judge Otero was one of the ablest and best judges the Territory of New Mexico ever had.

In 1855 my father was elected a delegate to the United States Congress against a powerful anti-American priest-ridden party. Just previous to this election, he had been appointed United States District Attorney by President Franklin Pierce, but he declined this honor. He had, however, served for a while as Attorney General of the Territory under Governor David Meriwether.

He served as a delegate to the United States Congress, representing the Democratic Party for three consecutive terms, 1855 to 1861 inclusive. He was a strong advocate for the 35th parallel line for a railroad to the Pacific, and he lived to see the realization of his hopes and pet measure in the construction of the Atlantic & Pacific Railroad, now the Atchison, Topeka & Santa Fé Railroad Coast Lines. During his term of service in Congress he also made an effort to have New Mexico admitted as a State, but failed, mainly owing to the Legislature's neglecting to call a Constitutional Convention. He was a strong advocate of the Kansas-Nebraska Bill presented by Senator Douglas.

President Abraham Lincoln tendered him the appointment of Minister to Spain, but he declined the same because he felt it his duty to remain in New Mexico, his home and that of his people. President Lincoln, upon the urgent request of the delegate, Hon. John S. Watts, Republican Delegate to Congress from New Mexico, appointed him Secretary of the Territory and Acting Governor in 1861, but on account of his Southern proclivities and warm sympathies he was not confirmed by the Senate, and so only served from April until September, 1861.

In politics, my father was always a strong Democrat, and was a delegate to the National Democratic Convention held at Charleston, S. C., in 1860, and cast his vote in that body for Douglas. He was what was known as a Liberal, Progressive and Constitutional Democrat. He never favored secession but his sympathies were with the South.

My father and mother were married at St. Louis on April 2nd, 1857.

Mary Josephine Blackwood, my mother, was born in the old St. Charles Hotel at New Orleans, La., on November 11th, 1840. Her father, Samuel Blackwood, was a lineal descendant of James Blackwood, founder of Blackwood's Magazine, published in Edinburgh, Scotland. Her mother was a Carroll of Baltimore and a member of the same family as Charles Carroll of Carrollton, Md., one of the signers of the Declaration of Independence. Her father settled at what was then known as Elliott's Mills, N. J., now Elizabethtown, N. J. He was a planter and a man of considerable wealth for those days, owning most of the land about Elliott's Mills. He visited Galveston, Texas, during the summer of 1840, and while there contracted a case of cholera and died. Her mother, accompanied by a negro nurse, travelled to New Orleans en route to Galveston, and while at the St. Charles Hotel, Mary Josephine, my mother, was born. The sailing vessel was about to leave so my grandmother, nurse, and baby took passage while she was still in a weakened condition, and the second day out she died and was buried in the Gulf of Mexico, leaving my mother, only a few days old, with the nurse. They never left the ship at Galveston, but returned in the same vessel to New Orleans. The captain, aided by the old negro nurse, soon got in touch with the family and an uncle, Judge Page of Virginia, hastened to New Orleans and took charge of the baby. A few years later Mrs. Timmons, my mother's oldest sister, took the child to her home at Charleston, S. C.

My mother's oldest brother was Page Blackwood, a very successful merchant, in business at St. Louis. Another brother, William Gardiner Blackwood, a young law student, was reading law in the office of Trusten Polk at the very time my father was studying in the same office, and they became warm personal friends and through this friendship my father met his sister, Mary Josephine, who happened to be on a visit to her brothers, and this meeting culminated a few years later in marriage. The following year, 1858, William Gardiner Blackwood was appointed a Judge of the Supreme Court of New Mexico, through the influence of my father, who was at that time a member of the United States Congress. Another brother was Major John G. Blackwood of Longstreet's Corps, McLaw's Division, French's Brigade, 18th Regular Mississippi Volunteers, C. S. A., before Richmond, Va., 1863-1864. He was a lieutenant on board the *Alabama* under Captain Semmes, C. S. N., which fought the *Kearsarge* under Captain Winslow, off the English Channel in June, 1864, resulting in the sinking of the *Alabama*. During the engagement he was struck by a piece of shell and his jaw was shattered so badly he had to have a silver jaw put in. After the war he took command of a sailing vessel and on his first voyage went around the world.

My mother was a most worthy representative of both of those distinguished families, the Blackwoods and Carrolls, in the beauty of her person, the grace of her manners, her brilliant intellect and the loveliness of her character. She attended school at Charleston, S. C., and graduated from the Sacred Heart Convent. She was quite a society woman and popular, well known and admired in Washington, New Mexico, St. Louis and Denver, as well as other points where the Otero family resided. She was lavish in her charities, and of a very refined taste.

By this marriage were born the following children: Page Blackwood Otero, born at Washington, D. C., January 14th, 1858; Miguel Antonio Otero (II), born at St. Louis, Mo., October 17th, 1859; Gertrude Vincentia Otero, born at Leavenworth, Kans., March 15th, 1865; Mamie Josephine Otero, born at Leavenworth, Kans., July 16th, 1867. Of these children, Page Blackwood married and had three children, all of them now residing at Los Angeles, Cal. My sister Gertrude died at El Moro, Colo., on December 11th, 1876. Mamie Josephine Otero was married to Henry J. O'Bryan at Las Vegas, N. Mex., on June 7th, 1888. Of this union there were two children:

Marie Aileen O'Bryan, born at Las Vegas, N. Mex., July

19th, 1889; Henry Duross O'Bryan, born at Denver, Colo., March 18th, 1892.

Henry J. O'Bryan died at Tacoma, Wash. My sister, Mrs. Mamie Josephine O'Bryan, died at Santa Fé, N. Mex., in St. Vincent's Sanitarium, on October 4th, 1928, from an automobile accident on the highway between Little La Majada Hill and La Majada Hill on Monday, September 24th, 1928, at about 3:00 P. M.

Myself, wife and one son, Miguel A. Otero (IV), all live in Santa Fé. My son married Katherine Stinson at Santa Fé, on November 28th, 1927.

Very soon after my retirement from the office of Governor of the Territory of New Mexico, which occurred on January 22nd, 1906, many of my good friends came to see me, and to insist that I write my memoirs. They, of course, knew of my early life on the frontier during the building of the Kansas-Pacific Railroad from Kansas City, Mo., to Denver, Colo., 1866 to 1871, and later the building of the Atchison, Topeka & Santa Fé Railroad from Granada, Colo., to Las Vegas, N. Mex., 1873 to 1879. They said: "We want you to include your very aggressive, fearless and businesslike administration while you were serving as Governor of the Territory, and as well the interesting history of your political activity, beginning a short time before the death of your distinguished father and continuing, practically, throughout your entire life."

Almost immediately after the death of my father, my life took a more serious turn. Unfortunately for me, I was named one of the administrators of my father's estate. This position interfered greatly with my own affairs and compelled me to act as wet nurse for the rest of the family, a thankless job at best, and one I have often wished I had rejected at the time of my appointment. Finally, I made a full and complete settlement of the estate and as guardian for my minor sister, by turning both positions over to my mother's and sister's attorney, Hon. William A. Vincent, receiving my discharge by the Probate Court of San Miguel County, N. Mex., coupled with receipts from all those in interest. My father might, and undoubtedly would, have become immensely wealthy had he lived a few years longer. He left no will, and as he was comparatively a poor man, both my brother and myself declined to take our shares, so everything went to my mother and sister. I was scarcely twenty-three years old when my father died, and at that tender age had to assume many responsibilities which were forced upon me, not at all to my liking or desire.

After completing my several terms in the office of Governor of the Territory, my first thought was to take a needed rest, and so I decided that an ocean voyage would be just the thing for me. I took my son, Miguel Junior, at that time fourteen years of age, with me, and he was truly a splendid companion. We secured passage on the steamer *Prinzessin Victoria Luise*, sailing from New York on Thursday, April 5th, 1906, for a Mediterranean cruise. After finishing the cruise, we continued our trip through many interesting places in Europe. We were gone several months, returning home in the month of September.

On our arrival in Santa Fé we were met by a large delegation of citizens with a brass band and many carriages and escorted to our home; and later in the evening I attended a large banquet given in honor of my homecoming attended by more than a hundred of the most prominent citizens from the Territory at large. And I might add that the Volstead Law was not then in force, and champagne flowed like water.

I had scarcely gotten settled when my same old friends again importuned that I take up the writing of my memoirs, but I hesitated for many years. Finally, after renewed requests, I became overpersuaded by a few of my closest friends, who argued that I was one of a very few, at that time living, who had actually taken part in "blazing the way across the plains," and that I owed it to the coming generations to allow them to read first hand my early experiences covering a most interesting period of our country's history, in the early settlement and development of the New West. I fully realized the enormous labor and time necessary to the undertaking, but I at last reluctantly consented to try it out. Many times during my trials and tribulations I have threatened to destroy my manuscript and give up the work, but somehow, as I progressed, it became more and more interesting to me, so I promised myself that I would finish it, if at all possible. In accumulating the necessary data I soon became convinced that one book would be much too large to handle with ease and comfort, so I decided to limit this volume. I chose, for many reasons, to complete it up to the date of the death of my dear and respected father, for we were devoted chums all during his lifetime, from my very earliest recollection until his premature death at the early age of fifty-two. Naturally, I depended largely on my father's good and wholesome advice, and soon after his sudden and untimely death, I found myself thrown altogether upon my own resources, but I soon learned that in this life one must depend largely upon oneself, and I was not long in learning my lesson, for I had gained a wonderful experience for one so young by my association with men who were much older than myself and I meant to use the knowledge thus acquired, judiciously, fearlessly and honestly.

My second volume, beginning with matters arising immediately following my father's death, will relate important events in my life, including my political career, and will cover more especially the nine years I served as the Governor of the Territory of New Mexico, under three appointments, two from President William McKinley and one from President Theodore Roosevelt.

I sincerely hope, my many readers and friends, after reading this book, may continue with the one to follow, for I intend to state absolute facts in connection with my three terms as Governor of New Mexico, let the chips fall where they may.

INDEX

Abbott, Emma, 255, 256, 257
Able, Cliff W., 119, 227
Ainslie, S. R., 41
Ainslie, Walter, 47
Alexis, Grand Duke of Russia, 50, 53, 54, 55, 56
Allen, Jim, 194, 196, 197, 198
Allen, Johnny, 202, 203, 204
Allison, Clay, 114, 120, 121, 122, 123, 124, 125, 126, 127
Allison, John, 122, 124, 125
Allison, William H. H., 116, 117, 118
Althof, Fred, 261, 262, 263, 264, 265
Anderson, Major Thomas J., 274
Angel, Santiago, 186
Anthony, Governor George T., 269, 274
Arbuckle, Mart, 114, 115
Armijo, Don Ambrosio, 87, 275
Armijo, Charles H., 91
Armijo, Jesus, 275
Armijo, Mariano, 87, 275
Armijo, Perfecto, 275
Armstrong, Jack, 191
Ascarate, Antonio, 57
Atchison, Topeka & Santa Fé Railroad, 1, 22, 65, 76, 88, 89, 93, 104, 129, 130, 147, 237, 244, 266, 268, 269, 273, 274, 279, 280, 283
Atlantic and Pacific Railroad, 244
Bobb, Eli, 91, 92
Baca, Amado, 57
Baca, Antonio, 57
Baca, Benito, 119, 150
Baca, Chata, 185, 186
Baca, Don Benito, 60, 61, 149, 150
Baca, David, 57
Baca, Domingo, 57
Baca, Eleuterio, 57
Baca y Sandoval, Francisco, 57
Baca, Don Juan Maria, 57, 60, 61
Bailey, Doctor, 222
Baird, Nettie, 120

Baldy, Louis H., 47, 50
Barela, Manuel, 192, 193
Barela, Don Mariano, 192
Barlow & Sanderson Stage Line, 63, 147
Barnes, Judge Sydney M., 205
Beattie Sisters, 120
Beckworth, 192, 193
Beeson, Chalk, 37
Bell, Ham, 71
Bell, John, 40
Bell, Mattie, 41
Bell, Thomas D., 119
Benedict, Judge Kirby, 158, 159, 160, 161
Bent, Charles, 144
Bent, Mrs. George, 169
Bent & St. Vrain, 142
Billy the Kid, See William H. Bonney
Bishop family, 41
Black Kettle, 15
Blackwell, Arthur M., 73, 75
Blackwell, C. M., 119
Blackwood, James, 284
Blackwood, Major John G., 285
Blackwood, Mary Josephine, See Mrs. Miguel Antonio Otero I
Blackwood, Page, 284
Blackwood, Samuel, 283
Blackwood, William Gardner, 284
Blake, Frank A., 119
Blake, Harry, 244
Bloom, Marion, 120
Boggs, Thomas, 58
Bonney, William H., 210, 211, 213, 214, 215
Bostwick, Judge John F., 278
Bowdre, Charlie, 210
Boyle, Sport, 200, 201
Bozeman, Louis, 210
Brinkley, Tom, 236
Brooks, Charlie, 153, 155, 156
Browne, Earnest L., 248
Browne, Millard W., 119, 207
Browne & Manzanares, 165
Brunswick, Colonel Marcus, 156, 157, 158, 164, 165,

167, 168
Buckskin, Charlie, 125
Buffalo, 12, 27, 28, 42, 43, 45, 48, 49, 54, 66, 67, 68, 69, 87
Buffalo Bill, See Cody, William F.
Bursum, Holm O., 107
Busch, Adolphus, 251
Calamity Jane, 21
Carr, Charlie, 109, 110
Carroll, Charles, of Carrollton, 284
Carson, Joe, 182, 187, 188
Carson, General Kit, 58, 59
Carson, Mrs. Valentine, 249
Castillo, Joe, 190, 191
Caston, Theodore, 186
Catron, Thomas B., 156, 159, 160, 238
Chaffee Light Artillery, 139
Chambers, Lou, 210
Chandler, Jack, 101
Chaves, Don Bonifacio, 219
Chaves, Martin, 215
Chick, Henry, 119
Chick, Lee, 119
Chick, W. H., & Co., 10, 25, 31
Chick, Browne & Company, 37, 41, 66, 70
Chisum, John, 157
Chivington, Major J. M., 47
Chunk, desperado, 122
Church, Jack C., 207
Clark, Mrs., 8
Clark, Julius, 120
Close, George, 98, 154, 155
Close & Patterson, 153
Clouthier, D. A., 119
Cody, William F., 15, 31, 32, 33, 51, 53, 55, 56
Cole, Charles O., 119, 195
Collar, Jacob, 40
Collier, John, 118, 119
Combs, Bill, 188
Conde, Fred, 171, 173
Conner, William, 40
Connolly, Governor Henry, 2
Cordova, Brigido, 112, 113
Cosgrove, Michael, 238
Cox, William, 259
Crawford, Andrew J., 119
Crawford, Jack, 173
Crawford, William S., 119

289

Crommitt, 236
Cullen, Robert K. L. M., 119, 205
Cummings, Nellie, 273
Cunningham, Dr. J. M., 89, 90
Curry, George, 103, 104, 105, 106, 107, 108
Curry, Jimmy, 106
Custer, General George A., 20, 27, 51, 53, 54
Daley, Dan, 153
Dambmann, Charlie, 260, 261, 262, 263, 264, 265
Davenport, Frank, 89
Davis, "High," 71
De Baca, Valentin C., 57
DeLaney, J. C., 106
Democratic National Convention of 1860, 283
Dennison, Sam, 108
Denver, Colorado, 9, 42
Denver, Las Vegas & Socorro Railroad, 258
Denver and Rio Grande Railroad, 76, 94, 129, 130
De Remer, J. R., 109
Dickinson, Colonel W. G., 276
Dietz, John, 86
Dirty Dick, 93
Dodge City Gang, 182
Dolan, James J., 106
Dolly Varden, 72
Doniphan, Colonel A. W., 144
Dorman, H. H., 63
Dorsey, John, 187, 188, 189, 190
Dorsey, Stephen W., 59, 238, 240
Douglas, Major, 4
Douglas, Stephen A., 283
Doyle, Joseph, 145
Duke, English bulldog, 80, 81
Dunlop, May, 248
Dunn, Noah, 191
Dutchy, 182
East, James H., 210
East Las Vegas, New Mexico, 182, 245, 246, 258, 259
Edwards, Rufe, 94, 97
Elkins, Mr. and Mrs., 259, 260
Elkins, Stephen B., 238
Ellsworth, Kansas, 9

El Moro, Colorado, 94, 98, 110, 148
Emory, Thomas, 210
Exchange Hotel, Las Vegas, 156
Faker, Charles, 124
Fall, Albert B., 107
Fernandez de Taos, Battle of, 144
Finley, Reginald, 119
Firing Out Club, 170, 171, 248
Fiske, Eugene A., 157
Ford, Bob, 178, 179, 180
Ford, Charlie, 178, 179
Fort Dodge, 73
Fort Harker, Kansas, 8
Fort Lyon, Colorado, 58, 59
Fort Wallace, 28
Franklin, Harry, 236
Fremont, General John C., 58, 144
French, Henry, 253
French, Pete, 154
Friedman, Moses, 29
Friend, Captain Edward, 208, 251
Frost, Clark D., 260
Gage, Dick, 26
Gallegos, Gertrudes, 99
Gallegos, Jose, 61
Garcia, J. S., 39
Garrett, Pat F., 210, 211, 212, 213, 214
Gibbons, Henry W., 73, 75, 91
Gildersleeve, Charles H., 157
Gillies, George M., 119
Gise, Cassius C., 119
Glasgow, Dr., 251
Goodlet, William L., 182, 188
Gordon, Dr. C. C., 250, 259
Granada, Colorado, 65, 69, 70, 71
Grant, President Ulysses S., 31, 209
Grau, Maurice, 264, 265
Greenstreet, William, 99, 112
Gross, Caroline Linton, 152, 247, 248
Gross, Jacob, 110, 111, 138, 151, 152, 163, 205, 236, 247, 248, 250
Gross, Blackwell & Company, 234, 248

Gross, Kelly & Company, 69, 73, 248
Grossman, Edward, 47, 50
Hagerman, Governor H. J., 107
Hall, Charlie, 136
Hall, Lee, 210
Hallett, Judge, 115
Hamilton, William, 119, 137
Harding, President Warren G., 107
Hardy, Belle, 120
Harkins, Mike, 87
Harper, Tom, 172
Harrington, Rufe, 98
Harris, Henry V., 183
Hart, "Teddy," 261, 263, 266
Hastings Sisters, 120
Hatch, General Edward, 207
Hauser, George, 137
Hauser, William, 137
Hayes, President Rutherford B., 209
Hays City, Kansas, 10, 11, 12, 13, 15, 32
Hazelton, George, 237
Hazen, William L., 174, 183
Henriquez, Mrs., 274
Henry, Tom, See Thomas Jefferson House
Herrera, Juan José, 223
Hickok, James B. "Wild Bill," 14, 15, 16, 17, 18, 19, 20, 25, 32
Hilty, Ike, 222
Hixenbaugh family, 105
Holliday, Doc, 216, 217, 218
Holmes, Rush J., 155, 205, 277
Hood, Al G., 137, 255, 273
Hood, Mrs. A. G., 241
Hopewell, Willard S., 139, 140
Houck, George, 167
Houghton, Oliver L., 119, 120
House, Thomas Jefferson, 187, 188, 189, 190
Howe, George, 168
Hughes, Bela M., 109
Humes, Charles T., 119, 174
Hunt, Governor Albert C., 99
Hutton, Captain, 262
Hyde, Alfred E., 210, 211

Indians, Apaches, 89
Indians, Cheyenne, 84, 85, 86
Indians, Navajo, 60, 89, 90, 145
Indians, Southern Apaches, 208
Indians, Utes, 89, 116
Inman, Colonel Henry, quoted, 55
Ingersoll, Robert G., 240
Irvin, Newton, 167
Jamarillo, Mrs., 215
James, Frank, 176
James, Jesse, 176, 177, 178
Jennings, Belle, 119
Jilson, Arthur, 127, 236
John, James M., 120
Johnson, Benjamin, 119
Johnson, J. L., 127
Jones, Albert H., 139
Jones, Frank M., 17, 20
Jones, Tom, 236
Kansas City, Missouri, 2
Kansas-Nebraska Bill, 283
Kansas-Pacific Railroad, 1, 9, 22, 25, 33, 42, 65, 93
Keene, Worth, 271
Keimle, Charlie, 137, 273
Kelliher, Michael, 200, 201
Kelly, David, 236
Kelly, "Dog," 81, 84
Kelly, Harry W., 73, 75, 94, 96, 97, 99, 100, 101, 107, 109, 115
Kemp, Tom, 36, 37, 38, 39, 40, 138
Kerens, Richard C., 238
Kihlberg, Frank O., 52
Kiowa, horse, 78, 79, 80, 92, 93, 249, 250
Kirkman, Captain, 106
Kirkpatrick, Ed., 172
Kisstler, Russ A., 131, 132, 202, 246
Kit Carson, Colorado, 22, 38, 40
Kitchen Brothers, 156, 158
Kitchen, Charlie, 156, 158, 167, 168, 169
Knickerbocker, Hattie, 248
La Constancia, New Mexico, 63, 64
La Garde, Dr. Louis A., 87
La Junta, Colorado, 94
Lane, Price, 254
Lane, Governor William Carr, 282

Las Vegas, New Mexico, 151, 156, 162, 167, 170, 171
Las Vegas Daily Optic, 132, 246, 255, 268
Las Vegas Fair Association, 244
Las Vegas & Gulf Railroad, 255
Las Vegas Gun and Rod Club, 173
Las Vegas Hose Company No. 1, 245
Las Vegas Hot Springs, 176, 266
Las Vegas Mining and Milling Company, 225
Las Vegas Telephone Company, 273
Laurence, John, 119
Lawrence, Jennie, 98
Leadville, Colorado, 138, 139
Leavitt, James L., 174
Leavenworth, Kansas, 8
Lee, Jesse, 105, 106
Le Fevre, Manuel, 146
Lewis, Jerry, 18
Liddel, Dick, 179, 180, 181
Lincoln, President Abraham, 2, 283
Lino, Antonio, 203, 216
Linton, Dr. Moses, 35, 152
Locke, Fred, 155, 156
Locke & Brooks, 156
Lockwood, William G., 156
Longuemare, Prof. Charles, 119, 220, 221, 222, 224, 226, 229
Lorne, Marquis of, 266
Los Lunas, New Mexico, 253
Louise, Princess, 266
Lull, C. E., 120
Luna, Jesus M., 157, 271
Luna, Solomon, 271, 272
Luna Tranquilino, 157, 270, 271, 272
Lunger's Club, 171, 172, 173
Lynch, J. W., 179, 180
Mann, Carl, 18
Manners, Captain, See Duke of Rutland
Manners, Lady Diana, 267
Manzanares, Frank A., 84, 273
Manzanares, Ofelia Baca, 150
Marcellino, Paul, 262
Marshall, Reverend Charles

H., 280
Marshall, General, 241
Martin, Jose Maria, 160, 161, 162
Martinez, Dolores, 134, 135, 136, 137
Martinez, Felix, 244
Mason, Barney, 210, 212
Masterson, Bat, 89
Mathers, Dave, 89, 182, 191, 196
Maximilian, Emperor, 12
Maxwell Land Grant Company, 105, 255
Maxwell, Lucien B., 157
Medina, Pablo, 78
Mendenhall, Hunter & Company, 263
Mennet, Adolph, 11, 41, 66, 67, 85, 86
Meriwether, Governor David, 283
Mexico Telephone Company, 241
Michaelis, Dr. T. M., 41
Milligan, Dr. M. M., 195, 222
Mills, Melvin W., 105
Mitchell, George, 94
Montezuma Hotel, 265, 275, 276
Moore, Jersey, 110, 111
Moore, W. Scott, 176, 177, 178
Morehead, James, 194, 195
Morehead, C. R., & Co., 8, 29, 248
Mulnix, Harry, 120
Mulvey, Bill, 16
Murphy, Pierce J., 119
McBeth, John A., 137
McCall, Jack, 18
McClave, Captain, 86
McCullough, John, 41, 89
McKay sisters, 120
McKinley, President William, 288
McManes, O. P., 105
McNair, Thomas Benton, 73, 75
McNulty, John, 239
Naranja, Cruz, 230
Navajo Frank, 98, 99
Naval Academy, Annapolis, 91
Neill, H. G. (Hoodoo Brown), 182, 201
Nettleton, George H., 76

Newby, Colonel, 145
Newell, Charlie, 78, 79, 82
Newell, Nels, 116, 137, 140, 222, 224
New Mexico Bell Telephone Company, 254
New Mexico & Southern Pacific Railroad, 77
New Town, See East Las Vegas
Nichols, Frank B., 119
Nickerson, Joseph, 65, 76
Nickerson, Thomas, 65, 76
Nixau, Madame, 264, 265
Nolan, Tom, 84, 119
Norton, Johnny, 36
Nuttall, Billy, 18
Oakley, Don, 222
O'Bryan, Henry J., 248, 285, 286
O'Bryan, Henry Duross, 286
O'Bryan, Mamie Josephine Otero, 285, 286
O'Bryan, Marie Aileen, 286
Old House, Santa Fé, 246, 247
Olsen, John, 48
Omohundro, Texas Jack, 51, 52, 53
Otero, New Mexico, 131, 132, 134
Otero *Optic*, 131
Otero, Judge Antonio Jose, 282
Otero, Emanuel B., 57
Otero, Gertrude Vincentio, 285
Otero, Katherine Stinson, 286
Otero, Don Manuel A., 30, 60, 64, 65, 274, 275
Otero, Don Mariano S., 60, 157, 237
Otero, Meliton S., 119
Otero, Don Miguel Antonio I, 1, 2, 3, 5, 7, 8, 12, 14, 51, 62, 63, 65, 89, 100, 101, 109, 126, 130, 131, 151, 152, 162, 205, 213, 219, 234, 237, 241, 244, 251, 255, 257, 268, 269, 270, 274, 275, 276, 277, 278, 279, 280, 281, 282, 283
Otero, Mrs. Miguel Antonio I, 2, 4, 283, 284, 285
Otero, Miguel Antonio, 1, 2, 14, 28, 29, 91, 96, 102, 107, 109, 127, 128, 148, 163, 164, 165, 195, 202, 207, 231, 234, 244, 250, 251, 252, 253, 268, 273, 277, 278, 286, 287, 288
Otero, Mrs. Miguel Antonio, 286
Otero, Miguel Antonio IV, 286, 287
Otero, Page Blackwood, 2, 5, 6, 14, 43, 50, 75, 91, 128, 137, 165, 227, 233, 248, 251, 273, 278, 285
Otero, Sellar & Co., 10, 14, 21, 25, 30, 31, 37, 38, 39, 41, 43, 50, 51, 57, 66, 69, 87, 88, 97, 109, 164, 233
Page, Frank, 185
Pancho, 121
Parker, E. W., 239
Parker, Thomas H., 109, 119, 163, 225, 231, 247, 260
Patterson, Billy, 94
Payne, Captain, 85
Pearson Brothers, 185
Peck, George R., 76, 77
Perea, Alejandro, 210
Perea, Jesus M., 157
Perea, Mariano, 157
Perry, Joe, 36, 94
Pickett, Tom, 210, 211, 240
Pinal, Father, 169
Pingree's College, 281
Poker Tom, See Thomas Emory
Polk, President James K., 282
Polk, Trusten, 281
Ponties, Bill, 91
Prichard, Colonel George W., 231, 242
Prowers, John D., 84
Radcliffe, Godfrey F., 174
Ramsey, Secretary of War, 209
Randall, William, 187, 188
Rath, Charles, 88
Rattlesnake Bill, 184, 185
Redmond, John, 253
Reymond, Numa, 238
Rifenberg, Grant, 103
Riggs, Frank, 123, 124
Riley, John H., 238
Rinehart, Indian Agent, 90
Riney, John, 104
Ring, William, 119
Robbins, Dr., 136
Robertson, Uncle John, 223, 229
Robinson, Lieutenant-Governor, 139
Robinson, A. A., 76, 77
Rogers family, 86
Rogers, Thomas, 105, 106
Romero, Desiderio, 212
Romero, Pablo ("Colorow") 212
Roosevelt, President Theodore, 107, 288
Rossier, Alfred, 119
Rough Riders, 107
Rudabaugh, Dave, 188, 202, 203, 204, 210, 211, 212, 213, 214, 215, 216
Ruder, Andy, 95
Russell, J. M., 206
Russell, Jimmie, 98
Russell, Sol Smith, 68
Rust, Dr. D. H., 248
Rutland, Duke of, 266, 267
Sandoval, Placido, 119
Sanford, General, 281
San Miguel National Bank, 152, 234, 235, 236
San Miguel Rifles, 207, 208, 209
Santa Fé Central Railroad, 140
Santa Fé Trail, 63, 147
Sargent, M. L., 76
Saunders, Jennie, 120
Savajeau, Alex, 277
Schaefer, Otto G., 273
Scheurich, Aloys, 59
Schomberg, T. M., 105
Schultz, Henry, 109
Sellar, John Perry, 8, 101, 102, 109, 137, 164, 165, 234
Sena, Andres, 241
Severance, Doctor, 222
Shanley, Pat, 69
Shaw family, 112, 113, 114, 115
Shea, Tim, 97, 98
Sheldon, Governor Lionel A., 105
Shelton, Charles, 253
Sheridan, Kansas, 25, 29, 33
Sheridan, General Philip H., 27, 32, 51, 52, 53, 149
Sherman, General William T., 209
Sherry Brothers, 47

Shout, Mrs. Anna B., 273
Simpson, Harry, 171
Simpson, Peter, 119
Singleton, William, 39, 40
Sitting Out Club, 248, 249
Skipwith, Dr. E. H., 259
Slocum, George, 119
Smith, Lee, 188
Smith, Sol, 68
Sorin, Reverend Edward, 128
Sosaya, Manuel
Southern Pacific Railroad, 244
Spangler, Michael, 277
Spear, John, 124
Springer, Charles, 255
Springer, Frank, 41, 255
Staab, Abraham, 157
Star Route Swindlers, 238, 239, 240
Starbird, Nelson W., 205
Steamboat, See Dolores Martinez
Steigers, Dr. Sol, 251
Stewart, Frank, 210, 212
Stewart & Norton, 36
Stockton, Alec, 119
Strawhorn, Sam, 15
Strong, William B., 77, 237, 269
Studebaker, J. M., 277
Stuntebeck, Father, 35
Sturgis, Henry, 165
Sutfin family, 151
Symington, Mrs., 275
Tabor, Grand Opera House, 255
Taos, New Mexico, 59
Tammie, Charlie, 103, 104
Tejanos, 62, 63
Tenderfoot Bob, See Bob Williams
Tetard, Emily, 248
Thayer, James, 281
Thomas, Edward, 5
Thompson, Bill, 17
Thompson, George W., 156, 157, 158, 168, 169
Thompson, Green, 95, 96
Thompson, Professor, 91
Thornton, William T., 157
Ticer & Company, 259
Tipton, Dr. William R., 186
Topeka, Kansas, 5
Trinidad, Colorado, 103, 112
Trinidad News, 165
Trujillo, Donaciana, 99
Turner, 29
Tutt, Dave, 15
Tuttle, J. J., 206
Two Lance, 55
United Lodge Hospital, 259
University, Notre Dame, 128
University, St. Louis, 34, 129
Varnes, 19
Vermijo Ranch, 60
Victorio, Apache Chief, 208
Vigilance Committee, Hays City, 13, 15
Vigilance Committee, Las Vegas, 181, 184, 189, 190, 192, 193, 196, 198, 199, 205, 206, 236
Vigilance Committee, Sheridan, 26
Villepegue, John, 1, 119
Vincent, William A., 286
Vinita Mail Service, 238, 239, 240
Waddingham, Wilson, 156, 157, 158
Waldo, Judge Henry L., 77, 156, 274
Wallace, Frank, 114
Walsh, Maurice J., 119
Ward, Frederick, 242
Ward, George W., 103, 104
Watkins, Charlie, 138
Watts, Judge John S., 2, 283
Webb, J. J., 188, 196, 201, 202, 204, 205
Wesche, Charles Emil, 183
West, James, 187, 188, 189, 190
Whigham, Harry, 105
White, Charlie, 216, 217, 218
Whitelaw, Frank, 223
Whiting, David, 1
Whiting & Otero, 1
Whitlock, 104, 105, 106
Wilcox, Lute, 167, 246
Wild Bill, See James B. Hickok
Wilder, Edward, 76
Williams, Bob, 210
Wilson, Billy, 210, 211
Wilson, J. E., 232
Windram, John, 70
Winters, David C., 120, 174
Wooten, Colorado, 148
Wooten, Richens Lacy (Uncle Dick), 59, 111, 141, 142, 143, 144, 145, 146, 147, 148
Wooten, Jr., R. L., 148
Wright, Robert, 88
Yeaman, Caldwell, 120
York, Captain, 94
Zealand, Father, 35
Zimmerman, F. C., 40

www.ingramcontent.com/pod-product-compliance
Lightning Source LLC
Chambersburg PA
CBHW030333240426
43661CB00052B/1616